FROM TITO TO MILOSEVIC

YUGOSLAVIA: THE LOST COUNTRY

Michael Barratt Brown

THE MERLIN PRESS

First published in 2005
by The Merlin Press Ltd.
PO Box 30705
London
WC2E 8QD
www.merlinpress.co.uk

ISBN. 085036552X

British Library Cataloguing in Publication Data is available from
the British Library

Printed in the UK by the Russell Press, Nottingham

From Tito to Milosevic

for Angela
with happy memories
of Sanna
　　　Michael

David & I got to Staffa
the following week

Contents

List of Illustrations   vi

Preface   vii

Chapter 1: The Trial of Slobodan Milosevic   1

Chapter 2: Sarajevo, April 1945   23

Chapter 3: Yugoslavs in Exile, Egypt, 1943-4   29

Chapter 4: War Relief Planning for Yugoslavia – Bari, Italy, 1944-5   39

Chapter 5: UNRRA Relief in Bosnia and Hercegovina, 1945-6   55

Chapter 6: UNRRA Rehabilitation, Belgrade, 1946-7   73

Chapter 7: Tito's Break with Stalin, 1948-57   87

Chapter 8: Workers' Self-management, 1958-74   97

Chapter 9: Socialism in the World, 1975-85   111

Chapter 10: Nationality and Nationalism, 1986-90   121

Chapter 11: Descent into War: Croatia and Bosnia, 1991-5   135

Chapter 12: Kosovo and NATO's War on Yugoslavia, 1996-9   153

Closure: What is Left of Yugoslavia after Sixty Years?   169

References   178

Index   189

List of Illustrations

Front cover: Tito with UNRRA Mission members, Belgrade, 1947.
Page x: Milosevic at the ICTY, the Hague, 2003. (*AP/Wide World Photos*)
Page 22: Sarajevo, 1945. (*Michael Barratt Brown*)
Page 28: Partisans in Bosnia, 1943. (*Michael Barratt Brown*)
Page 38: (1) Harrowing, Bosnia, 1944. (2) Tito with Fitzroy MacLean,
Ambassador Peake and General Steele, 1946. (*Michael Barratt Brown*)
Page 54: (1) Bridge over the Neretva, 1945. (2) Save the Children Fund Clinic,
Sarajevo, 1946. (*Michael Barratt Brown*)
Page 72: (1) UNRRA Tractor, Bosnia, 1946. (2) UNRRA Port Operations,
Trieste, 1946. (*Michael Barratt Brown*)
Page 86: (1) Golnik TB Sanatorium, Slovenia, 1963. (2) Workers' Council,
Rade Koncar, Zagreb, 1970.
Page 96: (1) Shipyards, Split, 1961 (2) Iron and Steel Works, Jesenice, 1970.
Page 110: (1) Motorcar Assembly line, 1980 (2) Combine Harvesters,
Vojvodina, 1980.
Page 120: (1) AVNOJ meeting, Jajce, 1944: Ribar – Croat; Tito – Croat; Pijade
– Jew, Rankovic – Serb; Dzilas – Montenegrin in the centre front row).
 (2) The six Republic leaders, 1991: l. to r, Montenegro, Slovenia, Croatia,
Macedonia, Bosnia-Hercegovina, Serbia).
Page 134: Bridge at Varvarin, 2000.
Page 152: Sixth Century Icon at Decani Monastery, Kosovo.
Page 168: Map of ex-Yugoslav States, 2000.

Preface

This book is in part a personal odyssey, but more importantly it is a celebration of the brave experiment in pluralist nation building that was Former Yugoslavia. It so happened that I watched it at close quarters for nearly the whole of the fifty and more years from its birth in the early 1940s to its death in the 1990s. The world of the media knows only of the internecine killings in Bosnia and Kosovo and the wicked acts of certain nationalist leaders, which have been made the moral excuse for a worldwide exercise of great power imperialism. It knows little or nothing of the hopes and fears of 25 million Yugoslavs from different ethnic origins and religious backgrounds who worked together to build a new society, or of the outside intervention that destroyed it.

The book begins with the trial of Milosevic, one-time elected Yugoslav President, before the International Criminal Court for Former Yugoslavia at the Hague, which is still in session as this is written. The trial is concerned with the events of the civil wars in Croatia, Bosnia-Hercegovina and Kosovo respectively in 1991-5 and in 1998-9. In telling this part of the story I have relied largely on my reading of all 30,000 pages of the transcripts of the proceedings at the trial. References in brackets in this and some later chapters of the book are to pages in the official transcripts. The book begins, therefore, at the end of Former Yugoslavia, because that is where most readers will know something of what has happened. It is my belief, however, that this ending cannot be understood without going back at least to the founding of the new Yugoslavia by Tito's Partisans in liberated territory during the German/Axis occupation of Yugoslavia from 1941 to 1945.

The next chapters are based on the historical monographs which I wrote for the UNRRA Yugoslav Mission in April-June 1947 after my three years in the country. These monographs were themselves taken from official reports of the Mission. Later chapters are taken from diaries I kept of my subsequent visits to Yugoslavia and from discussions I have had with my many Yugoslav friends. In drawing on books and reports about Yugoslavia I have tried to limit myself to those written by Yugoslavs or by those who worked in Yugoslavia but not as journalists. But I wish to confess my indebtedness to two American writers with special knowledge – to Susan Woodward, who worked in Zagreb from 1987-90 and was Special Assistant to the Chief UN Representative in Bosnia in 1994 (her two books appear in the References) and to Diana Johnstone for her book *Fools' Crusade*, based on the most careful study of the evidence in the Milosevic trial.

I have had much help in writing this book from Kay Carmichael, Ken Coates, Basil Davidson, Diana Johnstone, Milica Pesic and Phil Wright, who read the text at different stages of its development. My thanks to them all with the usual disclaimer of any attributions of responsibility for the weaknesses that remain.

The book is dedicated to those who helped me over the years to understand what Yugoslavia meant to them, and particularly to my friends, Mauricette Begic, Basil Davidson, Miladin and Maja Korac, Pedrag Matvejevic, Milos Nikolic, Milica Pesic, Nina Pirnat Spahic, Sylvie Skakic and to the dear memory of Eleanor Singer, Nada Kraigher and Robert Neubauer.

Postscript

After this book was written, the International Criminal Tribunal for Yugoslavia (ICTY) decided, in violation of international law and the rights of those accused, to impose counsel for Milosevic, denying the right he claimed to conduct his own defence. The reason given was the successive illnesses which Milosevic has suffered, which have delayed the hearings. Milosevic appointed Nico Varkevisser from Amsterdam as his assistant and to coordinate the work of the newly established Slobodan Milosevic Freedom Center at the Hague, an independent body within the Dutch Foundation 'Holland Yugoslavia'. At the same time, he appealed against the decision and refused to speak to the two English barristers, Steven Kay and Gillian Higgins, when they were asked to take over his defence after he completed his five hour opening defence in September 2004. As a result, no witnesses could be called, and the two lawyers asked to be dismissed. (See report from Ian Traynor in Zagreb, *The Guardian* 28.10.04.)

This attempt to deny Milosevic's rights was, however, overturned by the judges at an Appeal Court (Nikki Tait, London, *Financial Times*, 2.11.04). This was a great victory for Milosevic and a defeat for the prosecution. Some good sense had, however, emerged from a surprising quarter. According to the *Washington Times* of October 24, 2004, John Bolton, US Under Secretary of State, revealed the Bush Administration's desire to close down the Tribunal and made scathing remarks about Ms. Del Ponte, the chief prosecutor. 'There is a very real risk', Mr Bolton said, 'that the Tribunal's prosecutions will create new animosities.' He could say that again!

Milosevic at the ICTY, The Hague, 2003
(AP/Wide World Photos)

Chapter 1

The Trial Of Slobodan Milosevic

On most working days between September 2002 and February 2004 a visitor could enter a court house in the Hague and observe the trial of the former elected President of Yugoslavia, the Serb leader Slobodan Milosevic. The visitor would see on the bench an English presiding judge, Judge Richard May, flanked by judges respectively from Jamaica and Sri Lanka. On the left, the prosecution is led by a gentleman enjoying the name of Mr Nice. In the centre stand the witnesses brought by the prosecution. On the right Milosevic is accompanied by a guard, but without defence lawyers, only two *amici*, so-called, provided by the court as friends of the defendant. At the back of the court in boxes sit the stenographers and the translators – official translators of English, French and Serbo-Croatian and others from other countries. Above them a large screen is used for projecting images of photographs and documents presented as evidence of the criminal activities for which Milosevic has been indicted. For this is the main court room of the UN International Criminal Tribunal for Former Yugoslavia (ICTY).

By March 2004 there had been nearly 300 court days and over 300 witnesses to testify at this trial and to be cross questioned by Milosevic. And the trial of Milosevic is not the only one with which the International Criminal Court for Former Yugoslavia is concerned. In other rooms in the courthouse other Serbs would be facing trial for crimes for which they have been indicted in connection with the civil wars in Croatia and Bosnia between 1991 and 1995 and in Kosovo in 1998-9. Occasionally, the indicted Serbs will be joined by an indicted Croat or a Muslim.

Most visitors entering the court will have preconceived ideas of what to expect. Milosevic they will perhaps see as he is often depicted, a second Hitler who seized power in Yugoslavia as a Serb with the aim of creating a Greater Serbia and carrying out the 'ethnic cleansing' of Bosnia-Hercegovina, Kosovo and parts of Croatia. To this end his Serb army is said to have driven out of their homes hundreds of thousands who were not Serbs, but were Croats, Muslims and Albanians and to have murdered many thousands who had resisted. This was supposedly but the last stage of a barbaric history in which the different ethnic groups in the country had fought each other over the ages, only restrained by outside imperial powers – Turks, Italians, Hungarians, Austrians, Germans – and most recently by the iron hand of Marshal Tito. After much hesitation, so the story ends, the international community had at length sent NATO forces into the country to stop the fighting, ensure the independence of the Slovenes, the Croats, the Bosnians and the protection of the Kosovars, and to bring Milosevic to trial. It makes a good story, but is it true?

The documents circulated at the court state the terms of the indictment:

> Slobodan Milosevic is individually criminally responsible for the crimes referred to in Articles 2,3,4 and 5 of the Statute of this Tribunal as described in this indictment, which he planned, instigated, ordered, committed, or in whose planning, preparation, or execution he otherwise aided and abetted. By using the word 'committed' in this indictment, the Prosecutor does not intend to suggest that the accused physically committed any of the crimes charged personally. 'Committed' in this indictment refers to 'participation in a joint criminal enterprise as a co-perpetrator.' The 'joint criminal enterprise' included charges of 'genocide or complicity in genocide' – 'the destruction in whole or in part, of the Bosnian Muslim and Bosnian Croat national, ethnical, racial or religious groups as such, in territories within Bosnia and Hercegovina', as well as 'crimes against humanity, grave breaches of the Geneva Conventions and violations of the laws and customs of war in Bosnia-Hercegovina, Croatia and Kosovo'.[1]

A visitor who wishes to remain impartial and listen closely to the proceedings to reach his or her own judgement would have to bear in mind that there is another view that is not so widely held, but has much evidence to support it. On this view, the several, mainly Slav, peoples of Yugoslavia had lived together in peace for hundreds of years, except when they were invaded by Turks, Hungarians, Austrians, Italians, Germans and now Americans; that Tito's Partisans drawn from all the several Yugoslav communities had held down more German and Axis divisions in Yugoslavia in World War II than the British and American forces had done at the same time in North Africa or in Italy; that Tito's rule in peacetime was not a military dictatorship but a federation of peoples with large elements of political and economic democracy; that the country began to fall apart even before Tito's death because of demands made on it, as on many other developing countries, by the institutions of international capital, the IMF and American Banks; that the first acts of civil war came from Slovenia and Croatia, not from Serbia; that Milosevic was an elected President, whom the Americans called on to underwrite the peace in Bosnia-Hercegovina; that the numbers killed in the civil war have been greatly exaggerated; that it was mainly Serbs who were driven out of their homes in Bosnia and Croatia and that the "protection" of Kosovo has driven most Serbs out of their homes in Kosovo; but it has left the Americans with a massive military base in Kosovo, 'Camp Bondsteel', and opened Yugoslavia to capitalist investment.

On this view the main responsibility for the break-up of Yugoslavia and the subsequent civil wars lies with outside forces primarily German and American who fought out their own rivalry on the bodies of the Yugoslav peoples. This is the view which this author believes to be true on the basis of many years' experience in Former Yugoslavia. It is a view shared by many who have wide experience in Former Yugoslavia, including most particularly two authors: Susan Woodward, who worked in Zagreb in 1987-90, from which her book *The Political Economy of Yugoslavia, 1945-90* derived, and was the special assistant to the chief UN representative in Bosnia in 1994, from which experience came her *Balkan Tragedy*[2] and Diana Johnstone, whose book *Fools' Crusade* is based on the most careful study of the evidence in the Milosevic trial.[3]

But we must return to our imaginary visitor at the Milosevic trial before the International Criminal Court for Yugoslavia, to help him or her understand what is going on. The visitor will indeed be observing an historic event. This is a new form of trial. It is the first international trial of an elected head of state and of his accomplices since the Nuremberg trials of Hitler's associates. The trial before an international court of a UN indicted war criminal has created an important precedent, which might be followed in the case of others. Although the Yugoslav government at the time had expressed the wish to try Milosevic themselves, after his defeat in the elections of 2000, he was 'lifted' out of Belgrade to the Hague by NATO armed personnel.[4] To be named an 'indicted war criminal' already carried an assumption of guilt.

Under an agreement of May 9 1996, NATO had been made the official gendarme for the Tribunal. The methods employed in bringing prisoners to the Hague for trial has raised some questions about human rights. Special US armed units and others attracted by the very large rewards offered for a capture were employed to kidnap indicted Serbs, with instructions to shoot them if they resisted. Several examples were given by Diana Johnstone in her book *Fool's Crusade* taken from newspaper reports of indicted Serbs being shot when they tried to escape arrest and of others dying in their cells in the Hague. Slavko Dokmanovic, one time mayor of Vukovar, was indicted and seized in 1997 for trial for executing 250 Croat soldiers from a hospital in Vukovar in November of 1991. He was able to prove that he had been elsewhere at the time, and should have been acquitted, but was found dead in his cell in June 1998.[5]

Milosevic made much of such cases in his opening address at the second part of the trial, concerned with Croatia and Bosnia (pp. 11027 ff. of the official transcripts of the ICTY proceedings. Page numbers in brackets in this and later chapters will refer to these transcripts). Jilan Milutinovic, President of Serbia under Milosevic, gave himself up for reasons that are not clear, when his term of office came to an end, and was taken to the Hague to face the Tribunal by which he had been indicted.

What may have happened to Milutinovic is suggested by the story of what happened to Radovan (Ratko) Markovic, Milosevic's chief of state security. He was taken out of Belgrade where he was in jail and brought to the Hague. It had been expected that his evidence would finally pin the blame on Milosevic for "ethnic cleansing" in Kosovo. A special Jeremy Paxman programme had been organised on BBC TV for July 26 2002 to publicise this, but things did not turn out as expected. Markovic told the Tribunal that he had been tortured and offered asylum if he witnessed that he had committed criminal acts on the orders of Milosevic. In the event, in answer to examination he refused to do so, and said that the instructions fell entirely within the laws of war (p. 8765). It is a surprising aspect of the Tribunal's methods of work that the judge did not stop the proceedings and call for an inquiry into the truth of this allegation of torture. Markovic was returned to jail in Belgrade. On February 24 2004 he retracted in a Belgrade court the further confession he had made earlier, under promises of protection for himself and his family, of involvement in the death of Ivan Stambolic. Stambolic was a much loved one-time Serb President and protector of Milosevic, whom Milosevic had turned against to further his own ambitions.

The status of this court has at all appropriate times, and some inappropriate times, been challenged by Milosevic. The world media often compares Milosevic and the Serb armies with Hitler and the Nazis and the Hague trials with the Nuremberg trials. Milosevic ridicules this. In a civil war his forces never left Yugoslavia. It was NATO forces from outside that attacked a sovereign state. He denies that he gave orders for illegal actions or knowingly failed to prevent them. He insists that in both Nuremberg and the Hague it is victors' justice that rules. Indeed, he frequently complains that judge and prosecution (there is no jury) all come from NATO countries which invaded his country without UN sanction. He points to evidence that most of the pressure for the trials comes from outside the country. There is much support for his view.

The first chief prosecutor at the Tribunal (ICTY) was Richard Goldstone, a South African whose reputation came from his experience in the post-apartheid Truth and Reconciliation Commission. He did not reappear when the trial of Milosevic began, but before he left he compared what he called 'the

Bosnian victims' desire for revenge' with the black peoples of South Africa's satisfaction with the Truth Commission, suggesting that this was because of the greater degree of crime in Bosnian genocide.[6] By contrast, David Chandler in his 1999 book *Bosnia: Faking Democracy after Dayton*, based on a long period of study in Bosnia, concluded that 'The ICTY has little support within Bosnia …. Poll findings show that for Bosnian people of all three groups the question of war crimes is of little importance. Accusations of war crimes, so far, seem to have done little to develop community reconciliation.'[7] And there was no sign of that happening in the following years.

A New International Court

The history of the establishment of the International Criminal Tribunal for Former Yugoslavia is interesting. It was the particular child of both German and American foreign policy. Klaus Kinkel, the German Foreign Minister in August 1992, called for a tribunal to prosecute the Serbs for genocide. This followed the outbreak of fighting in Slavonia (a largely Serb populated part of Croatia) between Croat forces and the Yugoslav Peoples' Army (JNA), which was even at that time predominantly officered by Serbs. When the Tribunal's first president, Antonio Casese, was nominated, he referred to Kinkel as 'the father of the Tribunal'.[8] The idea of a Yugoslav tribunal had received essential support in 1993, after the United States government first became involved in the Yugoslav civil war. Casese's successor, Gabrielle Kirk McDonald, described Madeline Albright, President Clinton's Secretary of State, as the 'mother of the Tribunal' commenting that 'she had worked with unceasing resolve to establish the Tribunal' with the Serbs as its main quarry.[9] Mrs Albright had instructed Michael Scharf to draft the Tribunal's statute. At the time it was given a low profile. In commenting on it later Scharf wrote in the *Washington Post* that the Tribunal was 'widely perceived within government as little more than a public relations device … and useful policy tool …. Indictments would serve to isolate offending leaders diplomatically and fortify the international political will to employ sanctions or use force'.[10]

The Tribunal has no connection with the International Court of Justice, set up by the United Nations, or with the International Criminal Court, which is not recognised by the United States, at least for its own citizens. Milosevic again and again in his trial has insisted on the fact that the Tribunal has no legal basis under the UN Charter. He has some justification. The UN Security Council did set up the Tribunal, but under Chapter Seven of the Charter, which grants the Council power to 'take measures' and 'establish subsidiary bodies' in the interest of maintaining 'peace and security' (some would question that !). Under its statute the Tribunal's expenses were supposed to come out of the UN budget, but in fact it has depended on US and other governments' funding, on donations from George Soros and other private donors, with equipment and staff seconded by NATO members. Some $3 million came from the US in 1994-5 when the US was failing to meet its financial obligations to the UN.[11] Gilbert Guillaume, President of the International Court of Justice complained to the UN General Assembly in October 2000 that the Tribunal got ten times more money than his court and suggested that this was because 'various parties create new forums that will be more amenable to their arguments.'[12] 'Kangaroo courts' he might have called them.

In the court Milosevic stands alone with his guard behind him. He has no counsel, just his two *amici*, who ask questions to clarify points in the prosecution's case. One at least does not seem to be such a good friend. Milosevic had to complain (ICTY, page 10317) that the *amicus* Mr Wladimiroff had written an article in a Bulgarian journal *Kultura*, stating that if Milosevic was not caught on one count he would be convicted on others 'like any animal pursued in a hunt for game', as he rather crudely put it. Milosevic has insisted on defending himself. At one stage he was pressed to accept as his defence counsel Ramsay Clark, an ex-US Attorney General, who had been an outspoken critic of US actions in Yugoslavia. Milosevic would not have him, perhaps wisely.[13] For Clark, while calling Milosevic a 'war criminal', has stated that he was acting for him, which appears not to be the case. Milosevic has rather limited resources. He has a lawyer at the Hague to discuss each day's business with. He has the not always reliable use of a telephone in his prison to communicate with a back up team – some of the team in Canada, most in Yugoslavia – who inform him and his lawyer of the background of each of the prosecution witnesses, whose written statements have been made available to him in advance of their hearing. He has often had to complain that witnesses appeared in the wrong order, that there were too many 'protected' (i.e. *incognito*) witnesses and that the judge persistently interrupts him and does not give him as long for cross-examination as the prosecutor had been allowed for examination.

In fact, Milosevic was not indicted until 1999, just at the moment when NATO moved from its more limited attacks on Yugoslav forces in Kosovo to an all out bombardment of Serbia proper. This delay was not surprising because Milosevic had been called upon in 1995 by the United States' negotiators to underwrite the Dayton Accords, which ended the fighting in Bosnia. At first, the Milosevic indictment was concerned only with crimes against humanity and violations of the laws or customs of war in Kosovo. But when it became clear after 2001 that not half a million but only 3000 had been killed on both sides in Kosovo and that Al Qaeda had close links with the Kosova Liberation Army, Carla del Ponte, the Prosecutor, decided to add to the indictment similar charges in Croatia and the more serious charge of genocide in Bosnia.[14] She was the third prosecutor to be appointed and was said to show an almost embarrassing enthusiasm for what she called 'hunting down criminals' of the Bosnian war. It turned out that most of these were Serbs. Ms. Del Ponte's view was that Croats could be excused indictment because 'their own courts could deal with such matters'[15]

One indictment has not been considered, although a lengthy and carefully argued case was presented to the Tribunal by Canadian law professor Michael Mandel and a group of American lawyers, and that is an indictment of NATO for the bombing of Serbia in 1999 without UN authorisation. In a 2000 report reviewing the NATO bombing campaign Ms del Ponte concluded that 'NATO and NATO countries' press statements are generally reliable and that explanations have been honestly given'.[16] That egregious spin doctor Jamie Shea at a NATO press conference on May 17, 1999 said that he had no worries about prosecution. The prosecutor will start her investigation, 'because we will allow her to' and 'when she looks at the facts, she will be indicting people of Yugoslav nationality, and I don't anticipate any others at this stage.'[17] Charles Trueheart in the *Washington Post* quoted NATO officials saying that 'they had been assured by Ms Del Ponte that she would not carry that exercise far'.[18] And she didn't.

Only One Side Charged – Why mainly Serbs, not Croats or Muslims?
A few leading Croats and Muslims as well as the many Serbs have been indicted for war crimes and brought for trial to the Hague – a small number considering that there were many examples of actions by Croat forces in Gospic, Eastern Slavonia and the Krajina and by Muslim forces around Srebrenica, which would seem to be just as indictable as anything the Serbs were accountable for – in terms of sheer numbers being made to suffer, perhaps more indictable. A visitor to the Tribunal or anyone reading the transcripts of the trials is bound to ask why the difference. Fortunately for the Croats their leader Franjo Tudjman died before he could be arraigned as Milosevic's opposite number; and now the Muslim leader Alija Izetbegovic is dead. Milosevic is the great survivor, but for how long? He is an ill man and his trial seems likely to go on for many more months. Perhaps the hope of his prosecutors is that he will die before the Tribunal comes to make its judgement. In the event, despite Milosevic's continued illnesses, it is Judge May who has said that because of ill health, he will himself have to retire in May 2004, before Milosevic makes his final case for the defence.

Where leading Croats have been indicted there has been great difficulty in getting the Croatian government to hand over the indicted criminals. Even risking sanctions, the government refused to hand over General Janko Bobetko, but the general died before sanctions had to be imposed.[19] The most senior Croat still wanted in 2003 for war crimes in Yugoslavia, General Ante Gotovina, appeared at that time to be the subject of complex negotiations between Carla del Ponte for the Tribunal, the Croatian government, the European Union and the British Government. At issue was Croatia's application for membership

of the European Union, which was being blocked by a British ultimatum that
Gotovina be handed over to the Tribunal. The Croatian Prime Minister Ivica
Tucan, a Social Democrat and former Communist, was lobbying Tony Blair
at the end of September 2003 to take a softer line. Gotovina had been on the
run since 2001,when he was tipped off that he would be indicted. The Croats
maintained that he was no longer in Croatia.[20] But no one will be lobbying for
the Serbs.

The case of Gotovina is regrettably typical of some Croatian military leaders. His career was summarised in a full-page article in Le Monde.[21] From the
French Foreign Legion he became involved with a band of ultra right wing
thugs and criminals operating on the French Riviera around Nice and Aix-en-
Provence who sometimes serve as bodyguards for Jean-Marie Le Pen. In 1986
he was sentenced in Paris to five years for a jewel robbery but got out the next
year. After that his frequent trips to South America were believed by the French
police to be related to drug trafficking. He is understood by French Internal
Security now to carry a French passport and to have found refuge in south-
east France thanks to the network of earlier contacts from the French Foreign
Legion and from the extreme right in that region. It is unlikely that the ICTY
prosecution will push too hard for his appearance before the Tribunal because
he would not hesitate to tell the court that his 'Operation Storm' to drive the
Serbs out of the Krajina had the support of the United States.

It is more than lobbying and protection like this that the Croats enjoy.
According to Diana Johnstone they have at their service the most effective
public relations operated in the USA by Ruder Finn Global Public Affairs.[22]
When thousands of Serbs were forced to flee from Croatia over the Sava river
in May 1994, with many women and children failing to make it, British and
French representatives on the UN Security Council pressed for sanctions to be
applied to Croatia as well as those already applied to Serbia. This was repeatedly blocked by Mrs Albright, then the US representative at the UN – a point
emphasised by Milosevic in his defence (ICTY p. 10236). Ruder Finn's chief
Balkan operator claimed that his proudest moment was winning over Jewish
opinion in the US with his stories in 1992 of 'ethnic cleansing' by the Serbs in
Bosnia and of Serb operated 'death camps' – just like the Nazis.[23]

In the autumn of that year the International Red Cross reported 2,692 civilians held in temporary detention centres in Bosnia – 1,203 held in eight camps
by Bosnian Serbs, 1,061 by Muslim forces in 12 camps and 428 held by Croats
in 5 camps.[24] The 'mistake' which the Bosnian Serbs made, led by Radovan
Karadzic, was to invite the world press to visit the Serb run camps, and take
photographs. For Ruder Finn could then use these, including the famous picture of the 'thin man behind the barbed wire' at Omarska. It only became clear
later that this man and those with him were in fact outside the barbed wire,
but the photograph could be used to suggest to the world that the Serbs ran

camps like Nazi concentration camps.[25] All along, the Yugoslav wars have been as much propaganda wars as military struggles.

That is not to deny that Serb forces committed some terrible acts in Bosnia, which have led to sentences of life imprisonment on some who have been tried in the Tribunal's other courts at the Hague, for example on Dr. Milomir Stakic, the doctor at Omarska.[26] What is unacceptable is that these sentences should be passed on the decision of two out of three judges with no jury, and frequently on the basis of evidence much of which is hearsay. It is only right, moreover, that this should be set in the context of reports of similar horrors which have been perpetrated on the other side. Milosevic is adept at pointing this out. When he was questioning a witness from the Bosnian Association of Detainees who claimed that 200,000 non-Serbs had been held in Serb camps (ICTY p. 17429), he discovered from her that she herself had been held in a Croatian run camp.

Milosevic shows himself to be a smart and indefatigable lawyer, despite his ill health which has occasionally interrupted the trial proceedings for a number of weeks at a time. The techniques he adopts for cross-examination have been to discredit the good faith of the more important non-Yugoslav witnesses, to quote other western sources expressing alternative views and to question the veracity of local Albanian, Croat and Bosnian Muslim witnesses. Thus, he was at pains to expose the previous associations of Ambassador Walker, who revealed the so-called 'massacre' at Racak, which became the pretext for the NATO bombing of Yugoslavia: Walker's connection with the Nicaraguan 'contras', his friendship with Madeline Albright and honorary membership of a US-Albanian Friendship Society. Milosevic, further, drew attention to the connections with British intelligence of Paddy Ashdown who gave evidence of 'disproportionate' Serb military responses to KLA actions (p. 2318). He questioned the close relationship of one of the peace negotiators at the Rambouilet conference on Kosovo in 1999, Ambassador Vollebaek, with Javier Solana, at that time NATO's Director General (p. 7239) . He could also point to the pro-Albanian bias in a book written by Ambassador Petritsch, the chief negotiator at Rambouillet (p. 7297).

Milosevic opened his defence against the charges relating to Croatia and Bosnia-Hercegovina with a whole series of quotations from Western sources, exonerating him and accusing Croat and Muslim authorities of blocking a peaceful settlement, carrying out deportations of Serb populations and burning of their villages: acts as bad as anything of which the Serbs are accused. To answer the charge that the Serbs started it all, Milosevic was able to quote Cyrus Vance and David Owen, the chief UN negotiators in Bosnia: the first saying that it was 'premature German recognition of Slovenia and Croatia [by Europe and America] that led to the war'; the second saying that the 'United States … is responsible for the prolonged war in Bosnia' (pp. 10273-4). Thorwald

Stoltenberg, the other chief UN negotiator in Bosnia, is quoted as saying on December 12 1995 that 'President Slobodan Milosevic had played a key role in the peace process in Yugoslavia', the Serb side having in turn accepted all five peace proposals, which the others turned down. (p. 10312)

In the matter of the expulsion of rival populations, Milosevic was able to quote Lord Carrington giving a figure of '600,000 Serbs expelled from their territories in the then administered non-state borders of the republic of Croatia'. (p. 10254) In the expulsion from Krajina of 200,000 Serbs by Croat forces in 'Operation Storm' of July 1995, thousands of whom died en route, US General Charles Boyd, deputy commander of NATO, was quoted by Milosevic, confirming that the US helped to plan and implement the attack (p. 10241) and that 'what the Croatians called the "occupied territories" is land that has been held by Serbs for more than three centuries' (p. 10256).

When it came to comparing massacres on either side, Milosevic could give examples of the slaughter by Muslim forces of the Serb population of Bratunac on January 16 1992, just three days after a peace plan had been agreed in Geneva. Milosevic was also able to quote the International Red Cross denying the huge numbers of executions of Muslims claimed to have taken place at the hands of Serb forces in Srebrenica. The history books now say 7000 or 8000 died, but the International Red Cross reported that many thousands turned up alive in Tuzla and Sarajevo (p. 10260); and the Dutch blue helmets report said that 'there is no indication that action was taken in collaboration with Belgrade' (p. 10390). Zoran Ilic, Milosevic's predecessor as President of Yugoslavia, confirmed in his evidence at the Tribunal Milosevic's claim to have tried to dissuade the Serb commander Ratko Mladic from entering Srebrenica, which had been, although supposedly a safe haven, a Muslim base for raids on surrounding Serb villages. (p. 22611) Ilic added that Milosevic was outraged at the massacre, but Ilic went on to say that he was surprised when Milosevic apparently supported the training of Serbian paramilitaries in Bosnia shortly before the Dayton Accords, as Bosnian Serbs were falling back in the face of US armed Muslim and Croat forces.

Milosevic then drew a rather telling conclusion from all the evidence being brought to bear:

> The victims and casualties of the war against Yugoslavia were the innocent people from all three nations, all three ethnic groups. They were pushed into these conflicts because of foreign interests, other peoples' interests, but along with the full cooperation of their mindless leaders who led them to their deaths.' (p. 19279)

If this conclusion is correct, and I believe that it is, then two questions have to be asked: first, why the international community, that is to say the leaders of the United States and the European Union, ganged up against Milosevic and the Serbs; and, secondly, why world opinion went along with them. The answer to the first question will only become clear from an understanding of the whole story, revealed later in this book, of the rivalry of the United States, Germany, France and Russia for hegemonic power in Europe. The second question can only be answered by asking why journalists and others on the spot almost unanimously took the side of the Croats and Muslims and later the Kosovars against the Serbs. One reason has already been suggested, that most journalists and other foreign correspondents would arrive in Yugoslavia with no previous knowledge of the country, would be looking for a good story and would listen to whoever had the most effective public relations, and this would always be the Croats with the backing of the United States and Germany.

In Sarajevo, moreover, Muslim forces, when they occupied nearby Ilidza, drove the journalists out of the first hotel they were based in there. When the journalists were not in Zagreb, they settled in the Holiday Inn, situated in the central Muslim part of Sarajevo, under bombardment by Serb guns. The Muslims became the poor victims, and were not above firing on their own people and blaming the Serbs in order to win world support. On top of this, the story of Sarajevo as a multicultural city, which it had once been, was given heroic status, like the republican forces in the Spanish civil war. The Serbs were portrayed by influential writers like David Rieff in his book, *Slaughterhouse* and by his mother Susan Sontag,[27] as seeking to destroy the city's multicultural nature. In fact, Sarajevo's famous newspaper, *Oslobodzenja,* continued to refuse to take sides. The true situation can only be understood by looking at the whole history of Former Yugoslavia, which requires a whole book to attempt. A brief summary will be given here.

German and American Interests

Milosevic, in his summing up of the civil war quoted above, blamed 'foreign interests, other peoples' interests' for pushing the Yugoslav peoples into war; and we have seen that two of the chief UN peace negotiators, Cyrus Vance and David Owen, took the same view. We have to ask why they should have done that and why in particular the Americans and the Germans should have taken against the Serbs so strongly in a civil war in Yugoslavia – the Germans supporting the Croats and the Americans the Muslims. We have already noticed Klaus Kinkel calling for a tribunal to prosecute Serbs for their crimes. Kinkel had followed Hans-Dietrich Genscher as Germany's Foreign Minister, as a Free Democrat partner in Chancellor Kohl's government. The US negotiator for the UN in Bosnia Cyrus Vance referred to the Bosnian war as "Genscher's war". Klaus Kinkel is reported by his biographer as having said only a week after taking office in May of 1992, 'We must force Serbia to its knees'.[28] In the 1980s Kinkel had been head of the German intelligence service (the BND), which had long standing links with the diaspora of the Croat Ustashe, who had fought on the side of the Germans in the Second World War.

Germany was the chief instigator of European recognition of the independence of Slovenia and Croatia from the former Yugoslavia, when Chancellor Kohl persuaded Britain's Prime Minister, John Major, to fall into line, offering Britain in exchange exemption from the Maastricht Treaty social clauses and from adoption of the Euro. Announcing the reunification of Germany, Chancellor Kohl, as Diana Johnstone reports, had made a solemn promise:

'With its national unity restored, our country will serve peace in the world. In the future Germany will send only peace into the world. We are well aware that the inviolability of borders and the respect for the territorial integrity and the sovereignty of all states in Europe is a basic condition for peace.' 'But', he added, 'at the same time, we stand by the moral and legal obligations resulting from history.'[29]

Recognition of Croatia made Serbia an aggressor, and justified German arms being supplied in defence of Croatia's territorial integrity, while the 'obligations resulting from history' permitted sending German troops outside Germany to take part in the policing of Bosnia and arms to the 'Liberation Army' in Kosovo.

Chancellor Kohl's government was replaced in 1998 by a Social Democratic-Green coalition. What was their interest in destabilising Serbia? The same restraints on German military actions outside Germany remained, and were even strengthened by the pacifist convictions of many German 'Greens'. Their leader, Joschka Fisher, who became Germany's Foreign Secretary, had to retain the support of his less pragmatic, less 'realist' Green comrades. It was the peace movement in Germany, especially among the young after 1968, that made it possible for Europe to accept German reunification in 1990. It was Joschka Fisher's pacifist associations, despite his street-fighting past, that made possible the bridging of the dilemma for Germany between sending 'only peace in the world' and the 'obligations of German history'. Thus, in Diana Johnstone's view, were laid the foundations for what came to be called 'humanitarian intervention'.[30]

The concept of 'humanitarian intervention', which became the chief justification used by apologists for America's wars – those like Michael Ignatieff in *Warriors' Honour*[31] and Mary Kaldor in 'One Year After Dayton', *Dayton Continued*[32] – had a somewhat earlier history, according to Diana Johnstone. It went back to a 1992 study by the Carnegie Foundation under the presidency of Morton Abramowitz, who became an advisor to the Kosovo Albanian delegation at the Rambouillet peace conference in 1999 and champion of the Kosovo Liberation Army. His group of specialists in the early 1990s included US Secretary of State, Madeline Albright and US Ambassador Richard Holbrooke, the US negotiator with Milosevic over the Kosovo question.[33]

Diana Johnstone regards this group not so much as a conspiracy but rather as a small elite group who took it upon themselves to decide how the immense power of the USA was to be used. Madeline Albright is said to have asked Colin Powell, when he was chief of the US military staff, 'What was the use of having this wonderful army you are always boasting about if we never use it?'[34] The fact was that the military industrial complex of the USA needed the army to be used to sustain demand for their products. Their factories and their investments were the dynamo of the American economy. But why Yugoslavia when there are so many other places where the United States could, and did, deploy its armed forces?

One answer was given by Susan Woodward in her 1995 book *Balkan Tragedy*,[35] and has been endorsed subsequently by Peter Gowan in a 1999 pamphlet, *The Twisted Road to Kosovo*.[36] It goes like this. The collapse of the Soviet Union not only left NATO and its large US component without an obvious purpose, but left the whole of Europe open to the major Western European powers to unite and extend their influence eastwards, without the need for American support. Such a development would not at all have been in the interest of the United States, which proceeded to do all in its power to prevent it. NATO had to become an instrument for subordinating European ambitions to American interests. The combined European military force – Eurocorps – proposed in 1991 by the German and French governments, had to be brought under NATO and therefore under US command. Expansion eastwards had to take place as part of NATO in a 'Partnership for Peace' and should be extended to the Ukraine. Russia under Yeltsin was to be attracted into an American, not a European, economic and political embrace.

All these moves needed to be hardened up to serve American interests, so the argument continues. Germany after the two halves were re-united was a powerful force, conscious of what Chancellor Kohl had called 'the moral and legal obligations of history'. The German commitment to humanitarian intervention, then, was both economic and political. The Social Democrat Chancellor Schroeder, when he came to Kosovo to visit German troops at the end of NATO's war against Yugoslavia, was, he said, 'deeply moved in the context of German history in this region'[37] Since some of the Kosovars greeted him with the Nazi salute, Diana Johnstone wondered whether he was suffering from embarrassment, ignorance or amnesia. For some of those saluting will almost certainly have been sons or relatives, or even surviving members, of the SS Skanderbeg division recruited into Hitler's army, which had been responsible for mass murders of Serbs in Kosovo during the German occupation in 1941-5. There was no doubt, however, that Schroeder was taking seriously those 'obligations of history'.

What then are the 'obligations of German history'? They have to be concerned with the historic role of Germans, which include Austrians, in the defence of Europe, as their inheritance from the Holy Roman Empire. It has as ever to embrace the whole of Catholic Europe, including Franco-German solidarity, Poles, Slovaks and Hungarians, and of course Slovenes and Croats. But it stops at Russia and Serbia at the line drawn in AD 395 down the middle of modern Bosnia which divided the Western (Catholic) Empire from the Eastern (Orthodox) Empire. East of that line and south of the Danube are barbarians. The Greeks have to be allowed in, but this historic division between East and West, more than any anxiety about human rights appears to be what keeps Serbs, and the Turks, out of the European Union.

The big question in 1991 for the future of Yugoslavia concerned the response of the United States to this new greater Germany. While German involvement in the dissolution of Yugoslavia was evidently enthusiastic from the start, American involvement was at first hesitant. The US ambassador at Belgrade, Warren Zimmerman, had made it clear in January 1991 that Yugoslavia, having lost its special status as a bastion against the Soviet Bloc,[38] President Milosevic could not expect any support for the use of force to disarm the Croat paramilitary forces so as to stop Croatia's secession from the federation. Thereafter the Americans seemed at first disposed to let Europe settle the Yugoslav question with the aid of the United Nations. But when fighting spread to Bosnia the US ambassador encouraged the Muslims in March 1992 to renege on a UN peace plan, which had been negotiated for a tripartite solution within Yugoslavia, and to hold out for a unitary independent Bosnian state under Muslim leadership.[39] This new state would then have US support politically and militarily. Subsequent peace plans were all accepted by Milosevic, but not by the Croats or the Muslims.[40] Had they been accepted, the horrors of the Bosnian war in 1993 and 1994 would have been avoided, but from the American point of view Germany and the European Union would have got the benefit of major influence in the region.

US influence in Yugoslavia was certainly greatly strengthened under the Clinton Presidency with the encouragement by the US of a Muslim-Croat federation to offset the Serbs in Bosnia-Hercegovina, followed by American armed support for a Croatian military action to drive all Serbs out of the Krajina in north-western Bosnia. What changed US policy, according to Diana Johnstone, was that support for Bosnia's Muslim population and for the claim of the nationalist Bosnian Muslim leader Alija Izetbegovic for a Bosnian unitary state would serve to persuade Arab Islamic opinion in the Middle East that the USA did not only support Jews.[41] The Gulf War had only recently been 'won' and US forces were firmly, if not so popularly, established on land in Saudi Arabia as well as in Kuwait and in the air above the no-fly zones to the north and south of Iraq. It was also hoped that it would help to cement the US alliance with Turkey. The newly elected US President Clinton delivered himself of a remarkable interpretation of world history to the effect that 'the Serbs had already started two world wars and should be prevented from starting a third'.[42]

Susan Woodward and Peter Gowan would argue that the aim of establishing American supremacy over the expanding European Union was more important. In any case, the fact was that by the mid-1990s the US military-industrial establishment was moving towards the view that the United Nations was an obstacle to the extension of US military interventions through NATO, where these were required to maintain the new US military's declared policy of 'full spectrum world dominance'.[43] UN support had been won for the Gulf War because Saddam Hussein had manifestly aggressed against Kuwait. It might not always be so easy another time – as was proved in 2003 over war in Iraq. The UN's 'failure' in Yugoslavia could be used to demonstrate the absolute necessity for US action through NATO, which had to be beefed up to contain German ambitions after the collapse of the Soviet Union. Hence the involvement of the USA in the 1995 Dayton Accords, which ended the Bosnian war with the creation of a new state of Bosnia-Hercegovina shorn of the bits that Croatia annexed. These Accords were supposedly accepted by the Bosnian Serbs because of the entry of US planes to bomb the Serbian army HQ at Pale, but were perhaps more realistically explained by the invitation to the Yugoslav president Milosevic to underwrite the peace settlement. For this meant the ending of the damaging sanctions imposed on Serbia and the recognition of what was left of Former Yugoslavia.

Summing Up the Case Against Milosevic

It is impossible to come away from listening in to the Tribunal proceedings or reading the transcripts of the stories of hundreds of Bosnian Muslim and Albanian Kosovan witnesses without being convinced that terrible acts were performed in Bosnia by the Serbian armed forces, especially after the USA declared its support for the Muslims and Croats, and in Kosovo, especially after the NATO bombing began. Milosevic was able to make a good case for reprisals against the terrorist tactics of the Kosovo Liberation Army (KLA) before the NATO bombing, but once the bombing began he could not conceal the fact that the Serbs in Kosovo as in Bosnia responded to outside intervention with utter ruthlessness. It is not at all clear, however, that Milosevic was responsible or approved of these actions. Nor is there any evidence according to impartial investigators that the number of refugees or cases of rape were anywhere near the numbers reported, or that one should believe the wilder claims that acts of barbarism were committed. In cases cited of so-called Serb barbarity, Milosevic was able to show that decapitation of bodies and gouging out of eyes were the result of multiple bullet wounds to the neck after shoot-outs and of dogs and birds scavenging among the corpses.

Milosevic was particularly sharp in cross-examining poor Albanian peasants who had been brought as witnesses to the Tribunal. They certainly appeared to have been put up to tell their stories, often obvious falsehoods. They were made to contradict themselves and to tell contrary stories and were asked by Milosevic again and again whether some incident had been seen by them personally or was something they had heard about from others. On several occasions the judges had to intervene to complain of hearsay evidence being presented to the court (e.g. p. 7384). What was abundantly clear was the hatred which these peasants expressed for the Serbs, but this had been inflamed by media excuses for outside support given to Albanian separatism. They had suffered in a war because they became involved in an armed revolt backed by outside forces.

The feelings of the Serbs towards the Germans and Americans who had intervened in their country are more difficult to define. Hundreds of thousands of Serb families are still refugees from their homes in Bosnia or Kosovo but this is not necessarily blamed on outside forces, however much this would be justified. A certain apathetic hopelessness has descended – in strong contrast to the firm wish to put the past behind them and start building a new future which was the prevailing sense in 1945. Milosevic undoubtedly blames outside intervention for the worst horrors of the 1990s in his country. Milosevic's sharpest gibes were directed at one of the Prosecution's witnesses, the NATO chief of staff, General Klaus Naumann, concerning the political stance of the German government of Kohl and Genscher. It is impossible to read the transcript of the exchanges between Milosevic and Naumann without recognising Milosevic's ill-concealed hatred of the man.

This led at one point in Naumann's deposition to an extraordinary story, which he related as evidence of Milosevic's supposedly genocidal intentions in Kosovo. (p. 6991) As Naumann reported the occasion, he and General Wesley Clark were discussing with Milosevic the increasingly unbalanced populations in Kosovo as a result of the higher birth rate of Albanians compared with Serbs. Milosevic was said to have hinted at a possible 'solution'. This was that 'we could do what we did at Drenica in '45 and '46.' And on being asked what that was, the answer apparently came, 'We got them together and shot them'.

On the face of it this was a truly dreadful remark, which deeply shocked Naumann and Clark. When Milosevic came to defend himself in cross examination with Naumann, he asked whether Naumann knew who these people were whom they rounded up at Drenica, and explained that they were marauding bands which had been recruited by the German army occupying Yugoslavia to do the dirty work of 'cleaning up' villages that were harbouring Partisans (p. 7039). They were in fact rather more than that. They were what was left of the Albanians in the German army SS division, the Skanderbeg division. It was an utterly unacceptable suggestion from Milosevic as any sort of 'solution' for an imbalance in population, but it has to be understood in the light of the feelings about German generals that a patriotic Serb whose family had been active

Partisans was bound to have.

This is not to say that one approves or condones such wartime atrocities, but it is not adequate evidence to convict Milosevic of war crimes that a Serb with strong Partisan connections such as Milosevic can hardly forget when talking to a German general about wars in Yugoslavia in the 1990s that 50 years earlier several hundred thousand Serbs with Muslims, Jews and Romas were massacred by Croatian Ustashe allies of the German and Austrian forces, supervised in one notorious case by the man who became an Austrian President and General Secretary of the United Nations, Kurt Waldheim. On April 9 1945 I was myself shown mass graves in Sarajevo of those who had been executed by the Germans as they retreated from the city four days before. The Serbs were perfectly capable of retaliating. The miracle was that Tito's Partisans successfully united the overwhelming majority of the Yugoslav peoples, and this success story will form the heart of this book. Those who collaborated with the Germans escaped to form the diaspora with which Klaus Kinkel was working and which has been providing arms and propaganda for the new Croatian government, a government which once more flies the red and black checker board flag of the Ustashe that went into battle alongside the Nazi swastika against the Partisans in Yugoslavia.

One can hardly suppose that the judges at the Tribunal will take into account past sufferings of Serbs at the hands of the Germans and their allies in the Second World War, but they cannot avoid being influenced by the barrage of anti-Serb propaganda which preceded the trial of Milosevic and his fellow Serbians and which has not been stilled during its progress. This starts with the statement of charges. Quite different words are used in speaking of alleged crimes carried out by Serbs to those applied to Croats and Muslims. Only Serbs are said to have been involved in 'genocide'; the others committed 'war crimes'. Leading German government ministers have descended to racist language in speaking and writing about the Serbs as 'barbarians'. Milosevic is frequently likened to Hitler and the necessity of ending the Nazi regime cited as justification for bombing Yugoslavia.

The charge of genocide which is made against Milosevic and his associates requires that the prosecution proves a prior 'genocidal intent' in a 'joint criminal enterprise' to destroy an ethnic group in whole or in part. Much of the prosecution has therefore been concerned with Milosevic's reported statements and with the direct connection between Milosevic as President of Yugoslavia and the army officers and paramilitary forces under his ultimate command. The case against Milosevic is that he openly advocated a single state for all Serbs, that as ultimate commander of the Yugoslav National Army (JNA) and police force (MUP), he retired senior officers who disagreed with him and replaced them with his friends, that he authorised the transfer of JNA arms and units to Serbian forces in Bosnia and to Serbian para-military groups, that he encouraged the criminal activities of these groups such as Arkan's 'red berets' and of so-called Serbian 'crisis staff' in driving non Serbs out of their homes and villages in Bosnia-Hercegovina, that he knew about and did not stop maltreatment including murder of prisoners taken into Serbian concentration camps – all with the assumed aim of creating a wholly Serbian occupied territory in Bosnia-Hecegovina which could be annexed to Serbia proper in a new Yugoslavia.

Milosevic's case has been that all Serbs in one state did not exclude other ethnic groups living in that state, as could be seen from the large numbers already living inside Serbia – of Hungarians in Voyvodina and Muslims in the Sandjak (southern Serbia) to which many Muslims from Bosnia had fled; that the agreement reached between himself and Franjo Tudjman in 1991 for dividing up Bosnia-Hercegovina between Serbia and Croatia was designed to avoid war rather than to ignite it, and would indeed have averted war had it not been for the intervention of outside forces, mainly German and American, with their own agendas; that the retirement and replacement of JNA officers was a normal military process; that JNA arms were taken over by each of the Republics' Territorial Forces and the JNA was demobilised by Milosevic in May of 1992; that Milosevic repeatedly intervened in Bosnia to encourage Serbian forces to respect the laws of war (p. 20233) and to discourage para-military activity (p. 20244) and was frequently criticised by Bosnian Serb nationalists and by Serb nationalists in Serbia for not giving adequate support to the Serbs in Bosnia and Croatia.

It is extremely unsatisfactory in a court of law, as the ICTY purports to be, that so much verbal evidence is taken, much of it based on hearsay with very little documentary evidence to back it up. It has been particularly unsatisfactory that in the cases relating to Croatia and Bosnia many witnesses for the prosecution have been heard and not seen in court, their identity being concealed and being referred to by a letter and a number. This has been the case with many of the Yugoslav officials and police and army officers who have been permitted to give their evidence incognito. Arguing the case for the defence in these circumstances becomes very difficult for Milosevic. It is also unsatisfactory that evidence is sometimes presented in the form of intercepted phone calls, where the identity of the speaker has to be assumed to be what the prosecutor says it is and the circumstances likewise. An example of this occurs when a voice which we are told is that of the indicted Bosnian Serb leader, Radovan Karadzic, appears to threaten that 'Sarajevo will be gone and 200,000 Muslims killed'. (p. 15921)

Milosevic's case received some support from David Owen's statements in his book *Balkan Odyssey* that Milosevic did indeed support the various peace initiatives in Bosnia, but 'did not do enough', Owen says, despite being under the pressure of UN economic sanctions.[44] His case also received support from Zoran Ilic, one time President of the Serbian Party of Socialists (ex-Communists) and President of Yugoslavia after Milosevic's defeat in 2000. Ilic asserted that Milosevic was not responsible for the crime at Srebrenica, which remains the chief element in his indictment. Ilic insisted that Milosevic indeed sought to prevent the massacre (p. 22611). It may be said that this was just a Serb supporting a Serb, but since he followed Milosevic as president one would expect that Ilic would be anxious to distance himself, rather than give support.

Milosevic did not, by contrast, get support from Ante Markovic, a Croat and the last Prime Minister of Former Yugoslavia, who accused him of using the JNA to prevent by force the dissolution of Yugoslavia and of misappropriating funds to that end. (pp. 28000 ff.) Milosevic would not deny the accusation of using force to defend Yugoslavia. To do so was the duty of the JNA, which, Milosevic pointed out, was not dominated by Serbs at the top. (p. 10219) The army chief Kadijevic was half Croatian, half Serb, the air force chief Jurijevic was Croatian and the commander of the navy Brovec was a Slovene. Although in the end Serbs predominated in the JNA, Milosevic was right to point to the tradition in Tito's Yugoslavia of balancing ethnic backgrounds in official appointments. In any case Markovic's accusations about the use of the JNA were rebutted by Borisav Jovic, who was a rotating Yugoslav President when the civil war broke out, and who made it clear that as President of Serbia at that time, and not yet President of Yugoslavia, Milosevic had no control over the JNA.

The most damaging case against Milosevic made by Ante Markovic was that, while he did not regard Milosevic as a nationalist – rather, more interested in his own personal power (page 28042) – he did believe that Milosevic's aim was 'quite obvious: he was fighting for a greater Serbia'. However, in reading the transcripts, one has to remember that the prosecution was presenting Markovic's accusations against Milosevic – of giving orders to the army to defend the Krajina Serbs (p. 23037), of taking Serbia's share of Yugoslavia's financial assets for his government (p. 28012) and of ordering partial mobilisation (p. 28064) – as if all these things were done before and not after Croatia moved to secede in June 1991, indeed over a year after the April 1990 elections in Croatia had given Tudjman a nationalist majority in the Croat Parliament determined on independence. Perhaps the most telling revelation in the Serb's favour was Markovic's statement that Tudjman had made it clear to Markovic that the shelling of Dubrovnik and Vukovar by Serb/JNA forces 'suited him [Tudjman] in the sense of winning over arguments for his emancipation or for his secession and having Croatia recognised' (p. 28039). Croatia and Slovenia were recognised by Germany in December 1991 and by the European Union and the USA in April 1992.

Markovic reported to the Tribunal the discussions he had with both Tudjman and Milosevic after their meeting in March 1991 at Karadjordjevo when the two of them agreed to divide up Bosnia-Hercegovina between Croatia and Serbia. (pp. 28026 ff.) Both replied to Markovic's fear that there would be appalling bloodshed if they did that, by saying that they did not expect it. Muslims, they said, whose families had once converted from Catholicism would join the Croats; those who had once converted from Orthodoxy would join the Serbs. Milosevic with greater realism had added that the Muslims would get an autonomous enclave to live in. Markovic said that he had responded to all this by insisting that he would oppose any such move with all the power at his command, which he admitted was by then very little. He had resigned by the end of the year. On being asked whether he had told Izetbegovic, the Muslim leader in Bosnia, of his intention to oppose the division of Bosnia-Hercegovina, Markovic said that he had done so – though not immediately. That was strange because Izetbegovic was then regularly giving Markovic copies of intercepts of messages between Milosevic and Karadzic, the Serb Bosnian leader, concerning the arming of Bosnian Serbs (p. 28029).

The prosecution did not remind the Tribunal of it, but perhaps the judges will recall the fact that by the time Milosevic was helping the Bosnian Serbs to arm, the Croats were receiving massive supplies of arms from Germany and elsewhere.[45] Any justice that might come out of this trial will need to recognise that the tragedy of Yugoslavia cannot be blamed on one man or one side, but must involve condemnation of nationalists on all sides, and above all the complicity of the outside powers who were supporting them. What the trial cannot explain, by its very terms of reference, is how it came about that after nearly sixty years of extraordinarily successful development Tito's Yugoslavia fell apart and ancient divisions between different faiths and nationalities were revived. To understand that, we have to go back at least to the beginning of the Partisans' resistance to German occupation and to the German policy of dividing the Yugoslav peoples in order to conquer them. That understanding and recognition of the subsequent remarkable successes in reconciliation and rehabilitation achieved in Former Yugoslavia is the aim of this book.

Sarajevo, 1946

Chapter 2

Sarajevo, April 1945

I woke up in a strange room, wondering for a moment where I was. The sun was shining through the Venetian blinds of the tall apartment windows. As always I had left a window half open and I felt cold mountain air blowing in. Then I knew with a slight hollowing of my stomach – Sarajevo! I had got there. It was only just after seven. I had some moments to lie in this warm bed before having to get up and shave and dress to go to meet my interpreter and the Partisan liaison officer in the kavana down stairs. I had woken up in so many different beds in the previous weeks – thinking back from this morning, of Jajce, in a street half destroyed by German shelling, of looking out from a hotel above Mostar's lovely mediaeval bridge, of Split's shining bright stones reflecting the blue waters of the Adriatic, the bunk on a boat tossing across from Bari, the villa in San Spirito and the Hotel Imperiale in Bari and AFHQ in Caserta, where we had negotiated for months to get food into starving Dalmatia and Bosnia, back to Cairo and my hut on Maadi Camp and the Yugoslav refugee camps in Egypt at El Shatt and Tolumbat and all those preparations for relief units to go into the Balkans when at length the Germans withdrew. It had been a long haul, but I was actually here in Sarajevo in April 1945, a few days after the German army had left.

I tried practising the phrases of Serbo-Croatian that I might need to introduce myself, to explain the meaning of United Nations Relief and Rehabilitation Administration, which I represented. It had been dark the night before when we arrived in Sarajevo, but some message had got through from the Ministry of Supply, and we were expected. We easily found the house in the main street, still called Ante Pavelicova, after the Ustashe collaborator Premier of Croatia, but generally known as Alexandrova after the former Yugoslav king and soon of course to be named Titova. In Jajce some food supplies had got through the previous week from the Allied Military Liaison, but nothing would have reached Sarajevo. I had no idea when the Bailey bridges over the river Neretva, to replace those blown up by the Germans in their retreat, could be put in place to get food to central Bosnia. In the meantime, I hoped that some supplies could be ferried across the river.

Miraculously, there seemed to be water and electricity and a telephone in Sarajevo. I was told later that these essential services had been protected by the underground resistance in the City. I got up to look out of the window and realised that the trams were running down the centre of the street, and I could hear a newspaper boy calling the name of the new local paper – *oslobodzenje, oslobodzenje!* – liberation, liberation! – a fitting cry in the first week of a Sarajevo without Germans. Suddenly there was a deafening noise outside my window as the loud speakers opened up from Sarajevo radio with patriotic Partisan songs followed by part of the Beethoven symphony that was the Allied call – dudder der dum – and the day's news: the last units of the German army were leaving Bosnia, Soviet troops were outside Berlin, American forces were established in the Ruhr, an Allied Offensive had begun in northern Italy. It was the beginning of the end of four years of war, but what was I going to find had been left behind? From what I had already seen on my way up from the coast, I was expecting something near to famine conditions.

In the kavana I was greeted by our interpreter, a jolly little man, a professor from the Commercial College, whose excellent English made my efforts at Serbo-Croatian redundant. He was not a Communist but a Social Democrat and was soon replaced as our interpreter by others whose commitment to the Partisans had been deeper. I was sorry to see him go. He was an interesting man who had developed an 'interlinguistic language' which, unlike Esperanto, had in its mix Slav as well as German and Latin words. Our liaison officer was an army major, from the Department of Commerce and Supply, an obvious Serb, with a 1941 medal meaning that he had joined the Partisans in the first wave of resistance in Serbia after the German occupation of Yugoslavia. He had no English and appeared very impressed by my effort at greetings in Serbo-Croatian. He had good news: Fifty tons of flour was to arrive from Mostar on April 12 with an officer from Allied Military Liaison. It was planned to deliver it free to the 3,600 neediest people out of 20,000 in the poorest and oldest part of the city. This was Vratnik an entirely Muslim quarter of old houses that clung to the sides of the hills which rise up from the old centre of Sarajevo along the river Miljacka.

A further distribution was to be made to 12,000 people on the city's poor list and those who had lost the family breadwinner to the army or by death. 20,000 essential heavy workers were to be supplied on the railway, repairing the lines which had been torn up by the last German convoy, and those running the trams, electricity and water supply and sewerage which had been saved. It seemed that a Town Committee was up and running – from the Partisan Army and underground resistance movement, which were carrying out plans made well in advance for the day of the town's liberation. I began to think: 50 tons wouldn't go very far in a population of 160,000.

I was making notes of the population figures they were giving me. Sarajevo's pre-war population was 85,000, but this had been nearly doubled by muhadjirs – the Muslim word for refugees – who had crowded into the town and surroundings from villages which had been destroyed in three years of fighting. On liberation 90 tons of maize remained in the warehouses, which had been thrown open for looting as the Germans departed. Some of the looters were shot – to add more deaths to those the Germans had killed, suspected as being from the resistance. We were shown the mass graves of those whom the Germans had disposed of in trenches in the garden of the house which the German chief of police had occupied. Most of the town's records had been destroyed, but the book containing the town's poor list had been preserved, I was told, because its keeper ran out of the town with it on the last days of liberation; and even after liberation, it was said that he took it to bed with him.

Three kilos of flour were to be supplied to each person claiming at the Social Section of the Town Committee and six kilos each to the heavy workers through the cooperatives of the railway and town employees. This was something for 50,000 people until more supplies could be brought up from the coast and brought in from Serbia. There was still the looted maize and about 10,000 well-to-do people were supposed to have stocks to draw on. I was told that the surrounding villages had nothing left from the previous year's harvest and most had been unable to sow for this year. Cattle, sheep and goats had been destroyed. I could see that there was nothing in the market, absolutely no black market and all the shops were closed. Many people were in rags. Perhaps as many as 100,000 people in Sarajevo, 220,000 in the whole district – men, women and children – were in need, and nothing more was expected from the coast or from Serbia until early in May, at least a fortnight hence.

I had a trailer with my jeep filled with jerry cans of petrol – there was no such thing as a petrol station – spare wheels and tyres, tools, bedrolls and a certain amount of food, mostly American K rations, spam, condensed milk, chocolate, tea and biscuits. I gave some packs to our interpreter, offered some to my liaison officer, which he refused, and consulted them about where I could park the trailer. I had left it with the jeep in a garage in the basement of the apartment where I had slept, and I didn't want to drive around with it. The major assured me that nothing would be stolen. Partisan law was ruthless. Theft was punishable by death. After living in liberated Italy this seemed utterly incredible but it proved true. I didn't hear of a case of the death penalty, but stealing was unheard of in liberated Yugoslavia. There were policemen patrolling the streets, but quite few and far between.

Over Turkish style small cups of coffee, which I guessed was made from roasted chickory, I began to hear from my new contacts and others who had gathered around about life in the *suma* (the forest), to which many had fled for the protection of the Partisans, and from which they had just returned. They had been living under the trees, whole families in tents and huts deep in the forest where enemy planes could not spot them, fed on quite meagre army rations with what blankets and warm clothes they could carry. They were a mix of people from several communities and faiths, all of whom had done something to arouse the suspicion of the occupying forces. One Muslim family had adopted a little Jewish girl whose parents had been taken away, presumably to one of the extermination camps. Being able to walk freely and openly in liberated Sarajevo, despite the lack of food supplies, seemed to them to be very heaven.

Annexe to Chapter Two

[Excerpts from the official report of the UNRRA Regional Office, Bosnia and Hercegovina, written up in the Historical Monograph of the Regional Representative of the chief of Mission (MBB) dated April 1947]

The first two [UNRRA] observers for Bosnia and Hercegovina got their passes from JSCML, packed their jeep full of American Army "K" rations and bedrolls, and drove over the mountains to Sinj and on to Livno and Bugojno, and arrived late at night in Jajce temporary capital of Bosnia and Hercegovina. The first contacts were made with the ZAVNOBIH, in particular the Chief of the Department of Commerce and Supply, who was later to be the liaison officer with UNRRA in Sarajevo. It is difficult in writing the history of this period, after the passage of two years, to believe seriously the memories of this trip. To leave Split and drive a jeep from the lovely Dalmatian coast up the hairpin mountain passes into the barren rocky uplands of Bosnia is at any time an experience. In the first days of liberation, when the roads had not been repaired, and bridges were down, when none of the houses had been rebuilt, when Klivno was almost destroyed and Kupres had not one house standing, when the snow was still thick on the roads, when the forests had been untended for years, when no other UNRRA or ML persons had driven out of Split before along this road, when you knew little of the language and less of the sort of reception you might get, when stories were rife of wandering enemy bands of Chetniks and Ustashe, when the roadside was scattered with mines, guns and mined equipment – the journey by jeep was not only an experience, it was high adventure undertaken with great trepidation. But it was made, and friendly contact was established.

Sarajevo was liberated on 5 April. On 9 April the Acting Chief of Mission and SRO for Bosnia and Hercegovina drove over the mountains from Mostar to Sarajevo. The snow was melting but still thick on the roads, and on the pass above Nevesinje the bodies of dead soldiers were revealed by the thaw. Enemy equipment, shell cases, tin helmets, dead horses lined the road. The railway yards outside Sarajevo had been ripped up and torn by Allied bombing and German demolition, but the town itself, set amid the hills, was almost untouched. The electric light, telephones and water mains were all in working order, thanks to their defence by the town's underground Partisans. The trams ran along the broad streets between the pretentious government buildings of Austrian days. The little Muslim houses in the old part of the city climbed up the side of the surrounding hills, between the mosques and minarets and poplar trees. Veils and Partisan caps mingled in the crowded streets of the old Turkish bazaar.[2]

Partisans in Bosnia, 1943

Chapter 3

Yugoslavs in Exile, Egypt, 1943-4

It was really by chance that I went to the Middle East in 1942 and from there via Italy to Yugoslavia. I knew nothing about Yugoslavia when the Friends Ambulance Unit (FAU), which I had joined as a pacifist in 1940, found itself withdrawn from the Western Desert to Cairo after the German army under Rommel had been defeated by Montgomery and pushed back from Alamein in September 1942. I arrived in Cairo shortly after that historic victory. I had been sent out there from London where I had been working in the East End during the worst of the blitz and thereafter in other bombed cities in England. A colleague and I from the FAU Executive Committee had been sent to replace the chairman and vice-chairman who had died when their boat was torpedoed in mid-Atlantic. They were on their way to Cairo to make decisions on what the Unit should do as the war in North Africa ended. At that time we still had to go the long way round to Egypt via South Africa, because the Mediterranean was closed to Allied shipping. Our convoy was also attacked by a U-boat, but our ship was only grazed. We continued down the African coast with a heavy list to starboard, calling at Freetown, Takoradi and Walfish Bay, ending up at Cape Town. There we left the ship and proceeded by rail to Durban and then by flying boat to Cairo. The journey took three months and gave me my abiding interest in Africa. But that is another story.

After Alamein some of the FAU members who were in the Hadfield Spears Hospital Unit had gone on with the Free French Forces along the Mediterranean into Tunisia. Others were formed into a Mobile Military Hospital which followed the British Army up to Benghazi and Tripoli. A most successful unit was a Mobile Blood Transfusion Unit. Cairo remained a base for the FAU and its sponsors in the British Red Cross whose uniform we wore. As the fighting went across the Mediterranean to Sicily and Italy the question arose about the future work for the FAO in the Mediterranean theatre. The Hadfield Spears Unit moved on, but others came back to base. Judging from wartime autobiographies, much of any war seems to consist of waiting around for someone to decide where your unit should go.

Soon after I got to Cairo it had become quite clear what we should do. Greek and Polish refugees had begun to arrive in Palestine expelled from their homes or escaping from war and famine. They were later to be joined by Yugoslavs from the Dalmatian coast and islands, unable to carry on their normal fishing and harvesting and cut off by continuous fighting from inland supplies of grain. This was the result of the Sixth Axis offensive against the Yugoslav Partisan armies to dislodge them from the costal areas which they had occupied after the Italian capitulation in September 1943. The British Military Mission agreed with the Partisan High Command to evacuate to Italy all those who could not fight – wounded, aged, women and children – to hospitals and camps in southern Italy. The numbers were too great for local supply lines to cope with and 1500 were moved to Egypt in November followed by a further 24,000 in the early months of 1944.[2]

The Egyptian authorities were extremely nervous about having large numbers of Communists living among the Egyptian people – they had already had trouble with Greek resistance soldiers in Alexandria. So the Yugoslavs were placed in desert camps on the eastern side of the Suez canal, first at El Shatt and then at Khatatba. The first transit camp outside Alexandria was manned by army civil affairs officers and NCOs who had experience of administering East African camps for Italian POWs. The Yugoslav refugees were something different. They had their own committee organisation based on the districts from which they came and immediately protested at the way they were treated to the point that the camp commandant had to post an order on the staff bulletin board stating, 'henceforth refugees will be treated as if they were human beings'. It seemed a Godsend to the military authorities that there were voluntary society units available with some medical knowledge and military experience, to whom much of the running of the camps could be handed over.

Responsibility for the running of the camps was given by the military to a British civilian organisation under the Minister of State's office in Cairo, called the Middle East Relief and Refugee Administration (MERRA). This had already been involved in receiving and caring for the Greek and Polish refugees arriving in Palestine and for getting food by caiques into Greek islands abandoned by the German forces. It was also responsible for organising food and medical relief to go into Greece and Yugoslavia as soon as the German and other Axis forces withdrew. MERRA's director, Sir William Matthews, a one-time Public Assistance Board Chairman, had already been in touch with voluntary organisations in London with the aim of recruiting staff for such work. Until the time when the Balkans were liberated there would be much advantage in employing such persons in the refugee camps in Egypt. In the meantime there were the FAU members just returned from medical work with the British and French armies who could be assigned to the camps.[3]

I thus found myself, at the beginning of 1944, as the FAU officer in charge of relief work in the Middle East, with two immediate tasks which were engaging MERRA – the manning of the refugee camps in Palestine and Egypt and the recruitment of relief workers for the day of liberation in the Balkans. There were other voluntary organisations involved both in Cairo and in London besides the FAU, in particular the Red Cross and the Save the Children Fund. I became the chairman of the Personnel Committee in Cairo working in MERRA and liaising with the Council in London of the British Societies for Relief Abroad (COBSRA). I had to help with assigning men and women to the staffing of the camps and to work out with MERRA and the military authorities the type of units that were likely to be needed to go into Greece and Yugoslavia as soon as territory was liberated.

The result of my experience of working with the Yugoslav camp committees and of meeting the members of SOE (Special Operations Europe), who had established in 1943 the British Military Mission to the Partisans in Yugoslavia, was to create for me a serious crisis of conscience. I came to realise that I would have fought against the Axis invasion, partly because of the terrible stories of what the occupation forces had done, but chiefly because the Partisans had undermined my standard reply to all those who criticised my pacifist response to evil, which was that killing and all that war entailed would only generate more violence and more authoritarian regimes. Yet here were these camp committees, sub-camp committees, and tent 'street' committees discussing their organisation and reaching decisions in a manner which made our ideas about democracy look feeble indeed – and this was part of the organisation that, far from collapsing in the face of the most powerful military machine in the world, was in process of bringing it to its knees.

It was what I learned from my new friends in SOE, and particularly from James Klugmann, a well-known Communist, then a British army major in Intelligence, that most powerfully affected my thinking. There had been several Communist influences on my life. I was brought up in Oxford where my parents were close friends of the two Gillett families, who were Quakers like my parents, but several of whose children, whom I knew well, became Communists. I went to a Quaker school and at seventeen formally joined the Society of Friends. I seriously considered driving an ambulance in Spain, but continued my studies at Oxford and when I went down joined the Friends

Ambulance Unit. In 1940 I married Frances Lloyd, whose mother had strong Communist sympathies and was a close friend of Naomi Mitchison, sister of JBS Haldane, a well-known Communist scientist. I remained, like my father, a Christian socialist.

In Egypt at our desert camp, we had a political discussion group, which argued about new books that had appeared. One was the Trotskyist James Burnham's *Managerial Revolution*.[4] I was very impressed by his argument that in all previous revolutions in history those who revolted lost out. The slaves who rose against their masters became in turn serfs of their feudal lords. The serfs who rebelled became wage labourers for the capitalists. So now the workers who had overthrown the capitalists in Russia were ruled by a new class of managers. James Klugmann convinced me that it wasn't like that. What he called 'democratic centralism' really was democratic in the Soviet Union and this was also the basis of the Yugoslav Communist Partisans' strength. I had seen this at work in the camp committees and accepted the argument.

I gained an amusing insight into this when I took Col. Gordon Fraser of SOE to the camp at El Shatt together with two colonels of the Yugoslav High Command, Milentije Popovic and Vlado Dedijer (later an active member of the Bertrand Russell Peace Committee tribunals). The FAU staff at the camp had established excellent relations with the camp committees after the FAU had largely taken over responsibility from the British military authorities. They reported, however, that one bone of contention remained. The hygiene officer demanded that all the latrine tents should be kept as much closed as possible to prevent flies from entering and spreading disease. The Yugoslav camp committee asked that they be kept as open as possible to allow fresh air to enter. Answering my query about what to do, the Yugoslav colonels proposed an appeal to authority. Tell them that Mr. Winston Churchill the supreme commander of the British armed forces, who had sent his own son to fight alongside the Partisan armies, had issued an order requiring that all army latrine tents be kept closed except for entry and egress. The proposal was passed on to the camp committee and the FAU hygiene officer made no more complaints.

Life in a desert camp is not easy for anyone unused to the heat and the dust, and for people from the lovely sea-girt rocky coast and islands of Dalmatia it seemed to be a near approach to hell. With no fishing or work on the land and limited supplies of water there were real problems of how to fill in time and get the necessary laundering and cleaning done. The FAU members revealed remarkable capacities and resourcefulness in making use of the refugees' skills in building, woodworking and brick building and in weaving and sewing. More than this they were able to support the talents of folk singers and musicians in regular camp concerts and help others in producing a camp newspaper.

In fact, health conditions in the camps were not good. The Dalmatian islanders were not used to the hot dry environment and many of the children and nursing mothers were suffering from dehydration. It was decided to move them to a camp at Tolumbat, again in the desert but on the Mediterranean coast near to Alexandria. A British army unit which had been serving in Ethiopia was put in charge, with doctors and nurses from the British Red Cross and the Save the Children Fund (SCF). By good fortune the army unit included several officers who were quite sympathetic to the Yugoslav cause. Dr. Eleanor Singer, who later became my wife, was one of the SCF doctors and shared a tent with a local Alexandrine Red Cross nurse, whose relationship to Larry Durrell seemed often to require that the doctor who had a jeep should drive her into Alexandria.[5] Such were the strange associations that the war produced.

During this period James Klugmann had begun to explain to me about the situation in Yugoslavia and particularly the struggle that SOE had had in 1942 to wean Churchill and the British Foreign Office from their support for Mihailovic's Chetniks to support for Tito's Partisans. After the Germans occupied Belgrade in March 1941 Mihailovic had led some Serbian army officers and their followers, who had refused to lay down their arms, to distance themselves from the Germans but to lie low in southern Serbia until the Germans lost the war so as then to re-establish the Royal Yugoslav government, which had fled to London, and of which Mihailovic became Minister for War.[6] This policy of inactivity was the exact opposite to that of the Partisans who had set up a headquarters in Uzice in September of 1941. Such a policy combined with a hatred of Communism led Mihailovic and his Chetniks step by step to oppose the Partisans and by 1942 to begin to collaborate with the Germans and in 1943 to appear on their battle order. SOE knew all this because of the news they had from their officers sent in to Mihailovic and because German signals were being regularly intercepted by British intelligence at Bletchley. This is fully explained in the book *Special Operations Europe* by Basil Davidson, whom I got to know in Cairo and Bari, and who became a life long friend.[7]

It was, however, many months before the British could be persuaded to give Tito support and withhold it from Mihailovic, and then only because of the chance presence of one SOE officer in Cairo. As an historian Bill Deakin had worked with Churchill on his diaries and went personally to tell him what was happening. Deakin was dropped into Partisan held territory early in 1943, and some very limited supplies began to reach the Partisans by parachute in May 1943. It was not until the end of that year, after the Partisans had suffered terrible casualties, that any real help was provided and that was when the British had established a base in Italy and began in November to move wounded and refugees across the Adriatic.[8] Military supplies and liaison officers including Basil Davidson and Churchill's son Randolph could still only be parachuted into Yugoslavia. But that was regarded as a great victory

I once asked Basil Davidson why among those first parachuted into the Partisans there were so many Canadians. The obvious answer was that they were originally from Serbia or Croatia and spoke the language perfectly. But he added something that he said he had never written about and that was about how they were recruited. At SOE in Cairo he and others had remembered that in the Mutual Assistance Agreement signed between the British Government and the Soviet Union in July 1941, just after the Germans launched their attack, there was a clause about the exchange of intelligence. To meet the need for Yugoslav speaking British soldiers with Communist sympathies to go into Yugoslavia, expatriate Canadians of Yugoslav origin might be found, they believed, through Soviet agents in North America. Soviet intelligence was contacted and arrangements were made for Stephan Dedier, Vlado's younger brother, who was in the USA, to meet up with a Soviet agent who had the names and addresses of all Communist Party members in Canada. Stephan was taken in a car boot across the border into Canada to find men of the right age who might be prepared to enlist for military service in this way. There were many who were only too keen, including some who had already signed up for military service. Those selected for their mental and physical fitness were given the necessary training, including parachute jumping, and dispatched to Cairo.

While I had been in Cairo during 1943 and early 1944 the fortunes of war turned. The German armies suffered their first major defeat at Stalingrad in February and at almost the same time the British Eighth Army took Tripoli and moved on to join forces with US armies which had arrived in North Africa. In July the Allies landed in Sicily and within days the Italian fascist government fell. As British and American forces entered Italy, the Italian surrender was announced in September and German armies rushed in to occupy Rome and northern Italy. At the same time in Yugoslavia Axis forces carried out two major offensives – the Fourth and Fifth – against the Partisans, by then a regular army of several divisions holding much of central Bosnia. In extremely bloody fighting supported by unopposed aerial attack these offensives failed and when the Italians capitulated the Partisans were able to race towards the coast to seize the abandoned Italian arms.[9] I was told that when the Italian generals surrendered to the Partisan commanders in Split, they referred to their conquerors as 'signori banditi'. They were in fact three Belgrade University professors.

It was the Germans' Sixth offensive against the Partisan armies in January 1944 that drove them out of Split and the Dalmatian islands and led to the evacuation of refugees and wounded to Italy and Egypt. According to Sir John Rigg, British Minister for War reporting to the House of Commons on January 18, 1944, 'The Partisan army has at one time or another during this period engaged up to 15 German divisions, which might otherwise have been profitably employed elsewhere.'[10] By June of 1944 when the Allied D-day landings began in France, Churchill's tribute to Tito's Partisans was even more emphatic, since by holding these German divisions back in the Balkans they were not able to reinforce the hard-pressed German armies facing the Allied invasion. By this time Tito's Partisans were working in close collaboration with the British army and air force in Italy.

It has become the fashion of some historians to belittle the importance of the Partisans' holding action against what Noel Malcolm, for example, in *Bosnia: a Short History* calls four German divisions 'of low calibre', 'two reserve divisions of trainee recruits and one burnt out division withdrawn from Stalingrad, and a few more brought in ... after the surrender of the Italian forces.'[11] How many more was a few? The figure given by Sir John Rigg in January was fifteen, and in June Churchill informed the House of Commons just before the Allied landings in France that the Partisans' 'guerrilla army of over a quarter of a million men is holding in check fourteen out of the twenty German divisions in the Balkan Peninsula, in addition to six Bulgarian divisions and other satellite forces.'[12]

In my enthusiasm for the Partisans, I salved my conscience by leaving the FAU and proposing to report to the local army recruiting officer. My colleague Cyril Pickard in MERRA persuaded me that such an action would be very harmful to the cause of the relief programme which I was working on for Greece and Yugoslavia. I explained that I had obtained release from military service on condition that I served in the FAU. 'That is no problem,' said the Medical Corps colonel with whom I was planning the types of relief and refugee and hygiene and medical units, which would be needed when the Balkans were liberated. He could vouch for me. That seemed rather too easy a solution but I accepted it, and joined the staff of MERRA, which shortly afterwards was converted into the United Nations Relief and Rehabilitation Administration (UNRRA) Mission for the Balkans.

UNRRA was one of the United Nations' organisations being planned for the post-war world. As early as September 1941 agreement was reached among all the Allied European governments to plan for the relief needs of their countries on the day of liberation, and to this end an Inter-Allied Post War Requirements Bureau was set up in 1942 with technical advisory committees to consider the needs for emergency relief, food, clothing, transport, agricultural and medical supplies and to establish consistent bases for allocating supplies fairly between the several invaded countries. The Bureau had a staff of British civil servants under the direction of Sir Frederick Leith-Ross, and a not-unimportant role was played by the Yugoslav Royal Government representative, Dr. Rudolf Bicanic of Zagreb University. By June of 1943 the advisory committees had produced a Minimum Imports Programme for liberated countries which had the general support of the British Government.

Meanwhile the US Government's Office of Foreign Relief and Rehabilitation Operations (OFRRO) had begun to make similar plans following the US entry into the war in December 1941. Unfortunately, while Dr Bicanic in London had the confidence of Tito and his friends, and returned to Yugoslavia on its liberation, his counterpart in Washington did not. This was Mr. Constantin Fotic, the ambassador of the Royal Yugoslav Government in Washington, who was three years later sentenced *in absentia* by a Belgrade court to fifteen years imprisonment for aiding Yugoslav war criminals to escape to South America. This difference between London and Washington was to cause much subsequent difficulty for the UNRRA Mission in Yugoslavia. It was, moreover, in Washington that UNRRA's headquarters were established and the Bureau became UNRRA's London office.[13]

The declaration of the United Nations was signed on January 1 1942 but the UNRRA Agreement was not signed until November 1943. The first session of the UNRRA Council meeting at Atlantic City laid down the basic principles and procedures of the new organisation. They were designed to avoid the much resented 'conditions of relief' which were exacted after the First World War and found in their worst form as a political weapon against the USSR in the infamous Riga agreement. UNRRA would truly reflect the will of the United Nations. The Council of UNRRA consisting of all the member nations, and the Central Committee of the four big powers (China, UK, USA, USSR) meeting between Council sessions was responsible for directing UNRRA's work and for ensuring that proven needs were met fairly and equitably wherever they existed. New York State's Governor Lehman, director of OFRRO, was made first Director General.

While the principle of equitable distribution was to be applied between and inside receiving nations, responsibility for actual distribution was laid firmly on the shoulders of the Government or recognised national body which exercised authority within a liberated area. It was only necessary for the Director General 'to be kept fully informed concerning the distribution of supplies within any area' (Resolution 7, Para 4). However, in view of the uncertain military and political conditions expected in many parts of Europe immediately after liberation, paragraphs 7 and 8 in Resolution 7 envisaged that the Administration might be called upon by the military authorities or by the Government or national authorities to 'furnish distribution services through its own organisation and personnel' respectively where 'a Government or recognised national authority does not yet exercise administrative authority' and 'because of unusual circumstances.' With two governments claiming legitimacy in Yugoslavia – the Royal Yugoslav Government and Tito's Partisans' National Liberation Council – and with most, but not all, of Yugoslavia under Partisan control, these paragraphs were bound to create trouble. And in fact they led to at least three months delay in getting food into starving Dalmatia and Bosnia while the negotiations which are the subject of the next chapter went on between the military authorities in Washington and Italy, the Royal Yugoslav Government, Tito's representatives and the UNRRA US head office. We in the UNRRA Yugoslav Mission looked on in despair.[14]

Meanwhile, in Egypt UNRRA took over from MERRA responsibility for the refugee camps and for recruiting voluntary society personnel from the UK for relief work in Greece and Yugoslavia. By the middle of 1944 we had about 450 men and women working in the refugee camps and ready to move into Greece and Yugoslavia with the refugees just as soon as the Germans began to withdraw. About one hundred of the 450 were from the FAU. The work in the camps soon sorted out those who would from those who would not be suitable for relief work in the even more difficult conditions in liberated Europe. It also provided an invaluable introduction to the language and customs, and, especially in the case of the Yugoslavs, to the kind of 'democratic centralism' that would be found in a socialist Yugoslavia. This had already proved to be a bit much for some of the more anarchistic of the voluntary society recruits.

As our work in UNRRA developed, we were joined by new staff from the United States as well as the UK to add to our core of voluntary society workers. When our planning had reached the point where we needed to engage with the responsible authorities in liberated territories, personnel were assigned according to choice to Greece or Yugoslavia. Those for Greece went to Athens to set up an UNRRA Mission to work with the British army of occupation. Those for Yugoslavia went to Bari in Italy to make contact with the Allied Military Liaison for Yugoslavia and with representatives of Tito's Partisans in what was by then a National Council of Liberation (NCL). After the Sixth German offensive Tito's HQ had been moved to the island of Vis but there was almost continuous fighting throughout Yugoslavia except for eastern Serbia. Large areas of Croatia, Slovenia, Bosnia, Montenegro and western Serbia away from the main roads and railway lines were under Partisan control.[15]

Harrowing, Bosnia, 1944

Tito with Fitzroy MacLean, Ambassador
Peake & General Steele, 1946

Chapter 4

War Relief Planning for Yugoslavia, Bari Italy, 1944-45

I flew into Bari airport in the summer of 1944 in rather inauspicious circumstances. As we were making our descent, the captain announced that we should put our gasmasks on. A ship with cans of poison gas had blown up in Bari harbour. We were sitting on the floor around the walls of the plane and looked at each other with a mixture of horror and amusement. By this stage in the war it had become normal practice to use the case in which the army type gas mask was carried for packing one's most personal belongings, washing things, pyjamas and spare pants, etc.. None of us had a gas mask. Fortunately, the poisonous cloud had drifted out to sea and we landed safely. Allied Military Liaison had already been established at San Spirito a few miles up the coast from Bari, and we were directed there to occupy two neighbouring villas for our UNRRA Mission billets and offices.

I found James Klugmann in the SOE offices, which had moved to Bari from Cairo and was now the British Military Mission to the Partisans, and caught up with the news of the Partisan battles with the German army. Tito and his High Command were almost caught by a German parachute landing at Drvar and escaped to the island of Vis in the Adriatic. Despite the German deployment of crack parachute and glider forces and divisions numbering more than those facing the Allies in Italy, this their seventh Offensive against the Partisans was a complete failure. Some 50,000 soldiers from twenty German divisions were killed. Many Partisan wounded had been evacuated to hospitals around Bari, and military supplies were being dropped to Partisan forces engaging with German and other Axis divisions throughout Bosnia, Montenegro, Croatia, Slovenia and the Vojvodina. Generally the news was of fantastic Partisan successes (1). One day, however, when I walked into the SOE office, there was a pervading attitude of gloom among those present. I feared that some British parachutist had been shot down. 'No', they said, 'the case of whisky for Randolph had come loose from its parachute; it had crashed – and missed him!' This did rather an injustice to Randolph who was regarded as a very brave man, whose courage was certainly not of what was called the 'Dutch' variety.

What we in UNRRA had to do was to work out the implications of the agreement reached on April 3 between Governor Lehman and his senior staff and the Allied Military Liaison for Yugoslavia (AML). This agreement provided for UNRRA to act as the agent of the military authorities in providing for relief in the Balkans until such time as UNRRA could take over as an independent agency. Two Plans were envisaged for Yugoslavia – one for those areas under Partisan control and the other for those areas, mainly in Serbia and Macedonia, where it was supposed that Mihailovic and his Chetniks would be operating alongside Allied military officers. In fact there had been no consultation about this with the Royal Yugoslav Government nor, more seriously, with Tito. Sir William Matthews had only been consulted about the handing over of responsibility for the camps from MERRA to UNRRA and about the use of voluntary society personnel. But he was charged with the responsibility of managing a Balkan Mission of UNRRA to operate in liberated territory with two main tasks:

The first of these tasks was to carry out emergency health and relief functions under the directives of AML with a supply function

'to determine the persons to whom and the media through which relief supplies shall be distributed and to carry out the necessary supervision of the distribution of supplies with a view to ensuring equitable distribution and endeavouring to limit black market and other irregular activities'.[2]

The second task was to prepare for the future take over of responsibility from the military by providing executive personnel to assist with general planning and arrangements for takeover subject to overriding military authority in the military period. These personnel came to be referred to as 'opposite numbers'. Even in the military period UNRRA would 'take possession of relief supplies in the ports when and as determined by the Allied military authorities and administer their distribution under the direction and supervision of the Allied Military Authorities'.

This bypassing of the country government was based on the assumption noted in the last chapter that the government and other national authorities either did not exercise administrative control or had called on the military to furnish distribution services or because of 'unusual circumstances'. As far as we knew, although these assumptions might have applied in Greece and Italy and in Albania, they did not apply in Yugoslavia and would be deeply resented by the Partisans who had liberated their country largely single-handed and set up their own provisional government.

The problem for the embryo UNRRA Mission for Yugoslavia was complicated by the fact that, while the British staff drawn from MERRA, who had all had experience in Egypt of working with the Yugoslav refugees, were well aware of Partisan sensitivity to any failure to recognise their achievements, this could not be said of the recruits to UNRRA who had arrived from the United States. Those in particular who had come to set up the Distribution Division fully accepted that they, and not the Yugoslavs, would be controlling the distribution of relief supplies, whether or not this was under the general authority of the military. The April 3 agreement was their bible. They hadn't yet met any Partisans and regarded them with much suspicion.

Fortunately in June a reformed Royal Yugoslav government in exile in London under Dr. Subasic had reached agreement with Tito on a joint provisional government, recognising Tito's authority inside Yugoslavia and promising to give all support to the early liberation of the whole country and to the provision of relief to the most devastated areas. General Velebit arrived in London as a Partisan delegate, but no decision was reached on who from the Yugoslav side should meet with AML and the UNRRA 'opposite numbers' to begin planning for relief supplies to be delivered. One advance was achieved. AML agreed that UNRRA missions could have their own organisation in the country after liberation and could participate in policy decisions, even during the period of military responsibility, rather than being simply 'opposite numbers' to military personnel.

At the end of August authority was granted by the Supreme Allied Commander in the Mediterranean Theatre at AFHQ (SACMED), General (Jumbo) Maitland Wilson, for AML (now called ML- Yugoslavia) to start talks with the Yugoslav NCL at Partisan HQ on the island of Vis. Alan Hall, acting chief of the UNRRA Yugoslav Mission, was designated 'Chief Observer' and instructed by the Chief of the Balkan Mission to attend the talks as an observer with no power to negotiate on behalf of UNRRA. I accompanied him as his Executive Assistant. Before talks began, this order was countermanded by the British Foreign Office, which insisted that members of the Royal Yugoslav Government should attend as well as representatives of the NCL and that 'the talks should not be held on Vis as it seems to be too much playing into the hands of the Partisans and leaving the Royal Yugoslav Government out in the cold'.[3]

Talks were, therefore, planned to start in Bari on September 28, but on the very eve of their starting 'Free Yugoslavia', the radio station of Tito's Partisan

NCL, broadcast a statement to the effect that the NCL had decided to renounce UNRRA assistance because UNRRA 'had rejected the NCL proposal that aid should be distributed by the NCL and intended to establish a special organisation for supply distribution', despite the fact that the NCL was prepared 'to allow control delegates of UNRRA to look into the correct distribution of aid'. This obviously referred to the April 3 agreement between UNRRA HQ and AML. In spite of the broadcast the Partisan delegates from Vis arrived in Bari, shortly followed by those from Cairo and London, including representatives of the Royal Yugoslav Government. We still could not begin talks because the US and UK political representatives in Bari said that SACMED had not agreed. He had instructions from the Combined Chiefs of Staff (CCS) in Washington that the question of principle regarding equitable distribution of supplies and the admission of observers to check on distribution must first be agreed by the Yugoslav delegates. This was followed by a further CCS message that only the Royal Yugoslav Government should be involved and that there should be no discussion of the quantity of supplies, shipping or finance. This last message was evidently too much for SACMED who replied to the CCS that he would order talks to begin on October 3 on the original basis unless he received instructions to the contrary.[4]

On October 5 we all assembled at the Town Hall of Bari under a giant mural of Mussolini surrounded by officers in gorgeous uniforms carrying *fasces* like Roman legionaries, with the Adriatic sea in the background. The delegates from Yugoslavia were presented at their places on the conference table with a typed requirement in translation on little slips of paper for them each to sign agreeing to the two questions of principle. They had all been selected for their ability to discuss technical details and when confronted with this demand they requested time to refer to their higher authorities. The requirements, they said, represented their own principles, but they had no authority to sign on the dotted lines on the paper slips. Nonetheless, a week later after consultation among themselves the Yugoslav delegates presented their own draft agreement, accepting the principles of equitable distribution and admission of observers, with a limit of twenty persons, and proposed that the Yugoslav authorities should take over supplies at the ports and be responsible for distribution requesting immediate delivery to the coastal areas already liberated. On October 15 the Anglo-American political representatives meeting in Bari on their own agreed, only after heated argument as we were told, to a version of the Yugoslav text amended to allow for ML control at the ports and for a further twenty-five travelling observers.[5]

This might seem to be the end of the matter, but when the text was referred to SACMED, who passed it on to the CCS in Washington, he was told to hold his hand because it was now proposed that UNRRA should take immediate responsibility for relief supplies with no intervening military period in those countries which had not been occupied by the Allied armies, i.e. Yugoslavia. All UNRRA negotiations with Yugoslavs in future were to take place in Washington and none in Bari. There were three probable reasons for this decision. The first was that Belgrade was liberated on October 20 by a combined Soviet-Yugoslav force; the second was that Dr. Bicanic now in Washington on behalf of the Royal Yugoslav government wished to extricate Yugoslavia from the implications of the UNRRA-AML agreement of April 3. The third was a quite false report from an American UNRRA chief of distribution in Italy that the Yugoslav delegates had been antagonised by the ML staff in Bari and this was reflecting on UNRRA. In fact the Partisans tended to blame UNRRA in Washington for selling out to the military, and relations between the representatives of the NCL, ML and UNRRA staff in Bari were excellent.

I had already made contact with the senior medical officer at the Partisans' hospital near Bari, Colonel Robert Neubauer, who with his partner Nada Kraigher became life long friends; and I knew well several of the ML officers including the deputy commander. This British officer's attitude to his job was refreshingly frank. When I asked him why the ML shoulder flash was a phoenix, he replied: 'After the indescribable balls-up of ML will arise phoenix-like the inevitable fuck-up of UNRRA.' In fact from October 30 technical discussions did take place in Bari between ML and the Partisan delegates, which we in UNRRA were allowed to attend as observers. Agreement was reached on ML plans for organisation and delivery with a rough indication of the supplies involved. But actual delivery of supplies awaited authority from Washington. As I wrote in my official report, 'It is possible that, had UNRRA pressed in Washington at this time for the immediate signing of the military agreement instead of for independent operations, an agreement would have been reached and relief supplies would have gone into Yugoslavia some four months earlier than they in fact did'.[6] And, as we subsequently discovered, many hundreds of lives would have been saved and great suffering avoided from famine conditions.

While discussions took place in Washington about UNRRA plans for Yugoslavia in terms of the value of supplies and number of personnel – some $637 million and 261 staff were proposed by Dr. Bicanic – the CCS cabled SACMED on November 6 demanding even more stringent terms to be agreed by the Yugoslavs. These terms were to include unlimited numbers of observers and absolute freedom of their movement throughout the country, including observation of local production as well as of imported supplies, and with no promise of quantities or finance. Moreover, the reference in earlier texts to the heroic resistance of the Partisans had been cut out. A revised draft agreement was prepared by the Anglo-American representatives in Bari incorporating these new demands as tactfully as possible, and on November 11 the Yugoslav delegates were apprised of the CCS cable. They said that they were authorised to negotiate about an extension of numbers of observers, but these demands really went too far. They would give the impression that the Yugoslavs had only agreed to the principles of equitable distribution to get Allied assistance, when these were the very principles that had enabled them, after a bitter civil war, to bring about the unity of the Yugoslav people.

It was these demands that held up supplies during the vital winter months of 1944-5. The ports of Split and Dubrovnik had been liberated since mid-October and it was possible to plan seriously about port capacities and deliveries. By early November two ships had arrived in Bari harbour with 5000 tons of food and 2900 tons of port and engineering stores. By mistake the bills of lading were delivered at Partisan HQ in Bari in error for MLHQ. So the Yugoslavs knew they were there. Negotiations continued through November 12-14 in an attempt to find a form of words acceptable to the Yugoslavs and within the terms laid down by the CCS. The Yugoslavs were naturally anxious that the previous agreement with ML should hold, even if the promise of the quantities of supplies was not made binding. But on the unlimited number and free movement of observers agreement could not be reached. The Yugoslavs agreed to an increase in numbers, but not to free movement. An UNRRA suggestion appearing in the official report, I think made by me, to the effect that movements could be agreed at the time between ML and the local Yugoslav Commission, was accepted by the Yugoslavs but not by the Anglo-American side, as it was likely to be unacceptable to the CCS in Washington.

The deadlock in talks was duly reported to SACMED and on November 27 a cable from the CCS was received regretting the delay over 'a minor piece of drafting' and insisting that the Yugoslav delegates should be presented once more with the terms of the CCS cable of November 6. and if they 'were not prepared to accept our requirements, they must be told that relief cannot be provided'. This cable was reported to our negotiating body by Air Vice Marshall W. Elliot, the Air Officer Commanding Balkan Air Force, who had been in the chair representing SACMED throughout our discussions. Before our meeting began, the Air Vice Marshall took the head of the Partisan delegation to the window looking out onto Bari harbour and said quite quietly but I overheard: 'There are the ships with the food you need, and all the supplies currently available. If you do not now agree, they sail tomorrow to Greece.' The Yugoslavs knew very well that at that moment civil war had begun in Greece with the active involvement of the British army against the Communist resistance forces. They did not need to consult higher authority to say 'No!'

When the meeting began Elliot read out the cable again and added that if the Yugoslav delegates wished to disagree with its terms and to present their own document, they should do so at AFHQ, where they could realise who are 'the final arbiters'. 'In Bari', he went on, according to the official record, 'conversations had hitherto been conducted on the basis of negotiations.' It was now intended 'to impose an agreement' without which 'the Yugoslavs will receive no supplies.'[7]

That was the end of negotiations until mid-January 1945. But great concern was felt by all the delegates and telegrams were sent by the UNRRA Yugoslav Mission, the British Military Mission, the Commander of ML (YS) and by the British political representative in Bari to UNRRA HQ, to SACMED and to the British Foreign Office, pressing for the sending forward of the two supply ships to Split and Dubrovnik, from which news of hundreds of deaths from starvation along the Dalmatian coast were being reported.

These cables had one immediate response – from SACMED who instructed the Commander of the British Military Mission at Partisan HQ, Brigadier Fitzroy MacLean to inform Tito that SACMED wished to send relief supplies to the Dalmatian ports as an emergency shipment, having no bearing on the discussions concerning a relief agreement. This was in effect the contents of the two ships. Tito's reply expressed profound gratitude, accepted that distribution should be in accordance with the strict principles already agreed, recommended that all supplies be landed at Split and proposed to assign a designated special officer to sign for the supplies either in Bari or in liberated Belgrade and to direct operations through the already established local authorities in Dalmatia.

At a meeting on December 1 at AFHQ Caserta, which I attended with the honorary rank of colonel (I was twenty-six), so as to be admitted to the building as the assistant to Cyril Pickard from the UNRRA Balkan Mission, Tito's reply was considered. While we were waiting to meet one of SACMED's deputies, I noticed that there was a room labelled SACMED MAP ROOM, which people entered from time to time and left shortly after I heard a WC plug being pulled. When we did get to meet, there was much discussion. It was decided by SACMED's representatives that Tito's reply was unacceptable. Tito had not agreed to ML observation of distribution and had chosen Split and not Dubrovnik. Some argued that this was because Split was more favourable to the Partisans and some because it was less favourable. We knew that it offered greater access to the areas of greatest need. It was also suggested that the Yugoslavs could make use of some of the supplies only with technical assistance. This was true of the 'Bailey' bridges and perhaps some medical supplies, but from then on the 'distribution observers' also came to be called technical staff, although they were nothing of the sort. This was to cause much trouble later.

AFHQ ordered the two ships with their 7000 tons out of Bari harbour, and informed Tito that no supplies would be delivered until he accepted the CCS terms in full and sent a fully accredited delegate to Caserta to sign up. As a gesture of good will, Tito was offered 150 tons of food and medical supplies to be delivered to Split and Dubrovnik for distribution under ML supervision.

We made a formal protest to the ML commander from the UNRRA Yugoslav Mission followed by a similar protest from the British Military Mission (my friend James Klugmann). As a result the 150 tons was increased to 500, all to go to Split with observers from ML 'chosen for their tact and to be very carefully briefed.[8] Tito agreed and the 500 tons with an advanced party of ML officers reached Split on the last day of 1944.

This left the members of the UNRRA Yugoslav Mission extremely dissatisfied. Some had already resigned and gone home. Others threatened to resign, and all the Missions' divisions submitted letters of protest to the Acting Chief of Mission, while a petition was prepared for all Mission members to sign. On December 6 a cable was received from UNRRA HQ in Washington indicating that the earlier proposal had been revived for UNRRA to assume responsibility for Yugoslav relief with no intervening military period. We took the view in the UNRRA Yugoslav Mission that UNRRA would be unable to mobilise the necessary resources in time to meet the urgent need for food inside Yugoslavia without calling on the military for supplies and transport. We therefore proposed to the UNRRA Balkan Mission that we should use the good offices of my friend Colonel Neubauer, head of the medical section of the Partisan army in Bari, to take a proposal direct to Tito in Belgrade. This was that Tito should call for a meeting with a leading member of UNRRA HQ from Washington to meet him in Belgrade and agree on terms for delivery of relief supplies from military sources either by UNRRA or by ML.

This proposal could not be carried out because of adverse flying conditions between Bari and Belgrade. We thereupon proposed from the UNRRA Yugoslav Mission to the chief of the Balkan Mission of UNRRA in Cairo that a delegation should fly to London to see the UNRRA Director General, who was at that time in London. We believed that we needed to make it clear that the food situation inside Yugoslavia was desperate and that we were extremely doubtful whether UNRRA could mobilise in time the necessary food supplies and transport apart from those in military hands. We flew by flying boat from Cairo via Tunis and Gibraltar to Poole Harbour and I arrived one evening at my family home in Oxfordshire to the great surprise of my parents. I had the opportunity to contact my mother-in-law, who was working with the Britain-Yugoslav Friendship Association and to apprise her of the situation. She promptly contacted the editor of the *News Chronicle*, Aylmer Vallance, and the editor of the *New Statesman*, Kingsley Martin, so that, when we met at Claridges Hotel on December 17, some part of the story was already in the public domain.

I have an extraordinarily clear memory of the Claridges meeting. The Director General, Governor Lehman, sat in a deep chair in his room with his leg up in a plaster. He had broken a knee cap. He had around him several advisers from UNRRA and from the US State Department. One of them I recognised much later as looking just like Richard Nixon. Sir William Matthews, chief of the Balkan Mission, opened up explaining how serious the food situation was in Yugoslavia, that he had not been consulted about the military agreement, and how UNRRA was being looked to to meet the threat of famine. There were two alternatives to be put to the CCS: either they should relax their conditions and the army should be given the go-ahead or they should abandon the military relief period and ensure that UNRRA could obtain the necessary supplies. He favoured the first because the army had the supplies and the means of transport, but as soon as possible UNRRA should take over. The acting chief of the Yugoslav Mission turned to me to explain that the technical talks that we had with the Yugoslav delegates showed that they were wholly competent to receive the supplies and distribute them equitably. I went on to add that they had begun to blame UNRRA for the delays in getting food into the country and had been informing world opinion to this effect.

At this point my next door neighbour (perhaps Richard Dixon) whispered to me, 'You should shut up now, the old man has got the point.' The next day the Director General saw the Yugoslav Ambassador in London and General Velebit of Partisan HQ, and found that the Royal Government was not prepared at that moment to sign the UNRRA Basic Agreement, but that this should be done in Belgrade, when it was hoped Mr Sergeichic, the designate Yugoslav Mission chief would be in post there. On December 20 a telegram sent by the Director General to the CCS recommended strongly the twofold approach advocated by the Balkan Mission. This cable was at the same time supported by a cable from the British Foreign Office. The Yugoslav UNRRA Mission representatives were then asked to supply a plan of operation on the assumption of UNRRA taking immediate relief responsibility, including a list of supplies for a six month period and necessary shipping, mine sweeping, road transport, engineering, communications and other supplies.

We returned to Bari with this major task to perform. Making the list of requirements from the military authorities was not difficult. The work had already been done in the technical discussions with the Yugoslav delegates during the previous months. However, unity of thought on the size of the UNRRA Mission required, including the number of observers, was less easily achieved. The Transport and Distribution Division wanted a minimum staff of fifty, half of them distribution officers and observers, just for the limited area along the Adriatic coast with a population of at most two million people. The cable sent to UNRRA HQ included a figure of fifty for the Adriatic coast but implied that this was for the whole Mission staff of HQ and Technical and Supply personnel as well as of Transport and Distribution personnel.

Meanwhile, Marshal Tito had indicated to the commander of the British Military Mission that he would enter into an agreement along the lines already agreed subject to a limit of 100 to the number of observers to be admitted with

ML supplies. Clarification was then required as to whether this was a limit to the total number of ML and UNRRA personnel or only to the number who would be acting as observers as opposed to technical staff. On December 24 SACMED recommended to the CCS that in view of Tito's offer, agreement should be signed, as the delay was 'introducing an element of irritation into my relations with Tito'.[9] British forces were by this time collaborating closely with the Partisans in harassing the German retreat from the Balkans.

Some three weeks later agreement was at length signed between Marshal Tito and the British and American commanders of ML (Balkans) by which ML supplies were to begin to be delivered at once in Dalmatian ports and the total number of ML and UNRRA attached personnel to be admitted up to a limit of 300. Under the agreement supplies were to be handed over to the Yugoslav authorities at the available ports for them to carry out distribution through their own organisations; supplies would be billed to the Yugoslav authorities, financial settlement to be the subject of later agreements; ML was to supply technical advisers on engineering, relief, displaced persons and medical problems; facilities would be made available for ML and UNRRA personnel to observe equitable distribution throughout Yugoslavia; UNRRA to take over from ML as soon as it was qualified to do so; in the meantime UNRRA personnel would have their own line of command and the right to be consulted about deliveries.

The token delivery of 500 tons of food reached Split with a small contingent of ML personnel at the end of 1944. A further shipment of 1000 tons of food, clothing and medical supplies arrived at Sukurac (near Split) on January 20, followed by a tanker with 1400 tons of POL and a further ship with 139 trucks on February 9. Unfortunately, only thirty-six of these trucks were found to be road worthy. Further ships docked after some delays at Sukurac on February 15 and March 12 with a total of 5000 tons of food, engineering stores, textiles and medical supplies. At the end of January the main ML units arrived in Split and made immediate contact with the Yugoslav state commission for starting distribution in Split and its surrounds. The first eighteen UNRRA personnel joined them on February 7 after a very rough passage across the Adriatic in an LCI (landing craft – infantry).[10] It was not, however, until mid-March that trucks were repaired and supplies could be moved inland. So it had taken over six months from the first discussions with Yugoslav representatives in Bari for actual relief to arrive to meet what were famine conditions on the Dalmatian coast. This was not the end of the sad story of political considerations coming before humanitarian needs.

There remained the need for an UNRRA agreement to be signed for UNRRA to be able to take over the work of relief and rehabilitation from ML. A date for the takeover was fixed for April 15, after which it would be necessary for the UNRRA Mission to call forward supplies. Under ML authority what was delivered was what was available, amounting by April 25 to just 20,000 tons, which fell far below the monthly deliveries of 100,000 tons proposed in the technical discussions in November, let alone the much more ambitious programme of Dr. Bicanic in Belgrade. It was thought that the 50,000 tons planned by ML for April was the maximum which could be discharged at the two ports of Split (Sukurac) and Dubrovnik (Gruz) and much more than could be cleared from the ports, where storage capacity was no more than 20,000 tons. The trouble was that of the 650 trucks delivered by ML, 130 were quite un-roadworthy and half the rest were out of order owing to lack of repair facilities. Fortunately, the Friends Ambulance Unit trucks arrived in perfect condition and were put into service at once with Yugoslav drivers, while the FAU driver-mechanics set to at once to repair the ML vehicles. This, together with a typical Partisan mobilisation of men and women with carts and barrows, cleared the ports in time for the next deliveries in May.

The Yugoslav government called for a monthly programme of 160,000 tons. When Trieste was liberated and mines cleared, port capacities agreed with AFHQ for June and July were limited to 60,000 tons a month in Dalmatian ports, 45,000 in Trieste or Susak and 30,000 tons in Black Sea ports, whence barges could take supplies up the Danube. In the meantime, UNRRA still had to reach agreement with the Yugoslav Government concerning the basis of its own operations when ML departed. The matter was becoming urgent as ML was due to pull out by the end of March. The opportunity was taken of the senior Deputy Director General of UNRRA, Mr Hendrickson, being in Athens which suggested the possibility of his visiting Belgrade and meeting up with Commander Jackson, a newly appointed Deputy Director General who had been involved in the negotiations with SACMED and with Alan Hall, who had been confirmed as Acting Chief of the Yugoslav Mission. So it was that at length on March 24 1945, agreement was reached with the Yugoslav Government for UNRRA's operations in Yugoslavia.

The agreement was similar to those which Mr Hendrickson had signed with the Greek Government and before that with the Czechoslovak Government, with a few amendments (shown below in brackets), which tied in with discussions already held with the Yugoslav Government.

- The Government was to present monthly schedules of supplies required, after discussion with UNRRA officials, but agreement could not be regarded as a contract;
- Supplies were to be handed over to the Yugoslav government against appropriate receipts as soon as they reached the ports or frontier points of entry as agreed between UNRRA and the Government (not 'at such points as might be agreed from time to time');
- The Government was to keep UNRRA fully informed regarding the distribution of supplies (not as in other agreements – 'would consult

with UNRRA regarding …');
- The Government was to afford UNRRA representatives opportunity to observe the distribution at each stage (not 'to observe and examine into…') and to discuss distribution with the appropriate government authorities (not 'to make inquiries into and to consult with and generally satisfy themselves that distribution was in accordance with prin ciples agreed');
- Proceeds of sale were to go to the Government, not to UNRRA, and the Government was to provide enough local currency for UNRRA's expenses and provide a record of proceeds which 'within a reasonable time' were to be used for relief or rehabilitation purposes;
- The Government was to be entitled to request UNRRA to discharge or recall such of its personnel who violated standards of good conduct … ;
- Yugoslav subjects were only to be employed by UNRRA subject to the Government's authorisation;
- Not only the Chief of Mission but also his deputies and major assistants will be appointed in agreement with the Government;
- UNRRA will from time to time present the Government with a list of Mission members entitled to facilities and privileges;
- UNRRA was to take over from ML on April 15, but certain ML per sonnel to be agreed between UNRRA and the Government would stay in the country as long as required.[11]

This was a satisfactory end to a long negotiation and ended any talk of agreement between UNRRA and any other authority than the established Yugoslav Government in Belgrade, which was in effect Tito's government. What remained to be done was to get supplies into a starving country and to begin the tasks of repairing the damages of war. One result even of the limited deliveries of food to the Dalmatian coast was the return to their homes of the refugees from the camps in Egypt. The outstanding problem which remained harked back to the question of numbers of observers which had been the subject of so much discussion in Bari. This was the question of passes for travel throughout Yugoslavia. The 300 agreed passes had been issued in Bari or in Split to ML and UNRRA personnel.

The result of these issues was that so-called 'observers' were presenting themselves sometimes on the same day and asking the same questions of harassed Yugoslav officials wherever distribution was taking place. What was more disturbing for the Yugoslavs, the UNRRA Distribution Division had drawn up a complicated schedule of questions to be put to all those in charge of distribution with the aim of checking exactly where all the supplies were going. On top of this some of the ML personnel had kept their passes so as to spend some days holidaying on the coast before returning to Italy. The Yugoslav Government finally decided to withdraw all passes until lists of those entitled had been presented by UNRRA to the Government in Belgrade. Those of us who were already in the country had to make whatever local arrangements we could. But we were there actually in the country and able to report back on the conditions we found as the last stages of the war unfolded.[12]

It was, however, an ominous sign for those of us who were responsible for delivering the post-war relief and rehabilitation supplies to the Yugoslav people that we had met such resistance from the British and even more from the American authorities. The agreement which had been reached at Teheran and confirmed at Yalta between Stalin, Roosevelt and Churchill had given Greece to the British and Americans and Poland, Hungary, Czecho-Slovakia, Bulgaria and Roumania to the Soviets, but had divided Yugoslavia between the West and the East. We in UNRRA were caught in the divide. While Tito had been able to establish clear Communist political and military control over the whole of Yugoslavia except for Trieste, Britain and more especially the USA were evidently reluctant to abandon their economic interest.[13]

It was perfectly obvious to all who entered the country that the Partisans had not only carried on an extraordinarily courageous military struggle against the Axis occupation but in doing so they had begun to establish their own socialist state This was something quite different from what happened in the other East European countries where a communist regime had been imposed by the Soviet Union after earlier concessions had been made to right-wing elements to win the support of their western allies. Tito had also conceded the formation of an interim joint government with Dr. Subasic pending national elections, but the Partisans had already established such universal popular power through the Anti-Fascist Councils of National Liberation (AVNOJ) that the capitalist parties boycotted the 1945 election and the monarchy was abolished. Wherever the Partisans had established liberated areas, they had confiscated the property of German and other foreign owners and local collaborators. This included most of what industry there was, many banks and large commercial enterprises and the land of large landowners.[14]

This revolution was carried out by an army consisting largely of peasants. This was what Marx called the 'awkward class', which in Yugoslavia amounted to some 80 per cent of the population.[15] But in Yugoslavia there was a long tradition of working cooperatives – the so-called *zadruge* – in the countryside. About a million of the peasants were without land and they received land when feudal estates were broken up. All this was confirmed after the war by the new government in laws on nationalisation of industry and land reform. But it had been clearly envisaged in the resolutions of the first meetings of AVNOJ as early as November 1942. A year later a provisional government had been formed, representing all the different nationalities and faiths. Most Yugoslavs would tell you that they looked back on the Royal Government of the inter-war years as a brutal dictatorship, which was dominated by foreign interests and in 1941 had sold out to Hitler and the Nazis. And many had seen the Chetniks, the supporters of a Royal Serbian government, actually fighting side by side with German invaders. But that was now all over and the whole country was united in tackling the tasks of relief and rehabilitation.

Bridge over the Neretva, 1945

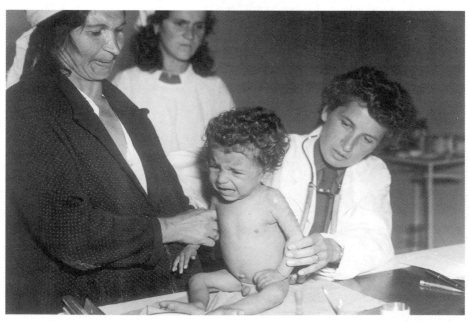

Save the Children Fund Clinic, Sarajevo, 1946

Chapter 5

UNRRA Relief in Bosnia and Hercegovina, 1945-6

By the end of 1944 the German occupation of the Balkans had been reduced by the Russian advances and by Partisan warfare to a withering arm, with the hand and fingers stretching south along the main road and rail communication lines. Between the fingers, in great areas of liberated land, Partisan detachments were being built up, in bitter fighting and with Allied help, into corps of a centrally directed army. Belgrade to the east, the Dalmatian coast and the islands to the west and Greece to the south were liberated as the fingers were cut off. Fierce attacks were being made all along the line of the fingers, and the hand withered but could not be withdrawn, so tight was the Partisans' grip. Only a very little of the life blood of the German armies flowed back to the eastern and western fronts where it was so desperately needed. It was the task of the Partisans – though it meant the destruction of whole areas, towns and villages, the blowing up of bridges, roads and railways and the loss of tens of thousands of men, women and children – to make that little as near to nothing as it could be made.

The very centre of the hand lay across Bosnia, and there the fingers stretched out along the deep passes. In the heart of the Bosnian mountains lay Sarajevo. There the German High Command planned the retreat of the German forces from the very house in which Archduke Franz Ferdinand of Austria had slept the night before he was shot by Serb patriots at the start of the First World War. The retreat from Sarajevo itself began in March 1945 and the German Balkan command pulled out the ragged remains that had been extricated from western Bosnia, Hercegovina, Montenegro, and from Albania and Greece of the famous Prince Eugen and other crack S.S. divisions. This was the end of the power of the Wehrmacht in Yugoslavia, and the roads on which the retreating army were caught by Partisan ambush and Allied bombing, and along which the first UNRRA representatives came, were a graveyard of tanks and guns and fallen beasts and men.

In April 1945 these UNRRA representatives drove in their jeeps in the wake of the Partisan armies over the snow-clad pass of Nevesinje, which had been cleared a month earlier than usual by the work of 1000 soldiers, through Kalinovik, which had changed hands over forty times during the war, and down into Sarajevo. And when they drove further inland from Sarajevo towards Belgrade, they climbed up the proud front of the great mountain plateau of Romanija and passed through Sokolac, Rogatica, Vlasenica – places that had changed hands forty or fifty times in all the fierce fighting in East Bosnia. They called the Romanija pass "dead horse pass" because of the hundreds of dead beasts which the melting snow revealed lying abandoned by the Germans on the side of the road. Everywhere they went the roads were the same, littered with abandoned equipment – tanks, guns, cars, buses, carts, disinfestors, helmets, papers, clothing. Here and there a German graveyard or the crosses above two American airmen told the story of desperate fighting. For many months live mines by the road side kept sensible drivers from straying too far.

The main road from the Dalmatian coast to Belgrade through Sarajevo was the one road for every UNRRA truck with food and medical supplies coming into the country, for many UNRRA members reporting for duty in Belgrade as well as for the UNRRA representatives in Bosnia. And the tyres of every truck and jeep picked up their quota of nails and cartridge cases, jagged pieces of metal and horseshoes. Along the sides of the roads charred piles of stone and silent hollow-eyed walls showed where mountain villages had once stood. The main impression of that ride was of lonely deserted hills. The UNRRA representatives drove their jeeps across terrifying temporary Partisan bridges and primitive ferries. On one occasion a ferry sank with the truck and its load and twelve people were drowned. They followed detours which forded the streams and everywhere they saw the ruins of the road and railway systems. I remember once finding a truck driver digging up the road so as to get his truck under a partly collapsed railway bridge.

The journey along the road from the coast tells the whole story, not only of the Partisans' struggle for liberation but also of the geography of Bosnia and Hercegovina. Up from Dubrovnik on the Dalmatian coast, which Bosnia and Hercegovina hardly touches, the road winds first among the rocks of the barren 'karst' country of Hercegovina, whence for generations the enterprising sons of peasants have emigrated in search of land. To get into Bosnia from the coast further north involves a similar rocky climb but on very poor roads up over the Velebit mountains into the barren Lika and the 'Krajina'(the militarised area), so called because Serbian families were settled there to provide a barrier between the Turks and the Austrians. [It was some 200,000 descendants of these Serbs who were driven out of their homes by Croatian ethnic cleansing in 1995.] Cutting down of forests over the years for shipbuilding has left these areas denuded and barren with occasional herds of sheep, the land broken up into patches of ploughed earth and a few deep landlocked valleys where tobacco, vines and corn are grown. In the south the Dubrovnik road follows the broad reaches of the Neretva valley into Mostar, rich with cherries, apricots and plums, vines and tobacco plants and all kinds of vegetables.

From Mostar going north fields of corn normally stretch right up the river to Konjic wherever there is a broadening of the valley between the high rock strewn sides to allow of earth on which the corn can grow. In the narrowest parts of the valley there are waterfalls to provide power for almost unlimited industrial development. Up from Konjic and over the heavily timbered mountains the road here climbs only to fall again to the valleys where sawmills should be humming busily, but where again there was never either land or work enough to maintain the whole population. Over the mountains past the great Jahorina mountain the road emerges into the broad Sarajevo valley at the source of the Bosna river and its confluence with the Miljacka. Here there are wheat fields and market gardens, but more important here is the junction of the main east-west and north-south railway lines and here should come wagons of black coal from Vares for Sarajevo factories, of steel from Zenica for repairing the bridges, of brown coal from Tusla for household use, and of timber for rebuilding the ruined houses. Here are the rich raw materials which combined with the water power of the rivers could increase industrialisation and solve the land hunger of these deficient areas.

The hills are poor again on the other side of Sarajevo until the road winds up the face of Romanija to the rich forests of pine and oak and beech and rolling pastureland, which is covered in winter by many feet of snow. In the summer little boys will run out to a passing car with straw baskets of wild strawberries for sale. In these villages before the war beef could be bought cheaper than corn. The cattle are nearly all gone, and with them the mountain huts where the peasants lived. The road winds down again this time to the river Drina, the eastern boundary of Bosnia. The land along the valleys seems green enough to the eye, but the earth here is sour from the minerals beneath. Only plums and a little corn can be grown here, but peasants were returning from exile in rich Serbia with nothing but a ramshackle cart, an old lame horse, an axe, a hoe and bags of corn to sow for next year's harvest and a little to eat until the new corn grows. Across the Drina lies the rich land which spreads between the great rivers Drina, Sava and Danube. Some of it is included in Bosnia, contained between the Drina and the Sava and lying along the southern bank of the Sava which forms the northern boundary of Bosnia. Here in a good year are great fields of corn, whet and roots, with villages full of pigs and geese and ducks – plenty for the poorer areas provided the government will buy the food and transport it.[1]

This is how I started my 1947 report on the work of the Regional Office of UNRRA for Bosnia and Hercegovina. The situation we faced was bleak in early April of 1945. As the German columns retreated along the mountain roads, peasant families returned to their own fields from exile in Serbia. They ploughed and sowed wherever they could, often at great personal danger among the many mine fields that remained from the fighting. As the last German train pulled out along the railway lines, tracks were pulled up, bridges blown and stations wrecked, completing the damage already done by Partisan attacks. The result, we were told, was in addition to 400 kilometres of road and 18,500 metres of road bridges destroyed, the total destruction in Bosnia of railway bridges and tunnels, with 80 per cent of locomotives and 60 per cent of wagons lost.[2] We could confirm this picture from what we found. ML engineers were hard at work putting up Bailey bridges all along the Neretva, and local people with Partisan help were making what repairs they could – cutting trees to make pylons, lifting bridges inch by inch on hand jacks out of the swirling waters where they lay crumpled and bent. Saw mills were everywhere gutted and wrecked. Coal mines and iron and steel works were idle.

Human losses were even more worrying. A quarter of the population of Bosnia and Hercegovina – some three and a half million before the war – were said to have been killed. 800,000 were refugees in other parts of Yugoslavia or within the boundaries of Bosnia and Hercegovina. In Sarajevo alone we found a population of 75,000 refugees above its pre-war 85,000 inhabitants. 100,000 war orphans were said to be left behind, 15,000 who had lost both parents. Houses, whole villages and whole towns had been destroyed – an estimated 175,000 houses, 1500 public buildings, 210,000 farm buildings completely destroyed or heavily damaged.[2] People had little clothing or bedding and the nights were still cold. We found one village, Kozara, where the women – there were no men; they had been killed in the Fourth Axis offensive – were ploughing almost naked by night, because they were ashamed to work by day. Everywhere we were told the same story, 'Nearly all our cattle are gone; we have no pigs or hens left. The Italians took them long ago.' The food situation was desperate. We found people in the hills eating grass and roots, acorns and berries and children at school every other day eating a gruel of beans and corn stalks.

I arrived in Sarajevo early in April of 1945, as I described in the second chapter, to set up the UNRRA office with nothing to show for the next two weeks but the 200 tons of flour that ML had delivered – for a population of 160,000 in the town alone and another 60,000 in the surrounding district. By the end of the month the first two Bailey bridges over the Neretva and the Rama ferry had enabled another 850 tons of food to get through. Rather more had been received in Hercegovina, but in the mountain districts around Sarajevo the situation was much worse. There were some supplies getting into the Dalmatian ports, but no trucks to bring the deliveries inland. We needed a thousand trucks and there were just 176 for the whole region – to meet the needs of over two million people. I proposed as an emergency measure to request that food should be flown into Sarajevo. I asked for 350 tons, but this rather grandiose figure was reduced to 100 tons – just to meet the needs of the child population. In the event, a flight direct from London of ten tons of milk, dried and evaporated, was authorised and arrived some weeks later.

It was utterly frustrating and embarrassing to make the visits to towns and villages that were required of us, to report back on the urgency of the need for food and the arrangements that had been made for its distribution. When I asked in one village of the local committee chairman whether he was ready with plans for distribution when supplies arrived, he replied, 'yes, we are quite ready and most ready of all are our stomachs!' It was especially embarrassing in my daily contacts with the local Ministry of Commerce and Supply because they knew the whole story of the delays in negotiating an agreement during the last months of 1944. At the same time, they were being most extraordinarily generous in supplying our UNRRA Mission with all the services we required – of cooks, maids, interpreters and permits for the purchase of controlled supplies, which included practically every household article. As we had received a whole truck load of food for Mission personnel permanently in residence and for those passing through, all I could do was ensure that the Yugoslavs we were working with regularly ate with us.

Early on in our time in Sarajevo we were invited to a showing of films of the early battles of the Partisans with the German army in southern Serbia to establish their first base in Uzice. There were terrifying pictures of blowing up bridges, firing on tanks and German planes straffing the Partisans stronghold. In the interval between films we began to talk with a group of Partisan officers. I had taken with me a book of photographs taken in London during the blitz and showed it to them. They were fascinated and absolutely amazed that London had suffered so much damage. It was a strange way to introduce ourselves, but it worked. We came to be invited to local celebrations, including one when Tito visited Sarajevo. I established a very useful connection with the Town's military commander and a very friendly relationship with the Bosnian President Ketsmanovic, an elderly and very scholarly man.

We soon began to be accepted as part of the local community and when Victory in Europe celebrations began at the end of April we joined in, and indeed led an enormous crowd in a march round the town carrying the Stars and Stripes and the Union Jack along with a Soviet Officer with the Red Flag. This officer told me that he had marched all the way from Moscow and I could believe it. He had an unfortunate limp, and as we walked arm in arm I found it hard not to copy it. Fortunately, my American colleague on my other arm had a strong stride and kept the three of us going. The fall of Berlin had been announced with a violent outbreak of gunfire all over the town. We feared that a group of Chetniks or Ustashe had been discovered and were being attacked, and were relieved to be met in the streets with hugs and cheers.

During May deliveries of food began to flow in larger quantities and we were able to see where it was all going. At each level of county, district and village the local committees were required to make a monthly return to the government of the Republic of what had been received and where supplies had been sent, and how much had been issued free and to whom. Few of them did this, but we found as we went round the country that careful accounts were everywhere being kept; it was just that nobody had time to copy these out for the government. As we usually had a Yugoslav liaison officer with us and always sent our reports to the Department of Commerce and Supply in Sarajevo, this was one way in which the information got back.

The questions we asked were pretty far ranging because we were anxious to report on the real needs of different districts as well as on the details of distribution. We always started with general questions about the economic situation: What was the population? What had it been before the war? What were the main occupations – peasant farming, cattle breeding, forestry etc.? What percentage of a normal pre-war harvestdid they have? What was the percentage loss of livestock? How many houses had been destroyed? Secondly, there were questions about food received and the proper execution of the State ration scale. How far could the district, town or village fulfil the scale with the supplies available? What proportion of the population could feed itself without help? What ration was received by heavy workers and how many were there? Thirdly, there was the question of price. How many people could afford to buy the supplies? What prices were charged? How did they relate to similar local supplies? How did people receive who could not pay? Fourthly, there were questions about other supplies. What had been received – tractors, tools, seeds, mules, medical stores? How were they all distributed? and how paid for? Finally, we asked about the main needs of the area – food, clothing, housing materials, tools, livestock, transport etc.[3]

In the middle of May we were given a particular task in Bosnia. UNRRA food arriving in Dalmatia was being given to Partisan soldiers by civilians, who were sorry for the plight of these serving men and women. Rather than prohibit this, the Yugoslavs authorities decided to arrange for equal quantities of UNRRA food to go officially to the army on the coast in exchange for Serbian food for starving Bosnians living near the borders of Serbia and Bosnia. I was ordered to go and investigate. On travelling east to the river Drina I found that, once more because of the lack of transport, of the 850 tons made available by the army at Lezhnica on the Serbian side of the Drina only 180 tons had arrived on the Bosnian side. There was no bridge and the ferry could not take a heavily loaded vehicle. There was a total of 3000 tons to be moved from further inside Serbia at Loznica. The grain was being carted up from the river to Vlasenica, and then taken in sacks on human backs to Sokolac for further distribution. It was obvious that the army would have to release light trucks to be ferried across the river. I managed to get a message to Belgrade with some details of the food situation in this eastern part of Bosnia. The food which had arrived would not last long, and more families were returning from Serbia all the time.

Here are the notes I made of the position in four districts:

Vlasenica. The nearest to Serbia but only 21 tons received for 25,000 population (half pre-war), less than a kilo per person and all were in need. Some fish available in the river. Children at school in the open air but eating only every other day.

Sokolac. Great destruction of life (3000 population out of 7000 pre-war), of houses and stock (80 per cent). People living in German bunkers. Stock breeding, not mainly a cropping country. Flour carried up on human backs from Vlasenica three hours away, and taken on from here to Rogatica, another three hours, and further to the rest of Romanija. Ration 100 grams daily, 200 for heavy workers. Very poor crop expected. Only 40 per cent land sown this year. Houses being built from local timber with axes. Other tools and transport needed.

Rogatica. 20,000 population (from pre-war 50,000). Stock breeding (80 per cent of stock lost) and forestry. Railway line not repairable for 4 months. Food all brought in on foot from Sokolac. 300 tons received, mostly grain, in three months, i.e.3-4 kg. per person per month for those in most need. Very little left. House building materials badly needed.

Visegrad. Present population 10,000 (half pre-war). Corn grown but little sown this year. Plums ripening. Terrible destruction of houses. Railway line rooted up by Germans on leaving. 400 tons of grain received from Serbia. Monthly ration in town 4kg. (10 kg for heavy workers)[4]

In June we began to cover two or more districts in each county of Bosnia and Hercegovina, but in the middle of June the problem of numbers and passes caught up with us. There was no record of who was in the country from UNRRA (and still some ML engineers) or where they were. The new chief of Mission, Mr. Sergeichic, agreed with the Yugoslav government to enforce a standstill on all movements until the picture was clear. I saw no reason to take any notice of this, as the military commander in Sarajevo told me that he was perfectly prepared to issue me a pass on an ad hoc basis, so long as I told him where I was going. I therefore informed Belgrade that I was planning to make a major trip around north and north-west Bosnia and would set off unless I heard to the contrary within three days. No answer was received. So I made my tour stopping off at Zenica, Zepce, Maglaj, Doboj and so to Bosanski Brod, then back to Doboj for Banja Luka. I did not go on to Prijedor and Bihac, which had only been liberated in May, leaving that for another trip, but returned via Doboj again to Tuzla and back to Sarajevo.

I was struck by the mix of different groups – Muslims, Catholic Croats, Orthodox Serbs (Pravo-slavs) – in these districts. Where I went was mainly Muslim country, except for Banja Luka, but with a mix of Serbs everywhere and in the north (Bosanski Brod) Croats. I found in the district committees which I interviewed, that there would generally be one from each faith to see me. I made a special point of asking because of UNRRA's anxiety about equitable distribution Much of this part of Bosnia is fertile, rich farmland, but still needed food until the new harvest came. UNRRA supplies were getting up on the long haul from the Dalmatian coast, but this would remain a problem until the railway from Trieste was repaired and a bridge built across the Sava and that was likely to be many months – it was in fact miraculously completed in November. Some supplies were coming by barge along the Sava, and this should make possible the delivery of urgently needed tractors, agricultural tools and equipment and stock.

After this trip, it became clear to me that I should go to Belgrade to report to the new UNRRA Mission chief and sort out the standstill on passes and my own position in Sarajevo. I shall never forget the first impression I had of Serbian towns and villages as I drove through fields being ploughed by tractor, streets full of smiling school children and farm animals – ducks and geese scattering away from our tracks, and when I stopped and asked for some water to drink, I was given delicious barley water and little cakes with plum jam. The contrast with our poor ruined Bosnia and its listless children and lack of food was acute. In Belgrade I found a city largely intact with shops and restaurants and hotels open for visitors. There were cars in the streets as well as buses and trams and military vehicles. The UNRRA office was in a big building near to the Post Office in the city centre. I was very anxious as to what I should find at UNRRA. I rather expected to be reprimanded for failing to carry out instructions and acting on my own. In the event I was warmly received by the new chief and, with a twinkle in his eye, he congratulated me on my enterprise and on my reports which, I was told, had proved most useful. It was a great relief, and I was told that I would henceforth be the official representative of the Chief of Mission for Bosnia and Hercegovina.

The battle with the UNRRA Distribution Division was ended. There had always been competing ideas about the Mission's structure according with the views of those who had been appointed in Washington or in London to different posts. There was a Relief Project Director concept, which assumed that UNRRA would direct relief projects with its own staff treating the Yugoslavs as something like colonial subjects. The director appointed went back from Bari to Washington with his staff at an early stage. There was a Distribution Director concept, which was changed into a Distribution Observer concept during the negotiations in Bari, but its director and staff retained the conviction that nothing short of a very hands-on control of distribution of relief supplies with a large staff would prevent the misuse of aid by the government as a political weapon.

This concept was only ended with the arrival of Mihail Sergeichic as chief of Mission and a more accommodating American deputy chief, Wilford Johns, who reduced the Distribution Division to a planning role working closely with the Yugoslav government department for special supplies. There was finally the Local Representative concept which most of the recruits to UNRRA from the UK supported. We saw ourselves as being responsible in each of the republic capitals for coordinating UNRRA relief supplies and technical staffs in association with the local government officials and a delegate from the central government department for special supplies. And this was how we were from then on to operate. After months of ad hoc activity I was at length recognised as the Representative of the Chief of Mission for Bosnia and Hercegovina and had a central government delegate to liaise with in my work.

Some ill will remained between some of the American and British staff of UNRRA. This was the result of the different ways in which we had been recruited. Many of the British staff, myself included, had come via Egypt and the refugee camps, where we had learnt to understand and to respect the democratic and egalitarian morale of the Partisan committees. The Americans had come straight to Bari and then to Split where they were billeted in the houses of rich Croats who were hanging out the Stars and Stripes and Union Jacks in place of the Swastikas of the past few years and both feared and hated the Partisans, about whom they told terrible stories. It took time for these Americans to get over this introduction and some never did. But there were some splendid Americans on our UNRRA staff who were just as enthusiastic as we were about what Tito and his Partisans had done in resisting the German occupation and were doing in rebuilding their shattered country.

I had already taken over for our UNRRA regional HQ a large villa in the centre of Sarajevo, which had been occupied by the Quisling president of Bosnia under the Germans and was still called after him the 'Villa Mandic'. I had an American deputy, a medical officer and a splendid American administrative assistant, who typed all our reports and received the stream of visitors we had with old world charm and efficiency. With our UNRRA staff and voluntary

society units we had a staff of local interpreters, including my brilliant interpreter, Madame Begic, and a large house staff. The two voluntary society units
were Dr Singer's Save the Children Fund Unit and a Friends Ambulance Unit
mobile bacteriological laboratory. For some time we also had representatives
of the World Typhus Commission until they were tragically blown up by a
land mine in their jeep carrying supplies of DDT to an outlying village. In addition, at any time we were the base for visiting UNRRA technical transport,
agricultural and engineering experts, visiting journalists and anyone requiring
a half-way stop-off between Belgrade and the coast. We rarely sat down for our
evening meal with less than twenty at our large dining room table, including
local Yugoslav officials for our visitors to meet. By September of 1945, regular
supplies were coming up from the coast. I could go with our Austrian cook
to buy fruit and vegetables in the market and the local wine merchant made
a special point of telling me when he had a new delivery of wine from Mostar
and Dalmatia.[5]

The two voluntary society units provided our most valuable contribution
to the relief and rehabilitation of Sarajevo and its environs in those days. Dr
Singer and her nurse took over the children's clinic releasing the Yugoslav
doctor for administrative work throughout the area. They saw thirty-five to
forty-five mothers with their children each weekday, treating all the diseases
of malnutrition and inoculating against infectious diseases. The nurse trained
young girls to take over the nursing care in the clinic and in the orphaned children's homes in the town. The chemist in their unit advised about nutrition
and supervised the distribution and use of the UNRRA milk powder that came
for all the schools and children's homes. The Bacteriological Unit was attached
to the hospital as a temporary laboratory and introduced the use of the new
sulpha drugs and antibiotics. At the weekends we all went out to local villages
with the jeeps and an ambulance and the laboratory for 'good will work', along
with blacksmiths, welders, mechanics and plumbers, to set up a health centre
and take the place of craftsmen lost in the war. I had my usual job of collecting
stones in the trailer to fill up the potholes in the road. The day's work would
end with glasses of plum brandy and singing and dancing in the streets.

It would be hard to exaggerate the shared sense of joy in singing and dancing the kola round a village square in those days, feet shuffling or stamping to
the beat of the accordion. Bystanders would soon be drawn in to the magic
circle where there was always a welcoming hand or arm to receive them. The
Partisans' kolas must have recruited thousands to their ranks. For who can bear
to feel themselves excluded from the circling band of young men and women
too, even with their hand grenades hanging from every belt. A rather cynical
journalist who visited us, one Penderel Moon, commented that he supposed
that all fascist regimes sang, to which we were quick to respond that not all
singing regimes were fascist. It really was 'bliss to be alive and to be young was

very heaven.' Our joy was felt all the more acutely because we were surrounded by all the evidence of a fearfully destructive military occupation, and not just in the direct effects of the fighting.

In her medical report to UNRRA written in May 1947 Dr Singer described what she saw in the following words:

> The children ... particularly those in the first decade of life were found to be definitely undersized and underweight. Dry skins, small amount of subcutaneous fat, atonic muscles and hair lacking in lustre were common findings. Anaemia, dental caries, gingivitis with or without pyorrhoea, and rickets were widespread. Mentally the children were on the whole docile and lacked the aggressive vitality of the well nourished child. The average child to be found in nursery school or orphanage was naturally livelier than the sick attending the clinic ....
> During the war milk was unobtainable in Sarajevo and outlying villages were scarcely better off with 80 per cent of the cattle slaughtered. It was clearly evident that war had resulted in an increase in the incidence of rickets since it was much more common amongst the under five year old children than in those over five. In the younger children it was still active, and crippling was frequently very severe.

The clinical report goes on to detail the effects of oral sepsis, intestinal parasites, goitre and endemic syphilis, and notes the very low incidence of upper respiratory tract infections and of allergic manifestations.

The report concludes with these comments:

> Yugoslav medicine has jumped from calcium to sulphonamides, from cupping to penicillin, from witchcraft to modern methods of therapeutics, with no intervening period of physiological or pharmacological understanding .... The work of the unit was warmly recognised by the Save the Children Fund and by UNRRA who both made good use of its experience and who demonstrated by reports and photographs the needs of Yugoslavia for food and medical supplies. It is possible that when the names of individual members of the unit are forgotten, the work will be remembered in Yugoslavia for the medical knowledge it brought and because it was a practical demonstration that friendly cooperation between people of different countries is really possible.[6]

It was a hectically busy summer for the whole UNRRA staff making visits to every county and almost every one of the over one hundred districts in Bosnia and Hercegovina with our liaison officer and an interpreter. We were received with extraordinary hospitality by district and village committees, representing the several communities, perhaps a Muslim chairman, a Catholic secretary and a Serbian orthodox treasurer. When we had to stay over night, I would be given the best bed in a rich peasant's house, a chicken would be killed, eggs brought, vegetables and fruit and loaves from UNRRA flour, all from different houses and not easily spared. There would be jokes about the UNRRA packets of army 'K' rations. Someone thought the packet of tissue paper (lavatory paper) was a tea bag and complained that the tea tasted of disinfectant. The Muslims rejected the tinned Spam, but everyone loved the chocolate.

Going up into the heart of the mountainous region on the Montenegrin border, I found myself in places whose names I recognised from the reports I had read of the German offensives against the Partisans – Gacko, Foca, Gorazde – all badly damaged in the fighting. Later, they were connected by a smart new road running from Dubrovnik to Sarajevo, but I had to climb up rough stone tracks in my jeep to reach them. Foca had become famous in Partisan history because of the 'Foca Regulations', elaborated in 1942 by Mose Pijade, the Partisans' idealogue. Foca's mixed Muslim and Serb population was then in liberated territory, but had earlier provided large numbers of Muslim recruits for the Ustashe contingents in the Axis forces. Winning support from these Muslim families was essential to Partisan success. In an area of food shortage everything had to be shared. Looting was a capital offence. Partisan army soup kitchens provided food for 3000 members of Ustashe families. The land of absentee landlords and proven collaborators was confiscated after court martial, but property rights were not challenged, richer peasants being required to supply tools and to take in refugees.

Somehow in these mountainous retreats more had to be produced – food, but also housing, furniture, boots, tools, arms, basic equipment for schools and hospitals. These were made in workshops hidden in the forests. The basis of the 'Regulations' to win local support was to work with the grain of local cooperative traditions and through local elected committees. Markets were not controlled, but prices were kept down by the release of stocks where profiteering was discovered.[7] The Foca model was to become one of the competing models in planning post-war development.[8]

Going north along the frontier with Croatia I entered territory shared mainly by Pravo-Slavs (Orthodox Serbs) and Croat Catholics. In Banja Luka my liaison officer, Major Babic, told me I had to stay with the Catholic bishop, who had collaborated with the Germans. I demurred, but I was told there was typhus in the town and was persuaded to accept an armed guard outside my room as well as the guard around the house. I learned afterwards that the major wanted to spend the night with his girl friend. In the event I ventured in to talk to the bishop about the history of Bosnia. When we had almost finished a bottle of excellent plum brandy, I thought to ask him about the future. Looking out of the window to the north, I said, 'The Germans have gone some days ago, now what happens to Bosnia?' The bishop took me to a map on the wall of his study which showed the line drawn north and south through Bosnia in AD 395 separating the Eastern and Western Empires of Rome. 'I don't know what will happen', he said, 'but I know what should happen. A great ditch should be dug along that line and the Pravo-Slavs (Serbs) transported to the east and the Catholic (Croats) gathered together to the west.' 'And the Muslims?' I asked, fearing the answer, but not expecting the viciousness of the tone when it came: 'In the ditch!'

As the autumn turned to winter in the mountains it was clear that what little had been grown in the summer months would last no time. Survival of many communities in Bosnia and in Hercegovina would depend on getting UNRRA food trucked up from the coast. Trucks had at last been found from British and American Army surplus in Italy and Trieste, and the bridges over the Neretva were completed. One minor tragedy of which I complained bitterly to Belgrade was that before they left the ML engineers had no opportunity to pass on their knowledge to the Yugoslavs or even to instruct them in the use of the spare parts and maintenance kits that they had put on order. For the time being all was well and there were 30,000 tons to be moved into Bosnia from the Dalmatian ports and from Serbia. It was a race against the winter. By November 20 all but the 5000 tons for the mountainous areas east and south of Sarajevo had reached their destination. I drove up into the mountains as the first snows fell on the last day of the month to speak to the village committees of Sokolac and Rogatica on the high Romanija plateau.

I had been up there several times during the summer, once for a special occasion. Governor Lehman the Director General of UNRRA was coming to visit Yugoslavia and I had offered to receive him in Sarajevo and bring Committee members of one of the most war damaged villages to meet him, with Bosnian dignitaries, at a banquet at our villa. The offer was accepted and I had agreed with the authorities in Sarajevo that the committee at Sokolac should be the one chosen. Unfortunately, the Governor's plane was delayed and he was not well on arriving in Belgrade. So the visit was cancelled. I had scoured the countryside as far afield as Mostar for food and drink for the occasion, and decided that the only thing to do was to take all that I had collected to the people of Sokolac. But I felt that I should consult with the Committee at Rogatica, who had responsibility for Sokolac and where destruction was as a bad as at Sokolac. They said that they were in fact down to the last two weeks of rations, but Sokolac had been promised, they insisted, and Sokolac should have the food and drink.[9]

It was a happy memory when I drove up into the mountains to see the Committees in November. But this is how I wrote up my visit at the time:

> They asked whether the trucks would come through. They had always been anxious about the winter. They had rebuilt some of their wooden houses, and had received some clothing, but all their reserves of food had gone. They said to me, 'We are glad you came. We know you will help. But we know too that we shall go hungry'. I drove back toward Sarajevo, worried and sick at heart. Black clouds hung over the mountain tops already capped with snow. As I reached the

head of the pass above Sarajevo, the sun came out through the clouds and lit the tops of the pine trees. The jeep skidded slightly in the slushy snow, and there they were down below in the dusk – big green trucks, a long winding convoy coming up into the hills. I could see them across the valley on the other road too. These roads had come alive with traffic – the same roads which I had travelled for six months alone, meeting only the occasional horses and carts of refugees return-ing from their exile in other parts of Yugoslavia or an odd UNRRA truck driver whom I always stopped to talk with, so glad did I feel of company in those wild hills, The battle of winter was won. I sat in my jeep and tears poured down my cheeks.[10]

I was able to make some later trips into the mountains to see how the distri-bution had gone. One time I was being driven by Vivien Imber, the nurse in Dr. Singer's unit. She had been visiting one of the children's homes. The jeep skid-ded on some gravel, hit the bank and turned over onto a ditch. She scrambled out, but my right knee was caught. She set off to the nearest hamlet hoping that it was friendly. There were still bands of Chetniks hiding out in the hills and she was very beautiful. After what seemed a very long time with petrol slowly dripping past my arm I heard voices approaching and Vivien's infectious laugh. Several large men soon lifted the jeep up onto its wheels and released me. They wanted no thanks; they had received food from UNRRA. I had torn a cartilage and had difficulty walking. I was given leave to fly back to England for an operation at UCH and the opportunity to be present at the birth of my son Christopher on Christmas Day 1945. Both my son and my knee did well. The surgeon said that I would have a little arthritis in the knee after fifty years. I have indeed got arthritis after sixty years, but at the time I hardly expected to survive fifty days returning to drive my jeep over those Bosnian roads with land mines on either side.

When I was back in Sarajevo some weeks later there was still great anxiety about the food situation. There was no rain and the long drought meant an-other poor harvest. An enormous effort had been made with mules and trac-tors brought in by UNRRA to plough up to 90 per cent of the land under crops before the war, but the maize withered and blackened in the hot sun without rain. UNRRA supplies had begun to include other foods besides grain – not only milk powder for the children but fats and sugar, pulses, cheese and meat and great quantities of army K ration packs, to make up a balanced diet for the whole population. Clothing, blankets, boots and shoes were coming in, some manufactured in Yugoslav factories from UNRRA imported raw materials. Many goods were now on sale in the shops as they reopened, but basic supplies were provided free to the old, the poor, war widows and the disabled.

All this in turn had been made possible by the repair of the bridges and the arrival of many more trucks and railway engines and wagons, wide gauge and narrow gauge, and the building of the famous 'youth railway' in the north east, which involved volunteers from all over the world and used UNRRA supplied bulldozers, compressors, rollers, dynamos, concrete mixers, portable saw mills, tools of all sorts and steel from the Zenica steel works, rebuilt with electric rectifiers with the specialist help of an engineer from the English firm which made them. It seems incredible looking back on it how much was done in such a short period of time, but the fact was that the whole population, men, women and children were set to work on the task of repairing the ravages of the war. No one who was not there would have credited the enormous enthusiasm and high spirits with which this task was assailed as a whole people seemed to go working, singing and dancing into a new world.

In UNRRA we had failures as well as successes. Trucks arrived which were unusable and without spare parts. Trucks and jeeps got stolen at Trieste and I knew all about 'Catch 22' before I read the book. This was particularly infuri-ating for the Yugoslavs because they were claiming Trieste as theirs and there was absolutely no black market inside their own country. When a long-awaited heavy workshop arrived from Italy, it was found to be worn and damaged, with parts missing and even covered with slogans denouncing the Yugoslav government. After every tour I sent in requests to Belgrade for urgently needed equipment for saw mills, tractor spares, radio and telephone equipment and other items that had to be imported. But increasingly through 1946 the stores began to fill with UNRRA supplies – aluminium for pots and pans, hides for the tanneries, wool for the carpet factory and other textile works, chemicals for the soap factory. We were just beginning to realise our title of 'Relief – and Rehabilitation'.

Telling the story of UNRRA became important both for the Yugoslav people and for those who were supplying this aid. We found 'UNRRA' painted on more and more imports – locomotives, wagons, trucks, mills – and a travelling UNRRA Exhibition came to Sarajevo and other major towns. Visits from for-eign journalists were sometimes a testing experience, when they came without proper passes or determined to prove that aid was being misused and UNRRA staff were communists or in the pay of the government. Some villagers were so frightened at the barrage of questions from one circus of Allied journalists that they feigned ignorance of UNRRA and claimed not to have eaten anything for months. For their pictures the journalists pasted UNRRA slogans and posters on walls and buildings unrelated to UNRRA. They unwittingly filmed military objectives. They refused to go on the trips we had arranged for them and finally the excellent dinner we organised for them with the Minister of Commerce for Bosnia and Hercegovina, at which speeches of mutual congratulation were made, only confirmed their view that we were government stooges.

The real test for UNRRA remained – ensuring enough food, especially in the mountain areas, for the winter. It was clear by the summer of 1946, as the war in Europe ended, that the harvest in Yugoslavia had failed again, not only in Bosnia but more widely, almost as disastrously as the year before. Despite the increased ploughing and sowing, the wheat crop was about 60 per cent of normal, the more important corn crop 30 per cent and potatoes 20 per cent. We were back where we had been a year earlier. Grain had to be got up into the mountains before the end of November. Corn from Serbia could not be matured and transported on time. UNRRA supplies landing on the coast were only meeting a quarter of what was needed. Some ships were diverted because, it was said, Yugoslavia had already received its quota. This was later found to be due to a 'clerical error' in the United States. When the ships did arrive there was a pile up at the ports and only the dispatch by Tito of a special commissioner to the Dalmatian coast, who mobilised every man, woman and child in true Partisan style, got the food loaded on to every kind of truck and vehicle and transported up into the mountains This included 7,500 tons of potatoes and seed wheat from Czechoslovakia for the next year. The whole operation required the most precise organisation of the movement of supplies from the east and the west of Yugoslavia. The ration had to be cut back everywhere, even in rich Serbia. But it was done and the result was the most remarkable tribute to Partisan principles of equality that could have been exhibited – and made a nonsense of all the doubts and fears that had delayed UNRRA's deliveries.

UNRRA Tractor, Bosnia, 1946

UNRRA Port Operations, Trieste, 1946

Chapter 6

UNRRA Rehabilitation, Belgrade, 1946-47

Belgrade had been liberated by Soviet and Partisan armies at the end of October 1944. I had visited UNRRA HQ there briefly on several occasions in 1945 and early 1946 and found a city quickly recovering from the German occupation and wartime shortages. By the time I arrived, in the summer of 1946, to take up the post of Executive Assistant to the Chief of the UNRRA Mission, Mihail Sergeechic, Belgrade had returned to normality with a much expanded population and construction sites everywhere, especially in the new suburb of Zemun down by the Sava. I was allocated an apartment in Dedinje, the smart suburb on the hills to the south of the city, where Tito and the leading members of the new government had villas. There was a standing joke at the time that demobilised Montenegrin Partisans had been told to 'buy a ticket for Dedinje' to find advancement.

It was a beautiful place with much open country not yet built on and fine views over the city. In winter one could ski to work over fields that were later carved out to make the football stadium. The villages were still near enough for peasants to bring their produce to our door for sale. I recall one winter evening with the snow lying deep around the house when a peasant woman knocked on our window with a hare for sale which she had trapped. We brought her in to warm her up in front of our log fire, gave her some soup and a glass of *rakija* , bought the hare and later jugged it for a party with UNRRA colleagues the next evening. However, in spite of trips out to the Danube and the Frushka Gora, I never came to love Belgrade as I had loved Sarajevo, its hills and Muslim quarter and market, and the Sunday *corso* and vibrant mixed population. There were walks in Belgrade on Sunday evenings around the Kala Magdan gardens at the confluence of the Sava and Danube rivers, which made one realise why the Turks had built their great fortress just there, but there was not the friendly intimacy of the Sarajevo *corso*.

When I arrived in Belgrade I was able to get some picture of what the Axis occupation had meant, not just for my little stamping-ground in Bosnia and Hercegovina but for the whole country. An Allied Conference on Reparations held in Paris at the end of 1945 had assessed the Allied losses of national property caused by destruction or pillage. Excluding the almost incalculable losses of the Soviet Union, these were estimated at a value of $54 billion, of which Yugoslavia's losses made up $9,145 millions, considerably more than Britain's $6,383 millions. In Yugoslavia the actual destruction had been calculated to include half a million houses, rendering one fifth of the population homeless. Over half the pigs, sheep and goats and poultry were lost. About half a million ploughs and peasant carts were unusable and 1500 tractors and tractor ploughs destroyed. Power stations, mines, heavy industry and timber works were hardly operating. Communications were particularly hard hit. Nearly a thousand locomotives were destroyed or removed and 500 severely damaged, while 30,000 rail cars were destroyed and 16,000 damaged. 80 per cent of all railway bridges were down and 28,000 kilometres of road damaged.[1]

Moving on from Relief to Rehabilitation was going to be a hard task for UNRRA. My job at UNRRA HQ in Belgrade was very different from that of a regional representative in Sarajevo. Trips out of Belgrade were rare – only to visit regional offices as they closed down, in Sarajevo, Zagreb, Cetinje and Ljubljana and to the Dalmatian port offices and Trieste, where the office remained open as the main port for the entry of UNRRA rehabilitation supplies. These were now our main concern, but there was still a threat of inadequate grain in the country. As the harvest had once more failed owing to a further year of exceptional drought, only half of a normal pre-war crop was available. We worked hard to persuade UNRRA HQ in Washington to include Yugoslavia in its emergency grain supplies programme, but opinion in the supplying countries, and particularly in the USA, had turned against Tito's regime. Churchill had made his 'iron curtain' speech at Fulton Missouri in March of 1946 and the war-time alliance was crumbling. Our main job became the defence of our existing programme and of the promised rehabilitation supplies against adverse criticism and threats of termination. We failed to get further UNRRA grain deliveries for 1947, and rationing was strict, though some Serbian peasants used their grain to build up their depleted pig numbers.

At the annual party given by Tito in November 1946, to celebrate the anniversary of the Partisan uprising in 1941, we were told that no bread was being served. Some of us murmured after Marie Antoinette, 'Then let them eat cake!'

We certainly tucked in to every other kind of delicacy before being introduced to Tito. He spotted Dr. Singer's *Titolik* medal for 'conspicuous gallantry', and asked what she got it for and smiled those clear blue eyes at her when she answered 'For driving the chief Yugoslav Army medical officer in my jeep round the hospitals for wounded Partisans in Italy'. She could just as honestly have added: 'For doing his hospital rounds with him and introducing him to new treatments including the use of the new drugs – M&B sulphonamides and penicillin.' UNRRA's relations with the Yugoslav government from Tito himself downwards were and remained extremely good despite the many disappointments and frustrations which we encountered. When one of the UNRRA road construction engineers was arrested for spying on the number and distribution of the Yugoslav armed forces, Tito had him released at once on condition that he was immediately repatriated.

Our regular relations with the government were not, of course, at that exalted level. Our main channel of communication was through the Zavod, the special department for foreign supplies, but this did not exclude direct contacts between UNRRA experts and individual ministries, as long as the Zavod was kept informed. It was not UNRRA's function either to frame the supply programme on behalf of the different departments of the government or to plan the distribution and use of supplies. But discussion between UNRRA's technical people and Ministry staffs was needed for four main purposes, to explain in detail the nomenclature of the largely British and American types of equipment available, to advise on actual availabilities as opposed to ideal programmes, to obtain adequate justifications for particular requests and to ensure early and correct answers to inquiries so that adequate substitutes and other second priority availabilities were not missed when first priority items were not available,

Queries only came up to the Chief of Mission's office for the Executive Assistant to deal with, when problems had arisen, though there were plenty of these. One rather amusing case was the demand we received to supply Dalmatian fishermen with cork floats, many of which had been lost with their tackle in the war. The message came back from Washington that glass floats were now normally used and could be supplied. 'No' said the Yugoslavs, 'Our fishermen could not use them and wanted cork.' Washington demurred despite repeated requests. I took the issue to the head of the Zavod and asked him whether Dalmatian fishermen never used glass. I had in fact seen them doing so. He came clean and acknowledged that the cork was wanted for bottling Yugoslav wines, but he did not think that this would be allowed. It seemed to me a perfectly legitimate rehabilitation requirement and I decided to get the chief to cable Washington insisting on cork. The cork came but in 3 mm. inch thick slabs and not 4 mm. Some time later I noticed that the corks in Yugoslav wine bottles were rather short.

One of the main problems facing UNRRA HQ in Yugoslavia was obtaining accurate detailed information on the distribution of supplies – grain and other foodstuffs, textiles, trucks, tractors, spare parts, mules, harness, tools, machinery and thousands of items of equipment – throughout the country. By far the biggest division was the statistics division and it had to deal with government departments which had little or no experience of bureaucratic controls. We brought into our office hundreds of Yugoslavs and trained them in statistical methods, but they had to rely on quite inadequate staffs in the republics, counties and districts where the supplies were ending up. This was a particularly serious problem for us, because we were constantly under attack with stories in the Western press of supplies being diverted to Russia, to the army or to favoured persons and groups. There was considerable resistance to our bringing in large numbers of inspectors, as I have already indicated. The regional officers, of which I was one, did their best to follow through the movement of deliveries that were reported to them in their regular meetings with republic ministers and officials, and there is no doubt that their spot checks and specific inquiries provided an important control on abuses. The total picture we could give to UNRRA HQ in Washington, however, never satisfied them.

The most time consuming case of unwarranted suspicions arose in relation to the low-flying planes sent in for DDT spraying in malarial areas. The planes arrived in July of 1946 already late for that season's spraying. They were found on inspection to be without the necessary spraying equipment and there was also a shortage of the right kind of DDT. UNRRA HQ in the USA insisted that they needed to send US pilots to train the Yugoslavs in low flying. In fact they knew all about that and only awaited the spraying equipment. We agreed to having an instructor come to explain the installation of the equipment, but this did not arrive until April 1947. In the meantime the US Embassy in Belgrade had circulated a story that the planes were being used by the Yugoslav and Russian armies, and this further delayed the arrival of the equipment. At length in May and June the planes were successfully put to use as part of a massive anti-malaria drive throughout Macedonia, the main centre of malaria in Yugoslavia.

Many of the UNRRA personnel recruited in the United States were recruited for direct medical, hygiene and relief work. While the several voluntary society units from the UK and Switzerland were welcomed and found useful work to do, those from the USA found very limited opportunities. The reasons for this were first that the voluntary societies' personnel came with vehicles and equipment for Yugoslav use and were prepared to get down to practical work. Those from the USA came as advisers or as they would say 'consultants'. This was the second reason. Once they had helped to draw up lists of supplies and explained their use, and made some visits to assess needs and check on deliveries, there was really no need for them to stay. Some were of Yugoslav origin and spoke the language, but only a few had expected, like the voluntary society recruits, to roll up their sleeves and get down to work with their Yugoslav fellows.

While the Yugoslav authorities were reluctant to receive many foreign personnel, they were very anxious to take advantage of the offers of places for training in the USA or UK or France. Unfortunately, disagreement between the Yugoslav authorities and the foreign embassies on who could be allowed out of Yugoslavia or allowed into the USA resulted in endless delays and the cancellation of the whole scheme in the case of the plan for sending twenty nurses to the USA. This scheme had taken up an absurd amount of time in the Mission Chief's office and unfortunately illustrated only too well the growing distrust between the Yugoslav and US governments. Other schemes for visits by doctors, health specialists and sanitary engineers were more successful. One group of medical experts whose work was enormously appreciated was the team of plastic surgeons from the UK. The fighting had left many soldiers with terrible war wounds and burns.

There had been an assumption at the beginning of UNRRA's planning that there would be the need for UNRRA to supply relief and repatriation and social welfare services. It has already been related how the Yugoslavs wanted goods and materials, believing themselves perfectly capable of organising their own service provision. This proved to be very largely true. A major survey of needs was made, but what emerged was a huge list of supplies of beds and bedding, blankets, clothing, boots and shoes, powdered and canned milk, jams and fruit juices and Red Cross packages for the large numbers in the many children's, old people's and invalids' homes that had been established throughout the country. These needs were indeed supplied together with many thousands of artificial limbs for the war disabled.[2]

The chief of the UNRRA Mission in Belgrade had two executive assistants, one Russian who spoke perfect English and the other myself. One special responsibility that fell to me was the entertaining of English-speaking guests. We had a brilliant public relations officer, but the chief liked to have me with him when he had VIPs to entertain. Thus I was present at the famous chess match between Tito and Fiorello La Guardia, the one time mayor of New York and the Director General of UNRRA after Governor Lehman retired. I was also present in Trieste when La Guardia tried to persuade the Army authorities to do something to control the pilfering of UNRRA supplies in Trieste docks. On a truly 'Catch 22' scale, whole jeeps were simply being cased up and dispatched back to the USA. La Guardia had a meeting with the Supreme Allied Commander of the Mediterranean Theatre, dressed as usual in khaki shorts. With much Italian gesticulation La Guardia demanded from the General, pointing at his shorts, something more than a 'boy scout agreement'.

A perfect illustration of the different attitudes of the Americans and the British to the Second World War and the Partisans' part in it occurred when I had to take two generals – one from the US HQ of UNNRA (whose name I am afraid I have forgotten) and General Gale from the British HQ – to lay wreaths at Avalah, the monument to the unknown soldier which was the object of NATO bombing in the 1999 war. I explained to them that the guard of honour would first come to attention lined up on either side of the walk up to the place where the generals would lay their wreaths side by side. Then the guard would shout 'Smrt Fascismu!' (Death to Fascism!), and the generals would be expected to reply 'Sloboda Narodu!' (Freedom to the People!). The American general looked worried and said '"Freedom to the People" is OK. We are all in favour of that, but what's all this about fascism?' 'That's what we have been fighting against these last five years', replied General Gale. 'Oh, yes, yes!' said the American. And I must say for him that he shouted his 'Sloboda Narodu!' with great verve, before walking up to lay his wreath.

Relations between the Yugoslavs and the British were generally good thanks to the aid given by the British Military Mission to the Partisans. The Britain-Yugoslav Friendship Society in London provided some aid and encouraged much more by its propaganda. The Society organised many visits to Yugoslavia by British MPs and journalists, who it was our job to entertain. These included an old friend of my family, Konni Zilliacus. They also included the British contingent to the International Youth Railway built in 1947 from Brcko to Banovici. Not all relations were easy, however. My offer to work on the railway was rejected, with a nice letter from the Youth Organisation saying that the offer would always remain green in their memories. Dr Singer's offer was also refused, although they badly needed doctors. We probably knew too much and speaking the language could not be so easily controlled.

There was, moreover, a long delay in processing my exit visa. I had in fact been threatened with exposure in Sarajevo on a trumped up charge of spying, designed to encourage me to spy on my next door neighbour, the British consul. Both our villas had armed guards outside and I guess that the local intelligence service knew more about his movements than I did. Despite all the public enthusiasm and popular cooperation, Tito's Yugoslavia had some of the elements of a police state. When in the end I came to leave Yugoslavia, I found that I had used up my exit visa by a visit from Rijeka to Opatija, at that time in the disputed territory of Venezia Julia around Trieste. I was stopped by the guards at the Trieste border and only the quite extraordinary fortuitous arrival at the frontier at the same moment of General Velebit, whom I knew well, got me out.

What had UNRRA achieved by the time we closed down the Mission and wrote our reports in April of 1947? Statistically, the answer was 1.275 million tons of food, 100,000 tons of textiles, 30,000 tons of medical supplies, 3,500 tractors, 20,000 horses, 9,500 mules, 4000 head of cattle, over a million tons of coke and coal, 150,000 tons of petrol, 250 locomotives, 800 wagons, 11,500 trucks and 2000 cars – to a total value of $415 million. It was an important point, recognised by the Yugoslavs, that not all the supplies had come from the

USA and UK. Some of the food and raw materials and equipment had come from other Eastern European countries, and especially from Czechoslovakia, paid for by UNRRA.[3]

One argument that was used in the West against the Yugoslavs was that UNRRA's aid was not recognised. This was manifestly untrue. The food sacks, the trucks, the locos and tractors and many other items were clearly labelled, and a travelling exhibition toured the main cities in 1946-7, describing the whole range of UNRRA's work. When I have been asked by Yugoslavs in subsequent years what I was doing in Yugoslavia before, and said that I was working with UNRRA, I have often had the smiling reply, 'Thanks to you I survived'. What many people outside the country could not accept was that a poor country like Yugoslavia had men and women everywhere who were perfectly capable of organising the distribution of relief fairly and efficiently without the help of personnel from abroad. It is my experience again that just the same situation exists in Africa, and the same colonial attitudes have reappeared in the United Nations operations in Bosnia today.

The question that should really be asked is, not what did UNRRA achieve, but what did the Yugoslavs achieve with UNRRA aid. This would have to include the rebuilding of railway lines, roads and bridges, and port facilities, between 70 per cent and 100 per cent destroyed throughout the country, the restoration of coal production half destroyed to two thirds of pre-war levels, of metals and chemicals likewise, the rebuilding of houses – 300,000 peasant houses, 200,000 town houses, 3000 schools and 500 hospitals and sanatoria. 9000 new cooperatives were established. One of my final pleasures was to be invited to attend the opening of the last railway bridge on the River Neretva that opened up the railway line into the interior of Bosnia from the Dalmatian ports. It reminded me of the struggle to get food into the country in 1944-5. In the end food rations were supplied to over 8 million people. Social assistance was provided to 2.5 million peasants, to half a million families without a wage earner, to over half a million orphans and half a million invalids, school meals to 600,000 and free milk to all children.[4] These were, of course, Yugoslav statistics, but subject to UNRRA monitoring at the centre and the regional surveys described in the previous chapter.

A mission from the United Nations Commission for Europe, which came in 1946 to investigate UNRRA in Yugoslavia, concluded that 'any person was able to get his or her fair share of supplies regardless of their purchasing power'.[5] This was only made possible by a sevenfold increase in the federal budget compared with pre-war levels and by massive transfers from the richer republics to the poorer ones. Not only was the aim to equalise living standards between the republics, but salaries and wages were fixed so that there was no more than a five to one difference between top government levels and those of the lowest paid workers. Of course, there were 'perks' for senior officials, including houses and special elite shops. I had such a house and I was able to buy a beautiful pair of high leather boots at one such shop in Belgrade.

In Yugoslav eyes the crowning achievement of the first years of liberation was that measures of relief and recovery had made possible the introduction in 1947 of a Five Year Plan, to double national income over 1939 levels and almost double income per head, through a fourfold increase of total investment and fivefold increase in industrial production and 50 per cent increase in agriculture.[6] Some of the detail of this plan seemed rather absurd, even specifying the number of pins and needles that would be produced by the end of the five years. But, starting from scratch with an undeveloped economy, such target setting could be understood. The National Plan simply consisted of an aggregation of what the republic, county and district authorities had submitted in consultation with the Central Planning Office. Targets were based on what workers and engineers, farmers and agronomists believed they could realistically do year by year in the five year period.

The Plan was based on eight principles for changing a backward agricultural economy into a modern industrial one:

- development, based on the country's rich natural resources;
- barter trade, without foreign loans;
- concentrating development in the previously most backward regions;
- increasing agricultural productivity, as labour moved from the countryside into the towns;
- predominant public ownership, but private enterprise encouraged in peasant and craft cooperatives;
- development of basic industries, including new industries in chemicals, aluminium etc.;
- great expansion of road, rail and river transport between the several republics;
- and a massive increase in education and training in schools, universities and technical institutes.[7]

In the first year, while I was still in the country, all the evidence suggested that the targets were being achieved. But there were huge problems ahead. The phasing out of UNRRA aid was to be replaced by barter trade agreements with neighbouring socialist countries – particularly Czechoslovakia and Hungary, but also with the USSR – and with West European countries – France, Holland, Switzerland and Belgium. Exports were planned to rise in 1947 to a value of $130 m. to meet imports of $420 m., the gap only partly covered by UNRRA aid. Exports in 1939 had amounted to $330 million, mainly tobacco, fruits and ores, and it was planned to double this figure by 1951.[9] In the meantime, how was the deficit to be covered and how could exports be built up to that figure? There were furious arguments among the Yugoslav leadership, first about whether to accept United States aid, second about the way to increase agricultural productivity and move labour from agriculture into industry and into mining the country's rich resources which could be the basis of expanded exports.

The Yugoslav Communist Party under Tito established its leadership of the resistance to enemy occupation on the basis of alliances with other parties and national groupings in face of a common enemy. In the 1930s the Party itself was very small: some industrial workers mainly in Croatia led by Tito and some intellectuals, mainly in Belgrade and Ljubljana, which provided much of the Party leadership. The alliances were very diverse, first coming from the several national groups, second from different classes – small-scale capitalists in Slovenia and Bosnia, peasant organisations in Croatia, rich peasant cooperatives in Serbia and Vojvodina. Excluded from the alliance were large-scale capitalists, large landowners and all collaborators with the occupying forces. Partisan struggles were fought in every part of the country not only as a war of liberation but as a social revolution. Collaborators had their property taken from them.

However, contrary to the views of many commentators, such as Misha Glenny or Neil Malcolm, the war was not a civil war or what Glenny calls a 'nationalist religious war' of 'Serb-dominated Partisans' forcing their Communist system on the rest of the Yugoslav peoples.[10] and [11] Tito was a Croat and while a majority of his generals were either Serbs or Montenegrins, among his closest associates Ivan Ribar (the first President of the National Liberation Council), Josta Nadj and Ivo Rukavina were Croats, Kardelj and Rozman were Slovenes, Apostolski was a Macedonian and Moshe Pijade was a Jew. Partisan successes depended on the principles of unity and brotherhood that they proclaimed and everywhere practised. Unity when the fighting stopped was achieved through the concept of a new Yugoslavia which, while divided up into several republics, was a federation of peoples not of states. Each republic contained peoples of different nationalities and religions. The exception was possibly Slovenia, depending on the inclusion or not of the Italian speaking people in the territory around Trieste and the large numbers of immigrant workers from other republics. A fair balance was obtained in each republic by the 'key' which allocated official positions according to the proportion of each national group in that republic.

Allocation of national resources could not be made on such a simple mathematical formula. The aim of raising the conditions of the poorest regions conflicted with the Communist principle of building on the most advanced elements in the working class, as Slovenes and Croats were quick to point out, since most of the 100,000 or so industrial workers were in their heartlands.

Transferring surplus labour from the land into industry and mining was not so easy. Urban housing and conditions of industrial work, especially in the mines, were not attractive, to put it mildly; and paying higher wages as an inducement reduced the surplus for reinvestment. Moreover, the Soviet solution for increasing agricultural productivity without benefiting the richer farmers, that of forced collectivisation, was contrary to the Partisan commitment to the peasants, who had fought valiantly in the war, and many of whom had just been given ownership of land as the result of the expropriation of large estates. Rhetorical phrases about rebuilding our country 'with our bare hands' came up against the realities of technical backwardness.

When UNRRA ended, there had been the expectation of some continuing form of international aid. Those of us who had been working with UNRRA expected to be transferred to one of the United Nations Economic Commissions. Some of our technical experts went to the European Economic Commission, or to FAO, WHO or UNICEF. Those like myself who had only some economic expertise and administrative skills found that US administered Marshall Aid had replaced the plans of the United Nations. Contrary to standard accounts of the offer of Marshall Aid, this was not at first rejected either by the USSR or by Yugoslavia. On the contrary Molotov turned up for the meetings in Paris with a large party of experts and detailed lists of requirements. Only when he found that the United States would be determining precisely how the aid was to be used did Molotov withdraw. I have some personal insight into what happened because the chief British negotiator was Oliver Franks (later Lord Franks), a Quaker and brother-in-law of my best friend in the FAU, Tom Tanner. His biography tells how Franks collapsed at the end of the negotiations.[12] This is said to have been from exhaustion. Another explanation, which he subsequently used, was that he realised that the Cold War with the Soviet Union was from then on inevitable. The Soviets had been deliberately excluded.

As for the Yugoslavs, their delegation continued negotiations for some days after Molotov left and was pressed by the British to stay.[13] They then decided to exclude themselves, but not on Stalin's orders. Tito continued to press for help from the IMF and to demand the return of the Royal Government's gold and dollar reserves, but without success. It was not perhaps helpful that Tito in 1948 persisted in his demand for Trieste to be incorporated in Yugoslavia or that Yugoslav planes shot down two American planes which crossed the border. But the Yugoslav leadership still believed in 1947 that aid from the Soviet Union could carry them through. They had signed up agreements for building industrial plants with Soviet technology, the output from which was to be shared equally by the USSR and Yugoslavia.[14]

The new International Communist Organisation, the Cominform, was based in Belgrade and some of the Yugoslav leaders believed that they were Stalin's favoured ones. Tito had no such illusions. In their struggles the Partisans had received no aid from the Soviet Union until the final joint march on Belgrade, and Stalin, out of loyalty to his British and American allies, had even for many years supported Mihailovic and the Royal Government.[15] Tito probably saw the Cominform in Belgrade as a Trojan horse. The decision was taken at the end of 1947 to rearm to defend the country's independence against east and west, and military needs had to be added to the reconstruction plan. Tito was right in his estimate, and after many alarums and excursions, Yugoslavia was expelled from the Cominform in June of 1948, thus breaking off all relations with the Communist countries. The break had been long expected but it was nonetheless traumatic.

It was not, however, the case, as is generally supposed, that the 'Yugoslav way' was only invented in order to deal with the situation caused by Tito's break with Stalin. The Yugoslav economic planners had from the first establishment of a Popular Front government decided to do things differently from the Soviet planners. Land was given to the peasants, although paradoxically the first result of the break with Stalin was that land was nationalised as an emergency measure to control food supplies and release labour for industry. Coercion of labour and the use of prisoners in the mines was another short-term remedy. But the aim of a decentralised economy, the central state being retained in the form only of a federal Parliament laying down laws for local authorities and enterprises to follow rather than directly administering economic activities, had already been promulgated by Edward Kardelj in a speech on April 25 1947, just when I was leaving Belgrade for England.[16]

One advantage for the planners, deriving from the decision to develop Yugoslavia's independent military capability, was that the obvious place to create an arms industry was Bosnia – furthest from the frontiers and near to iron and coal resources and an existing steel industry. One of the poorest regions in the country could thus be developed in this way. Yugoslavia is not the only country where the rich are more prepared to pay taxes for national defence than for redistribution to the poor. The diversion of resources for military needs, however, meant short rations elsewhere and a downward revision of many of the Five Year Plan targets. Thereafter, all grandiose national plans were abandoned in favour of Kardelj's regulatory system. Enterprises including hospitals, schools, universities and offices were granted powers of self-government with their own budgets within the law, as it was laid down in the new constitution of 1953. This is the subject of the next chapter.

Those who opposed this development and supported a Soviet style command economy were soon weeded out. The purge was applied throughout the country and at every level of government. Thousands left the country, many were jailed and some executed. An example of the purges was my dear friend Nada Kraigher, who remained an unreconstructed Stalinist to her dying day. At a reception in Ljubljana, where her cousin Boris had been made Economics

Minister in the Slovene government, she shouted across the room to him asking if he knew the price of eggs in the market. She was promptly arrested and jailed and only released on grounds of her ill health as the result of the intervention of her partner Dr. Robert Neubauer, who had been in charge of the Partisan hospitals in Italy and was the leading TB specialist in the country, indeed in the world. He became for some years a TB consultant to the World Health Organisation. Nada could laugh at herself. When she visited Georgia after Stalin's death and Khruschev's denunciation, she noticed that there was still a statue of Stalin in Tbilisi. 'So, at least', she said to her guides, 'you people recognise what a great man he was.' 'He was a monster', they replied. 'Then why do you keep the statue?' she asked. 'He was a Georgian, wasn't he?' was the response. Nationalism has much to answer for. And this will become a major theme in the next stages of the story of Former Yugoslavia.

Golnik TB Sanatorium, Slovenia, 1958

Workers' Council, Rade Koncar, Zagreb, 1960

Chapter 7

Tito's Break with Stalin, 1948-57

The most difficult political decision I have had to make in my life was to decide how to respond to Tito's break with Stalin.[1] When I abandoned my Quaker pacifist upbringing and became a Communist because of what I had seen and heard of Tito's Partisans, I had no doubts about the decision, only about how to carry it out. Later, when I decided to leave the Communist Party, I had no doubt about the decision; only about when to do it. But in 1948 to support Tito was to leave my comrades in the Communist Party and to support Tito against all the power and prestige of the Soviet Union. I knew much more about Yugoslavia than most people. There were things about Tito's Yugoslavia that I did not like – the spying and use of police power, the replacement by political appointments of many of the first local leaders I met in Bosnia. It was effectively a single Party system. I did not like the practice of '*protecsia*'. This was the protection of knowing someone who was a Communist Party member, who would vouch for you and give you precedence in having your business dealt with. In theory for some years after the war membership of the Yugoslav Party was secret, the aim being to emphasise the all-embracing character of the Popular Front. But everyone seemed to know who were Party members.

I could understand these things in the circumstances of war and immediate post-war state building and the undoubted leading role of Communists in the wartime resistance. The results, which I had seen with my own eyes after the war, of the needs of the people being met with an enthusiasm and efficiency that was heart warming were justification enough. Nobody who was there at

the time could doubt the genuine support for Tito, the widespread involvement of men and women in decision making and the universal commitment
to the tasks of reconstruction and development. There was a real sense of
participation and democratic accountability at the base, however secretive the
decision making was at the top. And I truly believed that in time this too would
be opened up.

There was a quite personal loss for me, if I abandoned Tito: not only the
impossibility for many years of seeing my Yugoslav friends, but the loss of a
book I had written on the struggle of the Yugoslav people to resist the Axis occupation and to rebuild their war-torn country after victory. My book was to
be called *Yugoslav Pictorial*, and had hundreds of beautiful pictures which I had
collected to illustrate the text (some of which are reproduced in this book). It
was sponsored by the Britain Yugoslav Friendship Association and was to be
printed by the British Communist Party press. It had to be abandoned and still
rests in its three green folders to this day for me to pore over nostalgically.

The arguments that were used against Tito by the Communist Party pro-
tagonists in Great Britain like my friend James Klugmann, whose book *From
Trotsky to Tito*[2] had much influence among Party members, appeared to me to
be quite unconvincing and in some respects untrue. It seemed to me incredible that James could write such a condemnatory book within three years of
his euphoric pamphlet *Yugoslavia Faces the Future*, published by the Britain
Yugoslav Friendship Association.[3] I condemned Trotsky for the same reason
that Bukharin confessed – that division could not be tolerated in the face of the
threat from capitalism and then fascism. But to accuse Tito of deviation from
the true faith and of being an agent of American intelligence seemed to me
quite unacceptable in the light of what he had done in uniting a divided people,
leading the most effective resistance inside Europe to fascist occupation and
beginning to build a new socialist Yugoslavia.

My distrust of James Klugmann's book arose from several doubts that I
had. The main evidence against Tito in the book was taken from the accusations made against other East European Communist leaders – Slansky in
Czechoslovakia, Raj in Hungary, Kostov in Bulgaria, Xoxe in Albania – that
they had links with British and American intelligence. I had some doubts about
these trials. I could hardly imagine our old family friend Konni Zilliacus as
an American spy, but it was as such that he was cited. Finally, a contrast was
being made between the apparent successes in reconstruction in countries
that had followed the Stalin line and some economic failures in Yugoslavia,
which were reported from Tito's own speeches. One thing I knew was wrong.
James claimed that the Yugoslav Communist Party was so secretive that you
could not even read about it in 1946 and 1947. That was when I was buying in
Belgrade bookshops copies of *Communist: The Organ of the Central Committee
of the Communist Party of Yugoslavia*.[4] I have a copy for January 1947 in front

of me as I write. And while Party membership was supposedly so secret, James seemed to know that there were only 160 Party members in the 4000 workforce at the Zeleznik works near Belgrade.[5]

The real dilemma was that it was a choice, not between Stalin and Tito, Soviet and Yugoslav socialism, but between an immensely powerful Soviet Union and a tiny Yugoslavia. Of course, I knew that there was spying and police power in a single-Party state in the Soviet Union, as much if not more than in Yugoslavia. I knew about the Moscow trials in 1937. My wife's first husband had been trained at the Comintern School and had to flee to China to warn comrades when Bukharin was arrested. I had read very carefully Bukharin's confession in her copy of the report of the trials. Actions which he had taken that caused disunity in the face of the threat of fascism had, he confessed, to be condemned. That was it – for Tito as for Bukharin, both of whom I admired enormously. Though I did not approve of the death penalty, and had then no idea of the thousands of others Stalin had killed, or of the millions sent to the Gulag, the threat of fascism was the justification; and it was the Soviet resistance to Hitler's armies that had ended that threat. No rewriting of history has been able to erase the simple fact accepted by all at the time – from Churchill and Roosevelt downwards – that the turning point of the Second World War was the Red Army's defeat of the German armies at Stalingrad.[6]

If we could sleep peacefully in our beds because of Soviet resistance to the threat of fascism, it seemed to be equally clear at that time that only the strength of the Soviet Union stood between us and the power of British and American capitalism. I had seen enough of the poverty and unemployment and misery caused by the failures of capitalism in the 1930s, and too much of the oppression of the colonial peoples in the British Empire at the same time, to have any faith in the revival of capitalist empires. Soviet empire seemed a better bet and held out the promise of a fuller life for millions of human beings everywhere.

When in 1954 Khruschev flew to Belgrade to re-establish relations with Tito, he is said to have greeted Tito with the words, 'All is forgiven. It was all the fault of Beria [Stalin's chief of police].' I went at once to see James Klugmann, to ask him how much was 'all'. 'Did that', I asked, 'include all the East European trials?' I was told peremptorily 'to keep my mouth shut'. I did not, and when the Hungarian revolt was suppressed by Soviet tanks in 1956 and Khruschev's secret speech was published in 1957, I knew I had to leave the Communist fold unless quite revolutionary changes occurred inside its leadership. There were no changes, though a few of us tried to make some. We failed and we left.

Looking back after fifty years and seeing the world as it is now, without the Soviet Union – under 'the full spectrum dominance' of United States capitalism, what do I think? I am glad that I got on with my job of teaching working-class activists, hoping one day to begin to build a socialist society. The 'ifs' of history are pure speculation. Had we in the British Communist Party and elsewhere on the Left supported Tito, could this perhaps have made possible a fully democratic development of socialism, not only in Yugoslavia but in the Soviet Union – before Gorbachev, by which time it was too late? I don't know how to answer. Only the Australian Party supported Tito. The rest of us were too frightened of losing what seemed then to be our only hope for a socialist future. I do not regret joining the Communist Party or my support for the Soviet Union in the 1939-45 war and in its subsequent rebuilding of a war-torn country, however unfashionable it may now be to say so. But I should not have supported Stalin against Tito in 1948.

What then were the results in Yugoslavia of Tito's break with the Communist bloc? There was a long history of dissent in Tito's relations with Stalin. If Vlado Dedijer's book *Tito Speaks* is to be believed, it was only by not going to Moscow on one occasion that Tito avoided elimination for his independent views.[7] Stalin gave no aid to the Partisans. But there is no doubt that for a time at least Stalin supported Yugoslavia's Five Year Plan. When that support was withdrawn, it was inevitable that Tito would look to the West, and most particularly to the United States, for loans to bridge the continuing gap between Yugoslavia's exports and the imports necessary for the country's industrialisation. His strongest card was the build-up of a military force capable of resisting a Soviet invasion such as occurred in Hungary in 1956 and Czechoslovakia in 1968. As a bulwark against the Soviet Union, Tito could hope to obtain loans from the United States, but he still wanted to preserve his independence through his trade relations with neighbouring states.

Stalin had already stamped firmly on Tito's suggestion of a Balkan Federation to include Bulgaria and Albania (later perhaps even Greece) as presenting for Stalin far too powerful a potentially independent socialist force. The trials and execution of dissident East European leaders, Raj in Hungary and Kostov in Bulgaria accused of 'Titoism', were soon to show that no breath of independence was to be permitted in the Soviet empire. Comecon, the Soviet trade bloc, did not include Yugoslavia. Existing trade agreements had, however, to be fulfilled and the drain of exports from the Yugoslav economy to pay for essential imports reduced availabilities of food and other goods for the already hard pressed Yugoslav people. The defence budget in 1949 was taking 22 per cent of national income. Wholesale prices and some retail prices were brought under direct state control. The introduction at the end of 1949 of the system of Workers' Councils can be seen in part as an attempt to gain workers' support for wage restraint and employment cuts.[8]

A desperate situation was only brought to an end in 1950 with the negotiation of loans from the USA to cover some two thirds of the Yugoslav current account deficit on foreign trade and with the receipt of IMF drawings and World Bank loans. At the same time, US export licensing controls through COCOM,[9] were largely lifted and Yugoslav sales to the west of copper and lead were permitted. The new freedom to manoeuvre made possible the long-planned decentralisation of government from the federal state to the republics and to the counties and districts within them and to the establishment of Workers Councils. Yet this decentralisation of economic and administrative powers was combined with a considerable strengthening of the political power of the Communist Party in place of the Popular Front. The Party became the Yugoslav League of Communists and the Popular Front was renamed the Socialist Alliance of Working People. None of this was to reduce the authority of the Party, as was made clear by the proposed introduction of a *'nomenklatura'* of some 90,000 persons.[10]

This strengthening of the Party membership and the proposed *nomenklatura* were the work of Alexander Rankovic, the Minister for the Interior, in charge of the secret police, Tito's hard man. It was not accepted; but the proposal was too much for Milovan Djilas, who may perhaps be called Tito's 'soft man'. Certainly, he was Tito's closest comrade in the Partisan's struggle and after the war became Yugoslavia's Vice-President. His criticism of the centralisation of power in the Communist Party and his public appeal in 1953 for the democratisation of socialist power in Yugoslavia led to his expulsion from the Party in January of 1954. When in 1956 he came out in favour of the Hungarian revolution, calling it 'the end of Communism', he was sentenced to three years hard labour in Mitrovica prison. His book *The New Class* was published in 1957 and led to a second trial and seven years imprisonment.[11] Djilas's argument was not just that the Party had become corrupted by power, but that this was the inevitable result of the required ideological unity and lack of criticism in a single Party state, which was central to the whole idea of national communism.

Djilas may have had rather exaggerated ideas of the benefits of social democracy in countries like Sweden, but he had a very accurate picture of socialism as it was developing in Yugoslavia. The much vaunted free associations of labour in industrial enterprises and work cooperatives were then, as he saw them, in effect no more than an extension of the ownership rights of the "new class" to be seen in their big houses, cars, privileged shops and rich life style. My friends told me that the brightest 5 to 7 per cent of children in school were being singled out in every region for Party membership. Workers' Councils certainly consisted of managers and engineers as well as union representatives, who would all be Party members. The trade unions' role was no more than the encouragement of more and better production. Even the post-war negotiating strength of workers, in work brigades and in a generally tight labour market, was being steadily reduced. What Djilas was jailed for was that he did not believe that this was only a temporary phenomenon, the result of economic shortages and the lack of educated workers.

At the time I firmly believed that he was wrong. What I failed then to realise was that the absence of opposition parties appealing to voters across all the republics meant that criticism of the leadership became concentrated in the several nationalist groupings. I recognised the need for opposition in Hungary. I too supported the Hungarian revolution and left the Communist Party in protest against the Soviet crushing of that revolution. But from my reading of books and articles that came out of Yugoslavia I came to believe that the Yugoslav model was democratic and potentially a socialist model. What was emerging in Yugoslavia was a planning system, no longer a planned economy, but one that was a mixture of liberal and socialist elements. Economic resources were not allocated by a central bureaucracy, but it could hardly be called market socialism because there was no competitive price mechanism at work. Susan Woodward, in her magisterial study of the *Political Economy of Yugoslavia 1945-1990* described it as being:

> based on the idea of democratic consultation and agreement among autonomous and self-interested but also cooperative property owners (governments and the work collectives with rights to manage social assets) on common rules for value and distribution.[12]

This was the compromise essentially reached between the necessary power of a central state to manage international relations and fiscal policy and the jealously guarded power of the several republics to manage their own affairs. It was equally a compromise between the necessary rules for providing for social needs and the freedom of groups of associated workers to look after their own interests. These were awkward compromises and the way they worked out in detail raised big questions, which the new constitution introduced in 1953 was designed to settle. In the meantime, there is no doubt that great energies were released. The country, in the words of one of Tito's most trusted lieutenants, Vukmanovic-Tempo, 'took on the character of one great construction site'.[13]

The 1953 constitution gave to local authorities the powers of political and economic organs of government. Not only in industrial and commercial enterprises and agricultural cooperatives but in educational, health and other social services workers in groups, large and small, were given a budget to spend in the way they thought best, albeit within a rigid framework of controls which all related to their integration with other workers in other enterprises and departments. The central state in effect withdrew from much of the management of the economy.[14] The fatal flaw, which became increasingly apparent as time went by and central control over fiscal policy was relaxed, was that the whole system depended on transfers from the rich republics – Croatia and Slovenia – to the poor – primarily Bosnia-Hercegovina, Macedonia and Kosovo-Metojia. Serbia neither gained nor lost on this arrangement. This transfer was achieved first by the common health and educational provision throughout the whole country and second by a General Investment Fund financed at first by federal monies and later by a direct capital tax on the richer republics, when the Fund came to be called the Federal Fund for More Rapid Development of Less Developed Republics and Regions. This tax was fiercely resented in Croatia and Slovenia and after 1975 could be paid in the form of direct Croat and Slovene investment in enterprises in the less developed regions.[15]

Susan Woodward has an interesting way of describing the respective progress of the more developed regions, which she calls the 'Slovene Model', the work of the two leading Slovenes – Kardelj and Kidric – in Tito's government, and of the less developed regions, which she calls the 'Foca Model', Foca being a particularly poor area in southern Bosnia-Hercegovina, famous for the Partisans' 'Foca Regulations', which I had learnt about when I had been there in 1945. According to the Slovene planners the whole country should follow their model, since it was economically the most advanced. Slovenia, as Woodward describes its economy, was:

> industrially advanced, a lean socialist core of skilled workers and commercially attuned manufacturers participating fully in Western trade [just across their borders in Austria and Italy], a settled labour reserve of private farmers and artisans, and a government of experts and local militia ….[16]

By contrast, Foca was typical of the least industrially advanced economies, few skilled workers, no 'commercially attuned' manufacturers, no foreign trade, not even a railway line nearer than Dubrovnik or Sarajevo, no 'settled' labour reserve of private farmers, but a large unsettled surplus of peasant labour on the land, few artisans and fewer government experts. The resources they had were of timber and minerals and water power and their own bare hands. These could be, and were, employed to great effect in the heroic workers' and youth brigades of the first years of post-war reconstruction. But such methods were costly and inefficient for long-term development. For that, outside finance was needed. It was obtained from the West after Tito broke with Stalin, but the more advanced regions – Slovenia and Croatia – claimed it. Foca had to develop as best it could after one or two major mining, quarrying and hydro-electric schemes had been introduced. That left them still with an underclass of unskilled workers and surplus agricultural labour. At the same time, a universal Yugoslav wide health and education service was producing bright young people whose only hope was to emigrate.

The progress of these two models worked itself out in the great advances of the 1960s carrying a backward, underdeveloped economy into industrialisation and modern civilisation, then stuttering in the 1970s, into disaster in the 1980s and destruction in the 1990s. The advance should not be underestimated. The targets of the first Five Year Plan were reached three years late, but by the mid-

1960s the statistics revealed a huge advance in national income of 9 per cent a year from 1953 to 1964, electric power output up five times, coal output more than doubled, steel production trebled, a fivefold increase in cellulose and in cotton yarn. Nearly a million new housing units had been constructed. The tonnage of freight moved by rail had doubled and by motor transport and by air increased six-fold. Over 9000 tractors, 9000 trucks, 28,000 motorcars and 48,000 motorbikes were coming off the assembly lines each year. Earnings from tourism had risen from $7 million to $98 million as more and more hotels were built along the Dalmatian coast and in the ski resorts of Bosnia and Slovenia.[17]

Although Susan Woodward's contrasting models of Slovenia and Foc'a may be too extreme – Slovene experts went to Foca and Foca's workers went to Slovenia – she is absolutely right when she argues that to understand the causes of the collapse of Former Yugoslavia it is necessary to look back to the origins of the planning system. We shall have to see in the next chapters how this encouraged and interacted with the emergence of the separate nationalisms, in the end to destroy the former Yugoslavia. But in the meantime the great experiment in workers' self-management was unfolding with much success. Life for the Yugoslav peoples really was improving, with high hopes for the future.

Ask any of the several Yugoslav peoples who were living at that time and they will agree.

Shipyards, Split, 1961

Iron and steel works, Jesenice, 1970

Chapter 8

Workers' Self-Management, 1958-74

In 1957 I left the British Communist Party, having failed along with other academics – Stephen Bodington, Maurice Dobb, Christopher Hill and Hyman Levy among others – to change the Party into a pluralist organisation from its normal democratic centralism, more centralist than democratic. I felt free – and would be allowed – to return to Yugoslavia. How much of pluralism and democracy would I find there? I had kept in touch with what had been happening in the country through reading the many books and papers and reports that were published during the decade I had been away. The opportunity for a visit came in 1959. I had become a founding member of the New Left in Britain; for the first two numbers of our new journal *New Left Review*[1] we received an invitation from the Yugoslav government to send a delegate to make an extended tour throughout the country at government expense and to report. I was chosen to go and duly found myself at Ljubljana station, greeted by my old friends Nada Kraigher and Robert Neubauer.

A few days' visit was not long to catch up with all that had happened to these dear friends. Although we had seen each other on a visit they had made to England, I had not seen Ljubljana for over ten years. My first impression was of the fine new blocks of flats and the many cars on the road from the old station. I might have been in Germany or Austria. Indeed, of course, I was almost in Austria. Shops were full of sophisticated dresses and shoes, of beautiful furniture and of all the electronic products I was used to – all made in Slovenia. The market was overflowing with fruit and vegetables and flowers. The streets were full of school children. The university was bulging with new students. Nada's publishing house had a long list of titles, in several languages. Robert's clinic and sanatorium at Golnik was greatly expanded. The stud farm of white horses at Lipica was re-established. The Slovene model was working. But what would I find in Foca?

First, I had to go to Belgrade by train – in a sleeper no less – to be briefed by my hosts in the English Department of the Foreign Ministry. Most of what they had to tell me I already knew from my reading, but what I saw was all new. Apart from Terasija and the city centre and Kala Magdan, I hardly recognised this greatly expanded city with the vast new development at Zemun through which I had been driven from the airport. Judging by the shops and hotels and restaurants and the traffic, the Slovene model was working here too. I could hardly wait for my driver who was going to take me south over the mountains and by way of Sarajevo to the coast and then up north through Bosnia to Zagreb and Ljubljana, to see how the parts of the country I knew best had fared.

The Serbian plain seemed little changed – a few more tractors and cars – but as we approached the borders of Bosnia reconstruction was very obvious. Banja Kovilaca looked once more like the little health resort it had been in Austrian times. There was a fine new bridge over the river Drina at Zvornik in place of the ancient ferry boats. Climbing up from Drinjac'a to Vlasenica and on to Han Pjesak and the forests of Romanija all was changed. In Sokolac, my special favourite, there were smart new houses as well as rebuilt log cabins. I stopped at the People's Committee to see if any of my old friends were there. They had all been replaced by bright young apparatchiks. Arriving in Sarajevo from the east little seemed to have changed – the trams, the mosques and great poplar trees around the Bascarsija, the old market place, the Hotel Europa and the main central buildings from Austrian times along the Miljacka and the old Muslim houses climbing up the hills on either side made me ache with nostalgia. Only when we travelled west did we see the great new blocks of flats along the road to Ilidza and the Vrelo Bosne, the source of the river Bosna, and now a smart tourist complex.

I had meetings in Sarajevo with Ministry officials, none the same as I had known, but all having fond recollections of UNRRA. The city had expanded along with the growth of local industry. In talks with a Sarajevo professor of sociology I learned that the urbanisation of Muslim villagers had not gone well. Most of the new arrivals to take up industrial jobs had been Serbs. The professor was very impressed with the work of the Austrian sociologist Ernest Gellner in explaining the difficulty of moving from an agrarian to an industrial society in communities like those of the Muslim Bosnians which had rigid social stratifications.[2] There were serious problems of unemployment and alcoholism among Muslim workers. But there were new carpets and local crafts in the Muslim market in the city centre, where I had hoped to stay. My driver, however, did not want us to stay in the city but had chosen a new hotel at the ski resort on mount Trebevic. I had to show him the way, with aching memories of times spent driving up in my jeep. It was certainly beautifully cool up there after our hot day's driving, and in a day's time we would see Foca.

The road to Gorazde was indeed much improved and a great memorial had been built to celebrate the bloody battles against the Fifth German offensive in July 1943. The mosques and churches and houses in Foca had been rebuilt, but the place still gave the impression of poverty. The most obvious change was the coming of electricity. Pylons now stood like giants striding the hills. We visited one of the new hydro-electric power stations at Jablonica on the Neretva river outside Mostar, and I was there instructed in the workings of the Yugoslav wage system, a central part of the new self-managed economy. This is what I had come to see, and I wanted to know how it worked.

A basic monthly wage was paid according to graded skills out of the net earnings of the enterprise, based on the previous year's earnings, from which were deducted federal, republic and local taxes and social insurance and some-times a contribution to the housing fund. To this was added, at the end of an accounting year, a bonus resulting from higher enterprise earnings out of in-creased sales or increased productivity in that year compared with the previous year. So the answer to a question about what you earn was often given by the seemingly meaningless number of '13 months', the extra month's pay being the bonus. At the power station, however, the answer came with very gloomy faces: '11 months'. 'How could that be?' I asked. 'We were fined', they said, 'because we were all asleep when the order came for us to switch on the generators to make our contribution to local supplies.' 'Better stay awake next year!' was all I could say.

Our next stop, Mostar, reminded me so vividly of my first arrival there and the way that Hamo, who later became one of our interpreters, attached him-self to us, speaking a mixture of German and English. I had no doubt that he had been attached to the Germans a few days earlier, but he was a likeable lad and a very quick learner, who seemed to have ingratiated himself with the new regime. We stayed, as before, in the Muslim quarter at the hotel next to the baths and just above the famous medieval bridge (the bridge the Croats would destroy in 1990). I ordered Zilavca, the local white wine and noted that the cork was the full 4 mm. in length, but the taste did not seem up to the delicious wine I had remembered. It was only the next day when we crossed the river on our way to Dubrovnik that I saw the huge new town of Mostar with schools and hospitals that had grown up on the Croatian side of the river.

Entering Dubrovnik from the hills behind the walls of the old city is always a thrilling experience. Nothing seemed to have changed in the city and port – a few more boats and a new hotel next to the Argentina by the sea beyond the port. Nothing else, but by great good fortune on our second night in Dubrovnik there was to be a performance of *Hamlet* at the castle, which provides the most nearly perfect backcloth to Elsinore that I could imagine. I was taken there by a Montenegrin journalist who confided in me during the first interval that I could have no idea of the agony that Hamlet suffered in considering the problem of revenge for his father's death in the way that he as a Montenegrin could feel it. This was because his grandfather's family had been murdered by Shkiptars (Albanians) over a land dispute and he had been brought up to believe that one day this would have to be avenged. In Tito's Yugoslavia this was unthinkable, but it still occupied his mind. (One day forty years later it would come only too horribly true.)

From Dubrovnik to Split, another familiar town, seemingly quite unspoilt, where I could sit in the shade of Diocletian's walls in the central square, read the paper, drink coffee, walk along the water front and revive memories of my first arrival here in 1944. But I had work to do. We visited the shipyard, very busy with orders mainly for export employing some 4000 workers. I was able to get a much clearer understanding of workers' self management. The workers met as a collective and elected seventy representatives, one or more from each department according to its size, to serve for two years on the Workers' Council. The Council had committees – for planning, personnel, safety, social standards, complaints, income distribution. The Council elected for one year (only two successive years of office being permitted) a Managing Board of ten which met with the General Director whom the Board appointed for four years together with fifteen department heads. Each department had a Department Workers Council with several committees. Finally, there was a supervisory committee to ensure that the yard was managed in accordance with its constitution and national laws.

It seemed as if the seventy workers' representatives, during their year in office, and especially the management board, must spend most of their time talking, but we were told that meetings were not more frequent than fortnightly. The Director obviously ran the yard with his department heads but subject to consultation and accountability to the workers, who could always sack him after four years. It was a striking fact that although white collar workers made up only about one in six of the work force, they usually made up some 40 per cent of the Council. Judging by the order book the system worked, but the rationality lay in a highly competitive world market, which would keep costs down and most particularly labour costs.[3]

After Split we drove along the lovely Dalmatian coast and then at Zadar turned inland and climbed over the mountains on atrocious roads to spend the night among the lakes at Plitvica, where my driver said that I had to stay in the splendid new hotel built to cater for tourists. I had wanted to go into Bihac because this was a predominantly Muslim area surrounded by Croats to the north and Serbs to the south, where the population had resisted the German occupation with great courage and I wanted to see how they had fared since I had last been there. But we had to press on to Zagreb, where we had appointments with government ministers. These proved to be very disappointing. I was wined and dined with splendid hospitality, but got very bland answers to questions about the poorer parts of southern Croatia. They would all benefit, I was assured, from the great expansion of the tourist trade. Zagreb seemed relatively untouched by the war and perhaps even more than Ljubljana reminded me of Munich or Vienna. We visited a coal-fired power station, which emitted the most appalling black smoke, but had immaculate blocks of new housing for the miners and an amazing range of cars, including many Mercedes, in the car parks.

Back in Slovenia I had one important factory visit to make. This was to the main Iskra electro-mechanics and electronics factory in Kranj just outside Ljubljana. I was led up to the manager's office where the Chairman of the Workers' Council was seated at the manager's desk (the manager was away) and welcomed me with the offer of a glass of plum brandy from a bottle in the desk, as if he owned the place, which in an important sense he did. Elected to the Council by the whole work force and to the Management Board as chairman, he shared with the representative from the local government authority the right to appoint the manager and exercise a veto over other managerial appointments. The local government authority in this case was the County. More important plants might be owned by the republic, less important by districts. During the chairman's term of office, which was for two years with the possibility of serving for another term, chairmanship of the Council, as with several of the Council's committees, was a full-time job.

I was interested to know how in this company they decided on the distribution of the income earned from sales, taking into account current wages and salaries and future investment. The chairman produced a large chart, which I had noticed reproduced on a very large scale on different walls in the factory buildings. It was headed 'Income Distribution: 1959' and had a first column showing items of income and disbursements and then four columns of figures, the first showing values in dinars, the second percentages of sales receipts and the third and fourth some calculations, as far as I could tell, of the percentages respectively of net profit and 'clear profit'. Total sales were valued at something over 6 billion dinars (about £6 million I reckoned). This had 100 against it in the second column and from this the second item – Cost of Materials – took 34.4 per cent. Before getting to a Net Profit figure, however, there were three more deductions – for Amortisation (3.3 per cent), for other Overheads (13.3 per cent) and for the Federal Turnover Tax (5.6 per cent). That left Net Profit of just over 2.7 billion dinars – just 43.4 per cent of sales receipts.

'How', I asked, ' was amortisation calculated?' The answer was that varying interest rates were assigned for the depreciation of different assets. Other overheads covered all expenses apart from labour – no rent was paid but these expenses included all the costs of telephones, postage, advertising, transport etc. The Federal Turnover Tax was set by the state according to the different products made at the factory, low on the most modern electronics, high on old types of electrical equipment. This tax, I knew, was the main source of central government income. Before coming to what was called 'clear profit', contributions had to be made to Social Needs. These would be for both county and district services and took nearly half the net profit (just over 20 per cent of the original sales receipts).

So what was left as 'clear profit' from which personal incomes could be paid was not much more than 1.4 billion dinars (22.7 per cent of sales) and even this did not all go to the workers. There were payments to be made to a Reserve Fund (1.5 per cent of sales), a Capital Assets Fund (2.1 per cent of sales) and a Social Welfare Fund (0.7 per cent of sales). In the end then there were 1,155 billion dinars for Personal Incomes. If there were 4000 workers, I calculated, that would be about £300 a year – less than £6 a week, compared with an average wage in the UK at that time of about £15.

And that was not in fact the end. As in the UK there would be income tax and National Insurance payments. So in Yugoslavia the federal budget took 11 per cent, Social Insurance 24 per cent and at Iskra there was a House Building Fund taking another 7 per cent out of personal incomes. A worker on average wages had a net personal income, after all deductions, of about £4 a week – a third of that of a UK worker. But the Yugoslav worker would have his house rent free, his holidays at a company rest home, free sports and recreational facilities; and most important of all goods in the shops would be much cheaper, partly because of lower labour costs, partly because indirect taxes would not be adding 10 per cent to 15 per cent to all prices.[4]

Before I asked whether the workers at Iskra were happy with all this, I asked whether they understood it all. I had worked quite hard to get it at all clear in my own mind. 'They understand it only too well', was the answer – 'Look at the charts on the walls! – and they would all like more control over their money and less taxation!' I seemed to have heard that one before. The company had done well the previous year and the pay-out was 13 months – a month's bonus over the wages based on the previous year. But it was obvious that all the deductions over which the workers had no control rankled.

The central government in Belgrade obviously got the message. By 1964 I read that the 'liberal reformers' had won the argument with the 'developmental economists', who were quite ruthlessly purged. Power was still further devolved from the centre down to the republics, but also down to each individual enterprise. The enterprise Councils were granted full ownership rights subject to regulation by the republics, with only the Federal Turnover Tax and international financial relations left to the centre. These reforms were introduced by stages and ratified in a new constitution in 1974. An even more important reform took place in 1964. This was to end all central controls on foreign trade. Each enterprise could thereafter enter into agreements for its own exports and imports.[5] What then was left of coordination between the republics and of overall national wage policies?

This was the question I asked everywhere on visits which I made with my family in the late 1960s and early 1970s, to meet up with our Yugoslav friends on the Adriatic coast at Cavtat, near Dubrovnik, at Piran near Trieste and on one long car journey from Split through Bosnia and up to Zagreb and Ljubljana. We could see year by year the enormous expansion of hotels all along the Dalmatian coast and we could also see that the workers in them were doing very well. So were other workers – in large scale agricultural cooperatives, vineries in Hercegovina, maize farmers in the Srem, hop growers in Slovenia. You could tell by the Mercedes cars standing outside the little villas surrounding the cooperative's offices. Elsewhere, in the countryside little seemed to have changed except that in the small towns and villages there were seemingly more young people hanging around apparently unemployed.

The answer to my question about national coordination in an increasingly decentralised form of government was that a great gap was indeed opening up between on the one hand what was called the 'social sector' of cooperatives and enterprises of 'associated workers', which included those in health and education, and on the other the remaining private sector of small owners mainly peasants and agricultural workers and a small number of privately owned businesses. This private sector possibly amounted to half of the population, but was largely in the underdeveloped south of the country and not in the developed regions of the north. As a result, the gap between the standard of living in the north and that in the south was steadily widening. The population outside the social sector was theoretically represented in the Socialist Alliance of Working People, but their influence was small.[6]

Was there no coordination? Our friends told us that there was in fact a quite powerful coordination exercised by the Party, the League of Yugoslav Communists. This was widely, and not always jokingly, referred to by my friends as a 'managers' club', because its members so often worked through the Chambers of Commerce for the several branches of the economy. Through these institutions common policies were worked out for the republics and also for the whole nation. 'Managers' club' gives a false impression, because the League of Communists, like the Yugoslav Communist Party, saw itself as 'the vanguard organisation of the working class' a mass party, as well as historically the leader of a national liberation struggle. 'Working class' has to be understood in a wide sense. At the Tenth Congress of the League of Communists of Yugoslavia in 1975 Tito made the following statement:

> The working class is the major force of the socialist revolution. Its revolution-
> ary nature is contained in its social being. But it is necessary to emphasise that
> the technical and other creative and working intelligentsia belonging to socialist
> production relations – within the framework of self-managed associated labour,
> and on the basis of the principles of distribution according to work – constitute
> an integral part of the working class.

The same Congress resolved that it was a clear obligation of the League of
Communists 'to work with determination and through organised activity for a
workers' majority in its ranks – wherever realistic conditions for this exist'.[7]

The main anxiety expressed by speakers at the Congresses of the League of
Communists concerned the emergence of a technical-bureaucratic class of
managers – Djilas's old criticism. Yugoslav Communists, after using the concentration of economic, political and legislative power to destroy the remnants
of feudal and capitalist power and to undertake the basic industrialisation of
the country, had chosen the road of social ownership and self-management by
the working people in place of state ownership and central management of the
Soviet economy. But self-management gave great power to those who became
managers. Moreover, the continuing existence of a competitive market, not
only for goods and services but also for labour and capital, created the opportunity for monopoly positions to be established and exploitation of labour
to survive, and indeed to revive. The process of transforming the state from
a force above society into an instrument of self-management and rule by the
working class led to successive measures of constitutional decentralisation, but
left in their wake big divisions between classes and republics.[8]

From my experience it would be wrong to underestimate the remarkable increase in the proportion of the population which became involved in political
and economic decision making. This was not only the result of decentralisation of government and of workers' self-management in the social sector, but
equally of the adoption of the delegate system of democracy in place of the representative system. Representatives, like local councillors or MPs, are in place
over a number of years until voted out and can choose how and when to report
back. Delegates are subject to recall and immediate report-back. Sent up from
one level of government to the one higher, from factories, workshops, offices,
schools, hospitals and other institutions, in Yugoslavia they were involved in
important discussions of policy; and very large numbers became involved,
since election was generally for two years with the possibility of re-election for
another term.

Self-management combined with the delegate system seemed to mean the
degrading of the role of trade unions. Workers were voting for managers, for
delegates and for trade union officials. It is sometimes argued that this must be
self-contradictory. But I was told by many friends in Yugoslavia that this was

quite sensible: some people are good at managing, others at criticising and still others at thinking about broad policy. Judged by results, the increased decentralisation of decision making had the effect of forcing the trade unions to play a much more adversarial role, as in capitalist countries. Strikes were reported in several parts of the country and in several industries.[9] But the big divide was not between classes in the normally accepted sense. It was between the social sector and the private sector, and between the north and the south.

Making democracy work from the bottom up instead of from the top down certainly involves more people in the process than a Parliamentary system with elections every four or five years; and this must be an advantage. It has one big disadvantage, which was especially serious in Yugoslavia. The delegate system provides a strong institutional base for particularist interests, whether industrial, occupational or regional.[10] Decentralisation gave increasing power to the republics, and this applied not only to government but to the League of Yugoslav Communists. The Leagues in each republic ceased to be branches of a national all-Yugoslav League, but became autonomous organisations within the League. In the absence of a political party system, they became in effect the basis for nationalist parties. Economic developments by the late 1960s were at the same time beginning to create a serious problem of disparate growth.

From 1968 unemployment began to grow rapidly, not so much in Croatia and Slovenia, but in Bosnia, Macedonia and especially in Kosovo. Much of this unemployment was concealed by the migration of Yugoslav workers to the booming economies of Western Europe, and especially to Germany. By 1971 it was estimated that there were one million Yugoslavs working abroad out of a total working population of thirteen million, The statistics showed that only just over half of the total population of working age were in regular employment. Half a million were registered unemployed and the rest, mainly in the countryside and in the south whose jobs in agriculture, in forestry, in construction work, even in textiles had only seasonal and irregular employment. The social sector, as it increased its labour productivity, was actually shedding labour.[11] How could this be?

One explanation offered was that workers in the self-managing enterprises, having every opportunity to increase their earnings by reducing the number of workers had no incentive to invest to create new jobs but were happy to shed labour. This explanation was proposed by American economist Benjamin Ward in the *American Economic Review* in issues for both 1958 and 1967 which gained wide currency.[12] It was refuted by those who pointed out that real wages had not risen but had actually fallen during the years of rapidly increasing unemployment.[13] The reason for this was that central government was very well aware of this danger to job creation, and had imposed an incomes policy restraining any such wage increases in the social sector. Kardelj had learnt from Ota Sik, Dubcek's Economic Minister during the 'Prague Spring' of 1968, who

had fled to Belgrade, that a sound theoretical basis for an incomes policy could
be established by calculating 'shadow prices' for labour. This was done by including in labour costs the 'dated labour' represented in the machinery used
by workers.[14]

The idea of dated labour had been developed by both Oscar Lange in
Poland and by Pierro Sraffa in England in the 1950s and 1960s from Marx's
concept of 'socially necessary labour-time'. [15] and [16] (This idea had caused
great excitement amongst those of us who belonged to the Society of Socialist
Economists in Britain). Workers in the advanced enterprises of the social sector in Yugoslavia should then only be paid for what they added to the 'dated
labour', and what they added was not necessarily any more than a worker who
had much less machinery at his disposal. As Kardelj put it speaking in 1971
to the Congress of Self-Managers: 'For the same socially acknowledged work
[i.e. Marx's 'socially necessary labour time'] approximately the same living
standard should be secured for the workers.' 'Trade unions were increasingly
expected', he went on 'to help coordinate the different interests which come to
the surface in the sharing of income and personal remuneration'. The basis of
this sharing should be 'the pooled production potential in the form of living
and *past* labour [emphasis added] and their part in the joint financial risk'.
Kardelj went on to speak of the 'clear insight' that workers could be given into
the value of their work at different levels of technology, which would lead them
to understand the needs of those at lower levels and of investment in new job
creating development.[17]

The second explanation for unemployment was Susan Woodward's – that
this was the inevitable result of imposing a 'Slovene' model on 'Foc'a' (ie. the
less developed regions). These regions were expected to supply raw materials
for Slovenia as well as for export, and at the same time to develop their own
manufacturing and processing industries for semi- manufactures – sugar, cellulose, cotton, steel, cement – a different plant in each republic and even sometimes each county. With far too many small and inefficient plants their costs
could not compete with what was available on the world market. Once foreign
trade was opened up, enterprises in Slovenia and Croatia began to look to imports for their semi-manufactures and even for some raw materials. The choice
of imported oil as the main source of energy had already reduced investment
in the local coal industry, which could not be restored when world oil prices
soared in 1973-4.[18]

This eventuality supported the third explanation for unemployment, favoured by those of us living in capitalist countries but deeply sympathetic to
Yugoslavia's attempt to build a form of socialism. This was that the fatal change
in Yugoslav political-economic policy was caused by the decision in 1964 to
open up the country to foreign trade, and, therefore, to permit the switch by
manufacturing enterprises from Yugoslav sources to foreign countries where

cheaper supplies could be found, thus increasing the quantities of imports, not only of machinery, but of semi-manufactures and raw materials and even of food. This undoubtedly had to be seen as the main cause of mass unemployment in the less developed regions, aggravating the general obstacles facing men and women in moving to an industrial from an agrarian society, especially where there were strong stratifications in the division of labour – landlords and masters, craftsmen, peasants and labourers – which were inappropriate for industrial organisation, and no overall national culture to provide the necessary social cement.

This was the great strength of Woodward's contrasting Slovene and Foca models. But the contrast was deepened by the increasing failure of the producers of Foca's raw materials to compete with foreign suppliers in providing the inputs to Slovene manufactures. World prices of primary commodities, the raw materials of industry, with the exception of fuel oil after 1973-4, fell steadily in the 1970s and this further weakened the economies of Yugoslavia's developing regions, but their development was already pre-empted by the freedom of Yugoslav manufacturing industries to buy in from outside. Woodward greatly exaggerates the continued role of raw material exports in Yugoslavia's foreign trade in the 1980s, but she is absolutely right in stressing that guaranteed markets in the Soviet bloc for some raw materials prevented Yugoslav producers from increasing their competitiveness and encouraged the fatally inefficient proliferation of processing plants for timber, cement, sugar, steel and minerals in every republic and even in several different districts.[19]

The rise of unemployment in Yugoslavia in the last years of the 1960s and throughout the 1970s appeared to be inexorable. According to official statistics job seekers' numbers rose from 300,000 in 1972 to 800,000 in 1979. But this figure does not include those underemployed on the land or in irregular, short-term work estimated during the recession in the late 1960s at another two million. The number of employed persons did rise steadily from 1968 to 1975 from about 8 million to nearly 10 million and nearly half of these were in the social sector, 4 million in the economic (productive) social sector. If just over half a million were unemployed, that would leave 4.5 million independent farmers and other private sector workers. Many of these would be underemployed, but quite a large number had emigrated temporarily to Austria, Germany or Sweden as guest workers. A Federal Bureau of Employment was actually established in 1960 to facilitate and control such cross border movements. Semi-official estimates by the Institute of Migration in Zagreb suggested that the number of these emigrants rose from 400,000 in 1967 to 800,000, possibly a million by 1971.[20]

Unemployment rates varied widely between the republics in the north and in the south. Whereas Slovenia's unemployment rate stayed at around 3 per cent right through to 1985 and Croatia's at around 5 per cent, that of Serbia,

Bosnia and Montenegro rose by the late 1970s to 15 per cent, Macedonia's to 25 per cent and Kosovo's to over 30 per cent.[21] The richer republics in the north – Slovenia and Croatia – simply blamed the south for laziness and failing to follow their principles of development, and the latter is largely Woodward's explanation. But we have seen that the southern republics simply could not compete with imported inputs for the supply of raw materials to the more advanced manufacturing enterprises in the north. There is another possible explanation. I have not been able to find figures for migrant workers from each of the republics, but anecdotal evidence from friends suggests that a large number left the north. They had many of the skills that Western European industry wanted and the northern borders touched Austria and Italy from which easy train journeys would take them further north. Croatia had, moreover, a long tradition of emigration mainly to the USA and Canada going back to the start of the twentieth century.

This trend to free movement of labour was associated with the free movement of goods and capital and was, indeed, likely to have been encouraged by the opening up of the country to outside investment as well as to foreign trade. By the early 1970s foreign firms were permitted to hold up to 49 per cent of the capital in Yugoslav enterprises. Such firms had to comply with all the rules about self-management and to accept other federal regulations such as the minimum wage and national incomes policies, but they could take their share in the profits and influence the source of inputs for manufacturing enterprises.[22] If some experts came in with the foreign capital it would not be surprising if some workers went in the opposite direction; and such exchanges were most likely to be taking place to and from the more advanced northern republics. It was becoming increasingly hard to distinguish Yugoslav socialism from the capitalist world in which it was becoming more and more deeply embedded.

Yugoslavia was facing the problems of all developing countries, and even some developed ones: how to protect their infant and/or old but inefficient industries in an increasingly globalised world economy, where the burden of indebtedness generated a vicious circle of decline. Wealth and power were becoming increasingly polarised, with less and less redistribution from rich to poor. Countries with the most technologically advanced industry or the cheapest labour or a combination of both could simply drive all others into a position of dependence, which the demand of the international financial institutions for debt repayment only reinforced. Possession of rich natural resources, apart from oil, offered no respite.[23] Yugoslavia's mineral resources – copper, lead, timber – were all vulnerable to synthetic substitutes. Nothing short of an alternative world trade system could have saved the Yugoslav experiment in self-management from creating in effect a class division between a developed north and an underdeveloped south.[24]

Car Assembly Line, 1980

Combine Harvesters, Vojvodina, 1980

Chapter 9

Socialism in the World, 1975-85

Tito had always hoped to maintain the independence of Yugoslav socialism from both Soviet communism and Western capitalism by establishing political and economic relations with sympathetic regimes. His hopes for association with neighbouring East European countries were ended by the trials and execution of East European leaders for the crime of 'Titoism'. When he turned to the West for aid he did not neglect to seek insulation from total dependence. This seemed to become a realisable prospect through the establishment in 1951 at Bandoeng in Indonesia of a 'Third Bloc' of 'non-aligned powers'. Leaders of several nations came together to explore the possibility of establishing not only a political force but also trading agreements which could cement their unity and increase their bargaining power with both East and West. All were nations of the Third World, with what were hopefully developing economies, not large enough alone for all-round industrialisation, but which with a wider market could hope to achieve the necessary economies of scale. In time their leaders came to include not only Tito, but Sukarno of Indonesia, Nehru of India, Ben Bella of Algeria, Goulart of Brazil, Qassim of Iraq, Nasser of Egypt, Castro of Cuba and Nkrumah of Ghana.

This seemed to be a sufficiently impressive list for me to include in a book published in 1963, *After Imperialism*, a proposal for a 'Third Force'; not so much a bloc, but what I called a 'Framework of Positive Neutralism', which I recommended to a probable forthcoming Labour Government in Britain.[1] My book ended with the recognition of the absolute necessity of finding a way to combine the interests of primary producers in developing countries who were trying to develop their industries with the interests of industrial producers who had the skills and could provide the equipment for the job. My proposal was for a scheme for long-term guaranteed purchases of both industrial and primary products as part of a multinational trade clearing system, which would avoid the check to progress constantly arising from international balance of payments difficulties. The benefits of such trade agreements had been made clear to me from the experience of the 'Bandoeng Powers', as the Non-Aligned grouping was called, and especially of the advantage for the Yugoslav cellulose/rayon industry in being able to develop on a scale that the home market could not have justified.[2]

The idea of a clearing union had been put forward by the Nobel laureate Professor Ragnar Frisch of Norway, who had been developing the use of the new computers for countries to draw up export plans which would optimise trade exchanges. He had advanced his idea of a 'Multilateral Trade Clearing Agency' at a conference in London in 1962 to recommend a Britain-Commonwealth-European Free Trade Area as an alternative to the European Common Market.[3] This conference, which I attended, was supported by Britain's leading Keynesian economists, professors Joan Robinson and Sir Roy Harrod. A further conference was held in 1963 at which I spoke and which encouraged Harrod to write an enthusiastic review of my book *After Imperialism* in the *Observer* newspaper.

However, my proposal found no favour with the incoming Labour Government of 1964. The book was reviewed by Dick Crossman, a leading member of this government, and damned with faint praise, saying that the proposal of a 'framework for positive neutrality' had been 'spatch-cocked awkwardly into the argument', when in fact it was of its very essence. This was not, however, the end of the matter. In the same year the failure of commodity agreements to increase the developing countries' export earnings from their primary commodities led to the first United Nations Conference on Trade and Development and the establishment of UNCTAD as a forum and monitoring centre for helping to advance the interests of these countries. At the Conference three Keynesian professors – Hart, Kaldor and Tinbergen – put forward a detailed scheme for a Commodity Reserve Currency, which would allow developing countries to use their stocks of primary commodities as a reserve asset in the same way that gold was used by those countries which held gold balances.[4] This was followed in 1964 at meetings of the United Nations Economic Commission for Africa and later at the Commission for Asia and the Far East by a proposal from a Hungarian FAO staff member, Dr Andreas Goseco, for a 'Supplementary Payments Mechanism' to promote trade among developing countries.[5]

All these proposals were killed stone dead by the determination in the

Western world, especially of US bankers, to retain their power, exercised through the World Bank and the IMF, to control international finance, and the equal determination of the Soviet Union, particularly after the building of the Berlin Wall, to retain its own economic empire based on the rouble. One by one the leaders of the Bandoeng Powers fell from power, though Nehru died naturally and Castro lined up with the Soviet Union. The others were overthrown by military coups in which the hand of the United States was only too evident – Sukarno, Ben Bella, Goulart, Nasser, Qassim and Nkrumah. Only Tito was left. By then he had really no choice but to accept what Susan Woodward called the 'Faustian bargain' of winning independence from the Soviet Union through accepting finance from the United States and opening the country to capitalist trade and capital investment.[6]

Thus it was, as discussed in the previous chapter, that workers' self-management in Socialist Yugoslavia was reduced year by year throughout the 1970s to the joint management of enterprises with the representatives of foreign capital, while national strategic planning came to be subordinated to the demands of the IMF. Then came the hike in world oil prices in 1973-4. Yugoslavia's position in the capitalist world economy was most seriously affected, along with that of so many other developing countries. The whole economy had begun to rely on imported oil, and the government was forced to borrow heavily to maintain fuel supplies. There was no problem for the country in obtaining loans from the recycled oil money. Yugoslavia was still seen in the West as a bulwark against the spread of Soviet power. But the foreign debt steadily grew and the pressure from the IMF to repay and to 'reform' the country's remaining socialist institutions grew in line with the debt. The first result was a further acceleration in the growth of unemployment. In Yugoslavia as a whole the rate went up from 15 per cent to 20 per cent, in Macedonia and Kosovo to over 30 per cent. Rates in Slovenia and Croatia remained unchanged at 2 per cent and 5 per cent respectively.[7]

The rates of unemployment in the southern Yugoslav republics and Serbia were higher even than the raised levels in the capitalist West. A sense of a common interest emerged in the late 1960s and the 1970s among socialists in Yugoslavia and Western Europe in studying the problem of unemployment. The post-war years of full employment in the West had come to an end with the oil shock. But the trade union movement remained strong in the UK, and Labour governments were in power for most of the years from 1964 to 1979. During this period much interest developed among the trade unions in the exercise of workers' control. I was present at the inauguration of the Institute for Workers Control in Britain, which began to hold conferences attracting not only academic socialists but large numbers of trade unionists – mainly shop stewards but also some trade union leaders – and even some Labour ministers, Tony Benn in particular. They were naturally interested to know more about the Yugoslav experiments in economic democracy.

At the same time, in Yugoslavia academics and others in government circles had begun to feel the need to reach out to socialists in the West to discuss common problems. An initiative from three Yugoslav theoretical journals *Socializm, Socialist Thought and Practice* and *Marksism u Svetu,* with the particularly enthusiastic activity of Milos Nikolic, led to the proposal in 1975 to establish an international conference 'Socialism in the World', in the form of an annual Round Table held at Cavtat in Croatia and of a journal of the same name, based on papers delivered at the Round Table. The aim of the Conference, according to the organisers, was 'to bring together Marxists and other socialist theoreticians, as well as fighters for socialism from different countries, movements and orientations, for the purpose of engaging them in joint theoretical discussions.' And they went on 'In that way these discussions can encourage the further creative development of the theory of revolutionary socialist transformation of the contemporary world'.

The journal would have the same goals, but the organisers warned that

'editorial policy will keep to the principle that the contributions which are published do not hold biased political qualifications, accusations and criticisms of any of the existing practical-political orientations within socialism as a world process.'[8]

The first Round Table meeting was held in Cavtat at the end of September 1976 and was called 'Socialism in the Present World'. The call for papers boldly announced that 'The history of the 20th century is prevalently marked by the world historical process of the disintegration of capitalism and the birth and development of socialism.' And it emphasised that 'socialist practice today is irrepressibly blazing its way to the world-historical scene through various forms and roads.' Issues for consideration were proposed as: 'Contradictions and transformations in contemporary capitalism and the problems of the revolutionary strategy of socialist forces; Socialist society and the role of the working class; The socialist substance of present-day anti-colonial and anti-imperialist revolutions.'[9]

About half of the participants came from the several republics of Yugoslavia and the rest from most of the European countries – east and west – and from the USA and Canada, India and Egypt. They included Ken Coates, my friend and colleague on the councils of the Institute for Workers Control and the Bertrand Russell Peace Foundation, who made a major statement on the dilemmas of the movement in Britain for workers' control in the struggle within the Labour Party to establish some serious control of the British economy through planning agreements which the big companies would be required to engage with.[10] Ken attended all the subsequent Round Table meetings and in a number of years I was able to join him. For me, as well as the occasion for meeting kindred spirits from all over the world, the Round Tables provided an invaluable opportunity to deepen my understanding of what was happening in Yugoslavia, to revive my grasp of Serbo-Croatian and to enjoy the stay in one of the most beautiful spots on the Dalmatian coast.

I had stayed with my family in Cavtat before. The town is built on what was left after an earthquake destroyed the original Greek settlement. A small raised peninsula sticks out into the sea with harbours on either side. I used to enjoy running through the pine trees round the peninsula and going up to the top of the hill at the centre where there is a beautiful marble chapel designed by the Croatian artist Mestrovic in the 1930s and dedicated to the memory of local fishermen. We picnicked and swam off the rocks in the idyllic peace that reigned before the place was developed. We stayed in B&Bs, buying fruit, vegetables and bread in the market for our lunches and eating and dancing in the evenings at the local restaurant. I found that, by contrast, the Round Table was held in a vast new and very smart hotel which had been built just south of Cavtat, its curved line of balconies rising like cliffs above the rocks and facing south over the sea. It had huge reception and dining rooms, swimming pools, indoor and outdoor, bars and terraces, with paths winding down to bathing stages by the sea. Most of the hotel was made available for the Round Table conferences – at the end of the season in late September, but the summer weather generally still held.

I have to say that at these meeting many of the set speeches were boring and often hard to understand, the simultaneous translators obviously struggling to make sense of what was being said. The great interest of these occasions lay in the discussions at meal breaks and in free time in the afternoons and evenings. Most of the sharper arguments took place at these times. We were able to hear something of the disagreements inside Yugoslavia that had led to the shutting down of dissident journals, and even the arrest and imprisonment of their editors. This was the case both with the Praxis group in Belgrade, with which we had had contact in Britain, and the Croatian nationalists, who had been heavily stamped on by Tito and with whom we did not feel great sympathy. As the years went by more and more critical voices were raised at the Cavtat gatherings by participants from Eastern Europe and even from the Soviet Union. The open discussion that had been for some time typical in Yugoslavia was becoming widespread, but within strict limits, since the idea of an opposition party was ruled out.

No one who had the opportunity to join the Round Table discussions at Cavtat in those years of the Cold War would fail to recognise the extraordinary nature of this event. In a world that seemed closed off by the antagonism of two giant blocs engaged in a perilous arms race, it was possible for those with a common interest in peaceful social development – from the United States, Canada and Latin America, from Western and Eastern Europe, from the Middle East, from India and Africa and even from China and Japan – to meet and exchange ideas and discuss their problems in an open way in perfect surroundings. It was an immense contribution that the Yugoslav League of Communists was making to the building of socialism in the world. The hotel itself offered a shining example of an enterprise managed by the workers. The cost of the whole venture, including the simultaneous translation and the publication of the proceedings in several languages, must have been a considerable charge on the resources of a small and far from rich country.

The information made available and the inspiration from the debates which those who attended could take back with them to their work in their own countries must have made a major contribution to the Peace Movement at that time, and in the years to come.

Most of those who attended the Round Table meetings were academics or journal editors, although some active politicians were to be found at each year's gathering, not only from Yugoslavia itself, but from many other countries. Those who attended from Britain included not only the MEP Ken Coates and the MP Stuart Holland, but also David Blunkett, then a local authority activist in Sheffield who was to become one of Mr Blair's staunchest allies in New Labour. It was not necessarily the case that all who came went away with a brighter vision of a socialist future. Some who came from Eastern Europe found new faith in democratic decision making which did not necessarily lead on to socialist solutions. If some seeds fell on stony ground, there can be no doubt that the Cavtat Round Table discussions made for deeper understanding of the problems and possibilities of achieving socialism. It was a brave initiative and typical of the breadth of interest and concern of Yugoslavia's Communists.

One year I was invited to go on from Cavtat to give a lecture at the Communist Party school at Kumrovec. My wife and I went together, calling first on friends in Zagreb, one of whom had served on the Central Committee of the League of Communists and come back to Zagreb to manage a large petro-chemical plant. He made a strong point that the future lay with the republics. Only through them could some control be established over the economy where, he believed, investment was going into unviable plants and enterprises, leading inevitably to unemployment. It was clear that his conclusion, while applying to Croatia, would not necessarily do so to the southern republics. While in Zagreb we had lunch with a charming old man who had been a colonel with the Partisans. He had heard that we had worked with UNRRA and he was anxious to thank us for the food which UNRRA had brought in that had kept his family alive at the end of the war. We felt embarrassed at such fulsome praise.

Our host very kindly drove us to Kumrovec, where Tito was born, in pretty, hilly country on the Croatian border with Slovenia. The Party's Political School had recently been established there next door to the Military School in magnificent modern buildings. We were wined and dined splendidly, and I was reminded of the similar beautiful schools of timber and glass built in Denmark and Sweden by their national trade union organisations. I had been billed as an expert on international trade. I decided to launch into a sharp criticism of the IMF and its belief that it was only necessary to open up the world's markets to free trade and free movements of capital for trade to grow to the benefit of the undeveloped as well as the developed countries. I showed that the enterprise zones established in developing countries by giant transnational companies had brought little or no benefit to these countries – all the profits went back to the TNCs and no development took place. Those countries such as South Korea which had successfully industrialised had done so by protecting their infant industries from foreign competition and maintaining strong central controls over their development. I did not rub it in that this was just what Yugoslavia was not doing.

I spoke slowly to help the simultaneous translators and over-shot my time limit, but what I said seemed, from comment afterwards, to have gone down well. Nearly all the students were young – in their twenties, we guessed – and some spoke good English and asked questions after the session was over. Both my wife and I commented that we were reminded of visiting a so-called 'Technical School' in Cuba, reserved for the very brightest children – the same bright-eyed enthusiasm, quickness and absolute assurance that they were born to rule, and among the girls as well as the boys. What was reassuring in both cases was that, although there were no black children in the Cuban school and few from Macedonia or Kosovo at Kumrovec, class origins were widely spread. Bosnia and Hercegovina was very well represented and we heard moving stories from young women and men from Muslim peasant families about how hard they had worked at their studies and then in the Youth Organisation to get the chance to come to the national Party school.

The last time I went to Cavtat was in 1988. There was much rather nervous discussion of nationalism and what it meant for the future of Yugoslavia as a federation of peoples, not of republics. I was invited to go on to Sarajevo after the Round Table meeting was ended. The Bosnian United Nations Association, which was chaired by a man I had known when I was with UNRRA, had organised a two day conference on nationalism. I made a very brief statement on the several arguments in the United Kingdom in favour of decentralisation of some functions of government to Scotland, Ireland and Wales, and in favour of independence for all separate from England in a European Union, which was a political federation and not simply a common market. My conclusion was that a state had to have a certain size and enough power to stand up to the giant international companies. It would be unwise to give up the powers of an existing state without replacing it with something as strong or stronger.

None of this interested the other participants, whose whole concern was with the effect on the many minorities within each of the republics of Yugoslavia of the rising tide of nationalism centred around the majority group in ethnic, religious or historic terms in each republic – Croats in Croatia, Serbs in Serbia, Muslims in Bosnia, Macedonians in Macedonia, Albanians in Kosovo. The possibility was even raised of some transfer of populations, an idea that horrified most of the participants but was raised quite seriously by the Macedonians. I found an interesting illustration of the problem when I walked up to the old UNRRA Sarajevo office in the Villa Mandic. I found that it had been converted into a centre for exhibitions financed from funds left over from the staging of the Winter Olympics in Sarajevo in 1984. To my astonishment I discovered that the curator was the granddaughter of our dear friend Nada Kraigher from Ljubljana.

I remembered that Nada had been very dismissive of the possibility of the Bosnians being able to organise such an international event as a Winter Olympics. It should, as all Slovenes maintained, have been held in Slovenia. In the event, Bosnia was chosen, but many Slovenes were recruited to help with the organisation, including our friend's granddaughter. It was a huge success and not all the Slovenes returned to Slovenia. Like many others, Nada's granddaughter had stayed on in Sarajevo after the Olympics and married a Bosnian of Muslim parents. They were obviously happy there with their charming little daughter, but when the break-up of Yugoslavia came, she stayed on for a time to fight for a pluralist Bosnia and her husband took the child to grandparents in Slovenia. Such was the fate of many families which called themselves Yugoslav, rather than as belonging to one or other of the several national denominations. It was the failure to develop a Yugoslav nationalism through all-Yugoslav non-governmental organisations other than those dominated by the Communist Party that proved to be Yugoslavia's tragedy.

AVNOJ meeting, Jajce, 1944: Ribar (Croat), Tito (Croat),
Pijade (Jew), Rankovic (Serb), Dzilas (Montenegrin)
in centre of front row

The leaders of the six republics, 1991
l to r: Montenegro, Slovenia, Croatia, Macedonia, Bosnia-
Hercegovina, Serbia

Chapter 10

Nationality and Nationalism, 1986-90

So much propaganda has been spread about the causes of the break up of Yugoslavia that it is hard for an inquiring but sceptical student to reach any firm conclusion. Yet the majority of world opinion has accepted the Croatian nationalist propaganda line rather than any other, to the effect that it was the result of Serbian nationalism stoked up by a demonic character named Slobodan Milosevic. It will have become clear to the reader by now that I could not, and I do not, accept any such simple one-sided explanation. What I had to think about after nearly fifty years' close association with Yugoslavs of many backgrounds and different ages was how it could come about that fissiparous separatist forms of nationalism broke out with such violence in 1990 in a country which had been born in 1918, reborn in 1943 and developed in many ways so successfully for over forty years.

I have to begin by repeating what I saw when I first arrived in the country in 1944. I had seen in the refugee camps and hospitals outside the country how Partisan soldiers lived and worked together like brothers, although they came from different parts of the country and from different backgrounds. When I started to travel through Bosnia and Hercegovina it was obvious to me that in every town and large village there were mosques and also churches, some Catholic some Orthodox. All were more or less in ruins as a result of the fighting with an outside enemy, but when it became possible to turn to such matters, the whole population would work together to make repairs. It was evident that people of different faiths had lived together for hundreds of years. They gathered in the evening at different *kavanas* according to their separate faiths, but in the general management of the local affairs they worked together. When I came to talk with their local committees, I found that if a chairman was from one faith, the secretary would be from another and all the different faiths might be represented on the committee. This was the origin of the '*ključ*', the key that, in post-war Yugoslavia, required representation according to the proportions of different faiths in any area.

I had lived and worked in Tito's Yugoslavia for three years and visited the country often enough thereafter to know that its several peoples could live happily together. I had then read the books of Bosnia's greatest writer, Ivo Andric, from which it was clear that it had always been so, except when invading forces sought to divide and conquer. Andric's great novel *Bridge over the Drina* is set in Visegrad just after the First World War. Serbs and Muslims live their separate lives side by side in peace and the young make friends across the religious divide. Writing under the German occupation of the 1940s, it seems as if Andric had to go back to 1919 to describe the hopes and fears of young people then, to make his comment of hope and fear on what he could see emerging among the Partisans. Towards the end of the book he has two young men sitting on the parapet of the great stone bridge at Visegrad. This bridge over the river Drina once marked both the frontier and the crossing point between the East and the West, between the Ottoman and Austro-Hungarian empires. The two young men are both studying at Sarajevo University. Toma Galus is a Serb and his friend Fehim Bahtijarevic a Muslim.

Galus is proclaiming the destiny of 'young and free nations, appearing for the first time on the stage of history, to express themselves directly. Modern nationalism will triumph over religious diversities and outmoded prejudice, will liberate our people from foreign influence and exploitation. Then will the national state be born.' And he goes on to describe

> all the advantages and beauties of the new national state which was to rally all the Southern Slavs around Serbia as a sort of Piedmont [the rallying centre of Italian unification] on the basis of complete national unity, religious tolerance and civic equality.
> His speech mixed up bold words of uncertain meaning and expression that accurately expressed the needs of modern life, the deepest desires of a race, most of which were to remain only desires, and the justified and attainable demands of everyday reality. It mingled the great truths which had ripened through the generations but which only youth could perceive in advance and dare to express, with the eternal illusions which are never extinguished but never attain realisation, for one generation of youth to hand on to the next like that mythological torch.
> His friend Bahtijarevic remains silent, even when Galus goes on to describe what

the new state will accomplish – in fermenting new ideas, encouraging new deeds, putting up great buildings, 'building new, greater and better bridges, not to link foreign centres with conquered lands, but to link our own lands with the rest of the world.

It is an ominous silence.[1]

As so often before, the achievement of a nation state, even one large enough to be economically viable for capitalist development, left most of the Yugoslav peoples after 1919 no better off than before and in many cases with the same foreign companies exploiting them on the lands and in the mines and factories. Would it be different after the Partisans' war of national liberation from 1941-45? That is Andric's unspoken question. All those who were there at that time believed that it would be different because the 'social dominated the national', in the perceptive judgement of Basil Davidson, reached after his wartime experience in Yugoslavia and long involvement in the struggles of African peoples for freedom.

Davidson wrote about this in a 1992 book entitled *The Black Man's Burden: The Curse of the Nation-state*. It offered a terrible warning to the "balkanised" states of the Soviet Union and of Former Yugoslavia:

> The jubilant crowds celebrating [African] independence were not inspired by a "national consciousness" that "demanded the nation" any more than were the peasants and their coevals in the nation states crystallised some decades earlier from Europe's old internal empires. They were inspired by the hope of more and better food and shelter. As long as the "social" held over the "national", this continued to be so. But it did not continue to hold that lead for long. Once the national sovereignties were declared, the arena was fixed for rivalry over the resources within that area; and the rivalry was bound to become abrasive and therefore divisive, if only because the resources were in short supply. This divisive rivalry was then discovered to be "tribalism", that is, the reinforcement of kinship and other local scale alliances competing against other such alliances.[2]

It was a perceptive warning for the peoples of Yugoslavia. In Tito's Yugoslavia the *kljuc* recognised the national differences but sought to reconcile them not only in the distribution of offices, but in the distribution of resources. Of course, I met many people who were unhappy with such an egalitarian arrangement. But it was generally accepted. In our UNRRA office in Sarajevo, we had among our Yugoslav interpreters and helpers a Jew, two Muslims, a Croat, a French woman married to a Muslim, two Serbs and an Austrian married to a Serb.[3] All worked and ate together happily. In Dr Singer's clinic women came from each of the communities and sat quietly waiting their turn without any one demanding precedence. We took all this for granted, as we would have done in England without asking whether someone was Scots or Irish or Welsh or English. It was natural in the United Kingdom which had been united some hundreds of years earlier, not less than a hundred years as in the case of Yugoslavia, and the UK had not been divided up by foreign occupation as had Yugoslavia in the lifetime of most Yugoslavs. We were well aware of the extraordinary success of the Partisans in bringing all the peoples of the country together in 'bratsvo y jedinstvo' (brotherhood and unity), the Partisan slogan.

The new Yugoslavia was founded at a historic conference held in liberated territory in Jajce on November 29, 1943, at which a Presidium of fifty-six members was elected and a National Council of Liberation consisting of six Serbs, five Croats, four Slovenes, one Montenegrin and one Bosnian Muslim and the following resolution was passed:

> In order to carry out the principles of sovereignty of the nations of Yugoslavia and in order that Yugoslavia may be the true home to all its peoples, and no longer an arena for the machinations of reactionary influences, Yugoslavia is being built up on a federal principle which will ensure full equality for the nations of Serbia, Croatia, Slovenia, Macedonia, Montenegro and Bosnia-Hercegovina.[4]

This vision of a united South Slav state was incorporated into the constitution of the new state by a Constituent Assembly meeting in Belgrade on January 31 1946 in the following words of the First Article:

> The Federal People's Republic of Yugoslavia is a federal people's state republic in form, a community of peoples equal in rights who, on the basis of the right of self determination including the right of separation, have expressed their will to live together in a federal state.[5]

We have to notice the distinction revealed in the two statements between nations, states and peoples. There is in fact an ambiguity in the Serbo-Croatian language – 'narod' is the word for both nation and people. But this ambiguity appears also in the English language, since many Scots, Irish and Welsh feel that they belong to a separate nation from the English, although most would recognise their common membership of the United Kingdom as a nation state. States became important when rulers sought to establish the territory over which they exercised sovereignty. Some were formed as federations of separate states like the United States of America which had nothing to do with separate nationalities. Others were formed as unions like the UK. A European federation would be a federation of nation states. Yugoslavia was formed in 1945 as both a union of peoples and a federation of states. Every state – so-called republics – contained a mix of peoples. Hence the constitutional recognition of a federal state and a community of peoples.[6]

The concept of nationality does not derive necessarily from where one was born but from one's parents' origins, their language and culture, often including their religion. So-called 'ethnic differences' imply different origins from long ago, often including difference in skin and hair colour. Only the Hungarians, Albanians and Romas in Yugoslavia (literally joint Slav land) are different in this sense from Slovenes, Croats, Serbs and most Muslims, who are all Slavs in origin. Serbs, Croats and Muslims (except for those in Kosovo) speak the same language – Serbo-Croatian – although some today would seek to argue that there are major dialect differences. The differences in religious background are more important. Most Slovenes and Croats come from a Catholic background. Most Serbs from an Orthodox (Pravoslav) background. Many people in Bosnia-Hercegovina are Muslims as are most Kosovars.

What Tito and his comrades did was to create a sovereign nation state out of many separate peoples, so that they came to call themselves 'Yugoslavs'[7] In 1945 I went to a memorial service in Sarajevo for a number of Partisan soldiers, who had died of wartime wounds. They were described as the best sons of our people (*najbolji sinovi nashega naroda*). I did not think to ask which "people" and in fact they came from several backgrounds. There had been funerals in several churches and mosques, but the memorial service was non-denominational. It was deeply moving after all these peoples had suffered from division and conquest in the war. There was still some sense, however, among the Muslims that they were treated differently from Serbs and Croats as belonging to a religion and not a nation.

To treat this problem, the 1974 revised Yugoslav Constitution recognised Muslims as a nation. Before the break-up, increasing numbers of Yugoslavs filled in their census returns under the heading of 'nationality' by entering 'Yugoslav', either for preference or because they were the offspring of mixed marriages. It would not be right to assume that all the others attended any place of worship – Catholic, Orthodox or Muslim – or followed any religious practices. By the 1970s Yugoslavia was becoming an increasingly secular society. Animosities between the several republics arose primarily from economic causes. As has been suggested in earlier chapters, the richer states in the North felt increasingly that they were having to subsidise the South without getting any benefit in return. Indeed the southern states were seen as a drag on their progress and Serbia in between as a much too powerful arbitrator.

It has to be added that there was a certain pecking order in most Yugoslavs' minds, exaggerated by growing economic inequality, with the Slovenes and Croats at the top, the Serbs in the middle and the Muslims, including especially the Albanians, at the bottom. Many Serbs told me that they felt just as strongly as the Muslims that they were looked down upon by the Slovenes and Croats. This was not something that could be called 'racism', even in the attitude of Serbs to the Albanian Muslims. The problem in Kosovo was that it was the location of the oldest and holiest centre of the Serbian Orthodox church but over the years had become increasingly inhabited by Muslim Albanians. What, then, was the cause of the growing sense of disunity that emerged so strongly in Yugoslavia in the 1970s?

Most explanations for the break-up of Yugoslavia start from the assumption that this was in large part the result of long-standing ethnic hatreds, always lurking below the surface. Some substance for this view can be found in an essay written by Ivo Andric. I quoted Andric earlier from his famous book *Bridge over the Drina*, at the end of which he sees a young Serb in 1919 dreaming of Serbia uniting the Southern Slavs as Piedmont rallied the Italians, but getting no response from his Muslim friend. In the essay, also written during the German occupation, called 'A Letter from 1920', Andric, a Croat who lived much of his life in Bosnia, foresees with terrifying clarity what might happen one day to Bosnia:

> And just as there are mineral riches under the earth in Bosnia, so undoubtedly are Bosnians rich in hidden moral values, which are more rarely found in their compatriots in other Yugoslav lands. But ... there's one thing that the people of Bosnia ... must realise and never lose sight of – Bosnia is a country of hatred and fear ... the fatal characteristic of this hatred is that the Bosnian man is unaware of the hatred that lies in him, shrinks from analysing it – and hates everyone who tries to do so. And yet it is a fact that in Bosnia and Hercegovina there are more people ready in fits of this unconscious hatred to kill and be killed, for different reasons, and under different pretexts, than in other much bigger non-Slav lands ... it can also be said that there are few countries with such firm belief, elevated strength of character, so much tenderness and loving passion, such depth of feeling, of loyalty and unshakeable devotion, or with such a thirst for justice. But in secret depths underneath all this hide burning hatreds, hurricanes of tethered and compressed hatreds maturing and awaiting their hour. Those who oppress and exploit the economically weaker do it with hatred into the bargain, which makes the exploitation a hundred times harder and uglier, while those who bear these injustices dream of justice and reprisal, but as some explosion of vengeance which, if it were realised according to their ideas, would perforce be so complete that it would blow to pieces the oppressed along with the hated oppressors.[8]

It is reported that the Bosnian Serb general Mladic quoted this letter in 1995 to the UN representatives in Sarajevo to show them that such hatred had always existed in Bosnia below the surface. If Andric was right, what was it then that supplied the trigger that released this explosion? Misha Glenny, who gained a wide knowledge of Bosnia as a BBC correspondent during the Bosnian war, took the view that 'Bosnia has always survived by dint of a protective shield ... internal stability was invariably guaranteed by an external power which mediated between the three communities' – the Austrian or Ottoman empires, the inter-war royal dictatorship or "Titoism"'. 'On the one occasion when this broke down', he goes on, 'between 1941 and 1945 the results were horrifying: a nationalist, religious war whose violence surpassed that of all other wartime conflicts in the region'.[9]

This is an absolute travesty of history. The years 1941-45 were the years of the Axis occupation of Yugoslavia when the Nazis sought to rule by dividing and conquering, arming Croat fascist Ustashe forces and using an Albanian SS Skanderbeg division to fight alongside German armies against the Partisan resistance, expelling Serbs from Kosovo and the Vojvodina and encouraging the massacre by the Ustashe of Serbs, Jews and Romas at Kozara and Jasenovac in 1941. Nor was this so different from the much earlier treatment of Serb resistance to the Turks, to the Austrians and Hungarians, not to mention the Venetian slave traders, who bought their slaves (Slavs) to sell to the Islamic armies in North Africa. That many Slavs in what is now Bosnia, Hercegovina, the Sandjak (Southern Serbia), Kosovo and Macedonia converted to Islam does not suggest mediation, but rather capitulation. No Croat would accept for a moment that the Serbian royal government between the wars were mediators. Only Tito in Glenny's list sought genuinely to mediate and it is fashionable to argue that after Tito died the break-up of Yugoslavia was inevitable. Tito is reported to have said to Averell Harriman at Kardelj's funeral in 1979 (the year before Tito's own death), 'Apres moi le deluge!'[10] I am not convinced that it was meant seriously. Tito had taken every possible precaution to ensure continuing unity with a rotating presidency. Perhaps Mrs Harriman could tell us whether there was not a twinkle in those clear blue eyes?

What then was the trigger that fired the terrible civil war in Bosnia-Hercegovina and later in Kosovo? Again the fashionable answer is the demon Milosevic who, according to his prosecutors at the International Criminal Tribunal for Yugoslavia 'acting alone or in concert with other members of the joint criminal enterprise, planned, instigated committed or otherwise aided and abetted the planning, preparation and execution of the destruction, in whole or in part of the Bosnian Muslim and Bosnian Croat national, ethnical, racial or religious groups, as such, in territories within Bosnia and Hercegovina ....' But this is said to have been 'from on or about 1 March 1992 until 31 December 1995'.[11] The break-up began long before that, as we have seen.

We had earlier to recognise the problems created for men and women moving from a structured agrarian society to an industrial society with a quite different division of labour. At sea in an unfamiliar world most people, and particularly those in less developed regions, looked for some social bonding. For a time the new Yugoslavia seemed to provide this, but as it ceased to hold together they fell back on a narrower nationalist consciousness. There is a long history of such nationalist responses, which Ernest Gellner examined so rigorously.[12]

We have in truth to go back further than 1989 to find the causes of Yugoslavia's destruction, back at least to the early 1980s. In the last chapter, I began to explore some of the reasons why Tito's Yugoslavia was falling apart. The reasons were mainly economic, though closely related to the whole political structure of post-1945 Yugoslavia. The gap in wealth between the north and the south, and most particularly between the two richest republics, Slovenia and Croatia, and the rest, instead of narrowing, was steadily widening. Unemployment rates did rise slightly in the late 1980s in Slovenia and Croatia to 5 per cent and 7 per cent respectively, but the rate in Kosovo leapt up to 40 per cent and in Bosnia-Hercegovina and Montenegro to 20 per cent. Even in Serbia and the Vojvodina the rate rose to 15 per cent.[13] These were intolerable figures. What made this situation even worse was the rate of price inflation. At 15 per cent in the 1970s, this rose to 40 per cent in 1981-3, thence to an average 200 per cent in 1985-8 and finally to 1300 per cent in 1989.[14] In effect the dinar became valueless. At the same time Yugoslavia had ceased to be a single market. Only a third of national output and a fifth of capital movements had come to circulate between the republics. The rest moved inside each republic or in the case of the northern republics between them and the outside world.[15]

In this situation of economic collapse, however, not everybody suffered. My friends in Sarajevo explained to me that they received dollars from rich relatives in the United States. That was unusual in Bosnia, but in Slovenia and Croatia many families and some in Bosnia-Hercegovina held savings in *Deutschemarks* or *lire* from working abroad as migrant workers or from their enterprises' export earnings or the earnings from tourism. There was in effect a dual economy, but one in which the south suffered most from the steady reduction in the federal arrangements for transferring income from the north to the south. At the same time, Slovenia and Croatia felt increasingly aggrieved because repayment of Yugoslavia's mounting foreign debt meant more and more of their manufactured goods going out of the country to increase earnings through exports. The contribution of the south had been sharply reduced by the fall in world prices of the raw materials that they produced. As more and more goods had to be exported to pay the debts, it was then the non-availability of goods in the shops that raised prices.[16]

I had early recognised that foreign debt was the problem, because this was what I believed was destroying the developing economies in Africa, which I was studying in the 1980s.[17] Low prices for their primary commodity exports and high prices for imports of oil and machinery resulted in deficits on their foreign payments' balances. These had to be covered by borrowing at raised rates of interest, and then the IMF moved in to demand guarantees of repayment and to require fiscal policies that were more restrictive. This is just what happened to Yugoslavia. The IMF first required increased exports, and since they required this of all primary commodity producing countries stocks built up and this brought prices even lower. The next requirements were reduction of government spending and of general government involvement in the economy, state industries to be privatised and markets for goods and capital opened to the world. Inflation was to be dealt with by repressing demand, which only led to more unemployment and less competitiveness. Wherever these policies were applied economic and political disaster followed. Small developing economies simply could not compete in a world of giant trans-national corporations. The correlation between high foreign debts and outbreaks of violence, even leading to civil war, was universal.[18]

When I put this argument forward in relation to Yugoslavia, it was said by Croat writers like Branka Magas that I had invented a 'debt bogey'.[19] In fact, Magas herself in the collection of her contemporary reports which she gathered together in her book *The Destruction of Yugoslavia* emphasised the damaging effects on the economy of foreign debt interest payments in 1983.[20] Such debt payments were absorbing a third of all Yugoslavia's foreign earnings, but the Croat nationalists held to their 'demon Milosevic' explanation of the Yugoslav collapse. Fortunately for my argument, it received support from a most authoritative source. Susan Woodward from the prestigious Brookings Institution in the United States, whom I have quoted earlier from her book *The Political Economy of Yugoslavia 1945 to 1990,*[21] had been appointed in 1994 senior adviser to Yasushi Akashi, the top UN official in the former Yugoslavia, special representative of the Secretary General Boutros Boutros-Gali. On the basis of this experience she wrote a sequel to her earlier book and called it *Balkan Tragedy.*

In presenting her 'Argument in Brief' Susan Woodward wrote:

> The conflict is not a result of historical animosities and it is not a return to the pre-communist past; it is the result of the politics of transforming a socialist society to a market economy and democracy. A critical element of this failure was economic decline caused largely by a program intended to resolve a *foreign debt crisis* [emphasis added]. More than a decade of austerity and declining living standards corroded the social fabric and the rights and securities that individuals and families had come to rely on'.

And in her conclusion she added:

> The primary problem ... lay in the lack of recognition and accommodation [by the 'international banking consortium'] for the socially polarising and politically disintegrating consequences of the IMF-conditionality program and approach to Westernisation. The austerities of policies of demand-repression led to conditions that could not easily foster a political culture of tolerance and compromise. Instead the social bases for stable government and democratisation were being radically narrowed by economic polarisation of rich and poor....[22]

The school of Milosevic demonisers could hardly argue with the Brookings

Institution, but my efforts to explain the role of the foreign debt and IMF policies were greeted with ridicule. When I was asked to contribute to the new Sheffield based journal *New Political Economy* in 1996 I wrote an article on this theme entitled 'The Role of Economic Factors in Social Crisis: the Case of Yugoslavia'.[23] It produced violent adverse criticism from an internal review, and was only published in the end in a newly invented category of articles entitled 'Commentary' followed by responses from Branka Magas and Ian Keerns in the next issue. I was accused of having retained too much of my youthful enthusiasm for Tito's Partisans and failing to recognise what came first – economic decline or political manoeuvring by the Serbs.[24] As for the first, I would rather be accused of such Partisan enthusiasm than of having to defend the adoption by the Croat nationalist government of the checker-board flag of the Ustase, which went into battle against the Partisans side by side with the Nazi swastika and German eagle. But no-one takes on the Croat propaganda machine with impunity.[25]

What Branka Magas is right about is that the political and economic problems of Former Yugoslavia were epitomised in the late 1980s in Kosovo, as they were to be once again in the late 1990s. Kosovo had for many years had a majority population of Albanians, mainly converted centuries ago to Islam, with a sizeable minority of Serbs and some Romas as well. The proportions have changed over time. In the late 1930s it was about 50:50 Serb and Albanian, but the Italians, when they occupied Kosovo in 1941, expelled several hundred thousand Serbs. Only a few returned after 1945. Kosovo is, however, a historic religious and national shrine for all Serbs. It was the heart of medieval Serbia. In Kosovo you can, or at least you could, see some of the oldest and finest Serbian Orthodox churches and monasteries, and Kosovo Polje (battlefield) is the site of the last heroic stand of the Serbs against the Turks in 1389, where the Turkish leader Murad was slain at the hand of a Serbian patriot.[26] It is the date of their defeats that people remember, as the English remember 1066.

Kosovo was not given the status of a republic in the founding constitution of Former Yugoslavia, but like Vojvodina, with its large Hungarian population, became an 'Autonomous Province' within Serbia. In both cases this was on the grounds that Albanian like Hungarian was not a Yugoslav 'nation' but a 'nationality', there existing Albanian and Hungarian states outside Yugoslavia. In the case of Albanians there were in fact a minority of Albanians also in another Yugoslav republic, the republic of Macedonia. At the end of the Balkan wars of 1912-13, a new state of Albania was created but without the Albanians in Kosovo or in what became Serbian Macedonia, the greater part of Macedonia being in fact Greece. A 'Greater Albania' was not acceptable either to the Serbs or the Greeks. This junior status of an autonomous province began to rankle among the increasingly well-educated Kosovars. They felt that their absence from the top table, when national (federal) decisions were reached, worked against them. The fact that teaching at school was in their Albanian language was an important source of pride but no help when it came to looking for jobs elsewhere in the country. And, as has been made clear already, in the 1970s Kosovo had the highest rate of unemployment in the country. Concessions were made after strong protests in the late 1960s, and in the 1974 Constitution the Province of Kosovo obtained in effect equivalent status with the republics.[27]

What set this back was the demand of the IMF throughout the 1980s for more centralised control of the economy and reductions in state spending. Combined with the withdrawal by the richer northern republics of redistributive subsidies to the south and a rising inflation rate, the result was not only increased unemployment, but wage levels below what workers could live on.[28] Albanians began to put the blame on Serbia and on the Serbs who still had key jobs in the Province, and to take matters into their own hands, threatening Serbs with expulsion. Such matters came to a head in 1989 when the miners at the vast Trepce mines complex in Kosovo went on strike, some of them on hunger strike, demanding the dismissal of three Serb officials. To show the complicated nature of the situation, we have to notice that Slovenian miners at first supported their comrades in Kosovo. The strike was settled by the dismissal of the officials complained about, but the Serbian Party in Belgrade reinstated them. Then Serbs in Kosovo began to complain that they in turn were being discriminated against. A petition signed by 60,000 Kosovan Serbs in 1987 asserted that genocide was being practised against them. The response of the Serbian League of Communists was to propose the rescinding of the concessions made to Kosovo's autonomy.[29]

It was in this volatile situation that Slobodan Milosevic entered the story. He had become chairman of the Serbian League of Communists in 1986 at the relatively young age of forty-six. He had a legal training but became a banker who believed in economic reforms, such as the IMF were demanding, but, as he argued, staying within a socialist and federal Yugoslav framework. He undoubtedly rose to power, replacing Ivan Stambulic as President of Serbia, by playing the nationalist card, transforming the Serbian League of Communists into the Serbian Socialist Party and going on to win Serbia's first post-war multi-party elections in 1990. In this he dished the extreme nationalists, Draskovic and Seselj. Diana Johnstone, who has written in her *Fools' Crusade* the most effective response to the demonisation of Milosevic, has emphasised that his popular appeal lay in his ambivalence.[30] On the one hand, addressing a Serbian rally at Kosovo Polje in April 1987, the rally which has been seen worldwide in the film *The Death of Yugoslavia*, he said that 'no one should allow them [the Albanians] to beat you'.[31] In saying these words, he broke the Titoist taboo as a leading Communist representing all the peoples of the country, by supporting a national (Serb) interest in opposition to those of other nations in Yugoslavia. With these words he became hugely popular in Serbia.

On the other hand, two years later, after extremely tough measures had been taken against dissent in Kosovo once more reducing its autonomous status, Milosevic spoke very different words on the same historic site at the 600th anniversary of the battle with the Turks,

> Equal and harmonious relations among Yugoslav peoples are a necessary condition for the existence of Yugoslavia ... Serbia has never had only Serbs living in it. Today, more than in the past, members of other peoples and nationalities are also in it. This is not a disadvantage for Serbia. I am truly convinced that it is to its advantage.[32]

Moreover, when he was himself labelled a nationalist, he condemned 'Serbian nationalism as a serpent deep in the bosom of the Serbian people.'[33] Rhetoric it may be but it contained an awful truth.

This is how matters stood in Yugoslavia in 1989, when the Berlin wall fell and revolution spread throughout Eastern Europe. Yugoslavia could hardly remain unaffected by events which led to the collapse of the Soviet Union. But the situation was different in Yugoslavia from that in other East European countries. It was not the protection of the Soviet Union that Yugoslavia lost, but the protection of the United States. And that protection had not so much maintained the Yugoslav socialist system intact as allowed its survival. But it was already under heavy attack from the capitalist international institutions. What United States' protection had done was to permit, and indeed to encourage, a large Yugoslav National Army to hold the country together as a bulwark against Soviet military power. Without that the country could split apart.

It would be wrong to end this chapter on the growth of separatist nationalisms in Former Yugoslavia without recognising once more that Tito's regime suffered from one fatal flaw. It was a one-party state. The absence of parties – apart from the one party, the League of Communists – that crossed the boundaries of the republics and the deliberate decentralisation of government meant inevitably that opposition to the Party line centred around the separate republics and took a separatist nationalist form. Economic democracy in the enterprises, both industrial and administrative, could not make up for the absence of political democracy. Even non-governmental organisations, trade unions and other voluntary associations tended to develop separately in each of the republics. There was very general freedom of discussion and debate in public places and in the media, but it stopped at freedom of political action.[34] When this did break out, it was immediately stamped upon as it took a national separatist form which challenged the very commonalty of Yugoslavia. When the economic basis of that commonalty collapsed, the whole political structure broke up.[35]

Bridge at Varvarin, 2000

Chapter 11

Descent into War: Croatia and Bosnia, 1991-5

There has been a plethora of books on the wars in Yugoslavia from foreign journalists and war correspondents with little or no previous knowledge of the country and its peoples who have inevitably picked up what clues they could find from the most persuasive English-speaking Yugoslav advocates of their own interests. These turned out mainly to be Croats. Although many of the journalists revealed remarkable courage in their pursuit of the truth, Zagreb remained after all a more comfortable base than Sarajevo or Belgrade. I have struggled through many of their reports and books, using my judgment from previous experience and from talks with my Yugoslav friends. I have had to rely heavily on the transcripts of the Milosevic trial, supplemented by the work of the two writers on Former Yugoslavia who, I have come to believe, approach most nearly to the truth, Susan Woodward and Diana Johnstone.[1]

We have to start in 1989. This was the year when Gorbachev, who had come to power in the Soviet Union and pulled the Red Army out of Afghanistan, met US President Reagan to end the Cold War. The Berlin wall fell and the Soviet satellites in Eastern Europe jumped at the opportunity of national independence as the way out of their political and economic weaknesses. Yugoslavia was not a Soviet satellite and despite the widening gap between the north and the south had considerable political and economic strengths. Susan Woodward from the US Brookings Institute opened her *magnum opus, Balkan Tragedy*, with the following words:

On the eve of the 1989 revolutions in eastern and central Europe, Yugoslavia was better placed than any other socialist society to make a successful transition to a market economy and to the West. It had, after all, been moving toward full global integration since its Communist Party leadership broke with Stalin in 1948. As early as 1955, Yugoslavia's borders were open to the movement of its citizens, foreigners and trade. Since 1949 it had regularly negotiated loans from the International Monetary Fund (IMF) and implemented marketising and decentralising economic reforms to satisfy IMF conditions ....Even after a decade of economic hardship and political uncertainty in 1979-89, the relative prosperity, freedom to travel and work abroad, and landscape of multicultural pluralism and contrasts that Yugoslavia enjoyed were the envy of East Europeans.
Two years later the country had ceased to exist, and devastating local wars were being waged to create new states ....[2]

How could it have happened? How did it happen? The standard explanation sedulously propagated by Croat nationalists was that a group of Serbian nationalists, led by Slobodan Milosevic, saw the opportunity to bring the other republics within a Greater Serbia by taking over command of the Yugoslav National Army and carrying out the genocide of non-Serbs who resisted.[3] Those of us who knew the country well knew that this explanation simply did not fit the facts. There were a lot of other nationalists about in other republics, even more extreme than Milosevic, looking for the opportunity to transfer power to themselves, if Yugoslavia broke up.

The best insight for me came from our young Serb friends who had demonstrated in Belgrade against Milosevic's attempts to control the Serbian press and television after he achieved the Serbian Party leadership in 1987, and particularly during his election campaigns for the Serbian Presidency in 1990. Our friends had suffered for this both in loss of jobs and threat of imprisonment, but they did not accept the story that it was only Milosevic and Serb nationalists who were to blame for what was happening to Yugoslavia. Some had to leave the country but some stayed behind joining with other like-minded writers and journalists from all the different republics to break through the communication barriers between the peoples of Yugoslavia, which the nationalist controlled media everywhere were creating. They sought to share information among themselves and to inform the outside world about the continuing inter-community associations that existed in the country. To this end they founded an organisation, AIM (Alternative Information Media), with offices in all the republics and in several west European capitals, including London, where I helped to establish their office. I was able to meet a group of them in 1992 at a summer school organised by the *Longo Mai* commune in French Provence. That this work continued right through the war in Bosnia and then in Kosovo is a tribute to the genuine belief in a pluralist socialist Yugoslavia that forty years of Titoism had implanted.

At the beginning of trouble in 1990 it seemed possible that a united Yugoslavia might survive the fissiparist pressures. Delegates from different parts of Yugoslavia, whom I met at a peace conference in Helsinki that year, spoke with cautious optimism. The new federal Prime Minister, Ante Markovic, a Croat who believed in a united Yugoslavia, had brought inflation under control and prepared a budget acceptable to the IMF involving the least possible changes in Yugoslavia's socialist federal structure and the least possible pain for the working people, despite the proposed loss of workers' property rights in enterprises in the social sector. But two major forces were working against him. The first was the new approach of the United States to Yugoslavia following the end of the Cold War. US Ambassador Zimmerman made it clear that Yugoslavia was no longer in a special category for access to financial support as a necessary ally of the USA against the Warsaw Pact forces. The offer of aid towards debt repayments which the IMF had promised to Markovic was withdrawn, and this aid was essential to his budget.[4]

Markovic's second problem was that after the dissolution of the League of Communists in May of 1990 multi-party elections were taking place in the republics before his own election was due, and the party which he had formed, the Yugoslav Reform Party, had no representation at those first elections. The effects, moreover, of his IMF dictated programme were already causing widespread anger among all those in the previously well protected social sector. What emerged when the votes were counted in the 1990 elections in Slovenia, Croatia and Bosnia-Hercegovina was not quite what the several ethnic nationalist parties in each republic had hoped for. Nowhere did they win an absolute majority of the votes. In Slovenia a coalition led by the ex-Communist Milan Kucan took power, and immediately declared Slovenia's sovereignty.[5] In Croatia Franjo Tudjman, another one-time Communist but standing on the strong nationalist position of the Croatian Democratic Union (HDZ) against the ex- Communist 'Party of Democratic Change', won 42 per cent of the votes. On a 'first past the post' electoral system this won him a majority in the Parliament.[6] In Bosnia-Hercegovina voting followed communal lines giving 30 per cent to the Serb party (the SDS led by Radovan Karadzic), 18 per cent to the Croat HDZ and 34 per cent to the mainly Muslim SDA, led by Alija Izebegovic.[7] In fact, the moderate Fikret Abdic defeated Izetgovic for the SDA leadership, but mysteriously withdrew. My Sarajevo friends suggested that Abdic hoped to be able to influence the SDA from outside. If that was his aim he sorely failed to moderate Izetbegovic's nationalist extremism, even failing to persuade him to alternate the Bosnian presidency with the Serbs and Croats, from which failure much disaster was to follow.

The elections in the other republics which followed were no more favourable to the extreme nationalist candidates. In Serbia, as we have seen, Milosevic carried his Socialist Party of Serbia, formed from the old Communist League, to an overwhelming victory over the more extreme nationalist Serbian Movement of Renewal led by Vuk Draskovic.[8] In Montenegro the Communists did not even change the name of the Party or their policies of self-management and won two thirds of the seats. In Macedonia also the Communists kept their name with the addendum of 'Party of Democratic Change', but gained only thirty-one seats against the thirty-seven won by a revived historic Internal Macedonian Revolutionary Organisation (IMRO), forming a multi-party coalition under a Communist leader Gligorov.[9] In Kosovo the Albanians simply boycotted the elections, leaving Milosevic's Serbian Party of Socialists unopposed. But the Albanians then declared a parallel state – which only Albania recognised. They then formally elected a pacifist literary critic, Ibrahim Rugova, as shadow President, surprising everyone even themselves.[10] Albanians had not been known for non-violence. But perhaps this seemed to them to be the only answer to overwhelming Serbian power. It did, however, leave space open for more militant elements, with foreign aid, to establish an illegal Liberation Army (KLA), of which more was soon to be heard.

The result of all these elections was that in effect, with or without the more extreme nationalist leaders, the peoples of Yugoslavia had been persuaded to choose to follow their particular communal interests. But these did not coincide with the boundaries of the old federal republics. Bosnia-Hercegovina was the most obvious case where there were Serbs and Croats as well as Muslims, but Croatia had large numbers of Serbs inside its borders. Serbia had even larger numbers of Muslims as well as Hungarians and Albanians. Macedonia contained a sizeable minority of Albanians. Tito's balance of republics and nations had been upset. It could not be put together again. The only force interested in doing so was the Yugoslav National Army (the JNA), whose very mission was to defend a federal socialist Yugoslavia, and whose leaders did for a time found a League of Communists – Movement for Yugoslavia with several hundred thousand members. But this was gravely compromised because nearly all these were Serbs.[11]

The army was very soon put to the test. Each of the republics had, as part of the Yugoslav system of defence against a possible Soviet invasion, a Territorial Defence Force, and these Forces were mobilised and given extra arms by the new nationalist governments. Tudjman, the new head of government in Croatia, had long argued that Bosnia was historically a part of Croatia and that Croatia was a republic of Croatians.[12] He had also adopted the Ustashe flag and symbols of the war-time Croatian state created by the German occupation. The Serb populations in Croatia rose in protest, especially where they found that the authority of Serb officials and police in the mainly Serbian parts of Croatia – the Krajina and western Slavonia – was being challenged. When the Croatian parliament asserted its right to secede from Yugoslavia, the Serbs of Krajina declared an Autonomous Region of Krajina around Knin.[13]

One result of the elections in Slovenia and Croatia had been that the JNA ordered that the arms of the Territorial Defence Forces should be handed over. The Slovenes kept most of theirs and obtained illegal imports of arms from Hungary. Most of the Croat armoury was seized, but Tudjman obtained arms from the Slovenes and from arms dealers world-wide, financed by Croatian communities in North America, with whom Tudjman had maintained contact over many years.[14] By January 1991 the JNA decided to fix a deadline for the Slovene and Croatian Territorial Defence Forces to hand over their arms. The Federal Presidency representing all the republics was hopelessly divided. Ante Markovic had by then lost all power to impose his will in support of the JNA and a united Yugoslavia.[15] Most of the republics had abandoned all his reform programmes and were busily renationalising privatised companies. At the same time, and more importantly, Ambassador Zimmerman had publicly announced to Belgrade that the US would not accept 'the use of force to hold Yugoslavia together'.[16]

At this point the Americans appeared to waver. Secretary of State James Baker visited Belgrade declaring his support for Ante Markovic's reforms and opposing the secession of Slovenia and Croatia, favouring a confederation in place of federal Yugoslavia.[17] This was a crucial moment in United States foreign policy. The US response to Saddam Hussein's invasion of Kuwait had just been launched with the attack on Baghdad. Continuing European support in the UN, including that of the Russians, for 'Desert Storm' – the war against Iraq – was essential for the Americans. Serious destabilisation in Europe following a break-up of Yugoslavia had to be avoided. It was time, as many voices in the US were claiming, for Europe to tackle its own problems; and if they couldn't, some were adding, the US would take over. The European Union decided to act. On March 13, 1991, the European Parliament passed a resolution declaring 'that the constituent republics and autonomous provinces of Yugoslavia must have the right freely to determine their own future in a peaceful and democratic manner and on the basis of recognized international and national borders'.[18]

This ruled out the use of the Yugoslav Army, but left unclear the meaning of national borders. In the case of Croatia what was the nation – the nation of all Croats or the Yugoslav federal republic of Croatia? In fact, it was well known by then, according to Susan Woodward, that Germany had joined Austria, Hungary and Denmark in at least covert support for independence for Slovenia and Croatia. Conservative elements in the German press – the *Frankfurter Algemeiner Zeitung* and *Die Welt* in particular – were running a vicious campaign against 'the Serbo-Communist power called Yugoslavia' which 'should have no place in the European Community', and even the left-wing *Der Spiegel* was depicting Serbs as 'non-European' barbarians and Yugoslavia, like the old Austro-Hungarian Empire, as a 'prison house of peoples clamouring to escape'.[19] Into this excitement of emotion, just a week after the European Parliament's declaration there entered Slovene President Kucan in Bonn having talks with the German Foreign Minister, Hans Dietrich Genscher. The British Government under John Major did not favour the break-up of Yugoslavia, but this was the time when the European Community was discussing the terms of the Maastricht Treaty for the future of the European Union. Major did not wish to sign up for the Social Clauses or for Monetary Union. German Chancellor Kohl offered him exemption from these clauses, if he would agree with German policy over Yugoslavia.[20] Thus was the future of the poor in Britain and in Yugoslavia condemned.

On June 25 1991 Slovenia unilaterally and illegally proclaimed her independence – illegally because by the Final Act of the Helsinki Conference agreements the OSCE had ruled that changes in frontiers could not be made 'without the consent of the governments and peoples concerned', and of course the Yugoslav government and peoples had not been consulted.[21] Croatia followed suit the day after Slovenia. The next day Markovic signed an order for the JNA to take action in Slovenia. The JNA forces inside Slovenia attempted to secure the international borders, but found a much more effective resistance than they had expected.[22] A troika of European Foreign Ministers negotiated a ceasefire on July 4 and the Slovenes claimed a great military victory against the Yugoslav National Army. Ken Coates, at that time an MEP and convenor of the Parliament's Committee on Human Rights, had to remind them that the victory was a diplomatic victory in winning European support for their cause.

While the Slovene secession happened with very little loss of blood, the same could not be said for that of Croatia. The key question was of foreign recognition, after which actions by the Yugoslav army to hold the country together could be treated not as a civil war, but as aggression. This could have no legal basis because Croatia like the other republics was only an administrative unit of Yugoslavia and, also like the other republics, comprised a number of different peoples, in Croatia at least a third of them Serbs. Nonetheless in early July the German Parliament (the *Bundestag*) voted to recognize Slovenia and Croatia.[23] Fighting in Croatia between Serbs and Croats then worsened dramatically. In August 1991 the European Union sought to reduce hostilities by establishing an International Conference for Peace in Yugoslavia under the chairmanship of British Foreign Secretary Lord Carrington and an Arbitration Commission presided over by a French Judge, Robert Badinter.[24]

In fact this Commission did not arbitrate but issued opinions on criteria for state recognition. These 'opinions' were, to put it mildly, somewhat surprising. Instead of noting and recognising the historic constitution of Yugoslavia as a federation of peoples or of relying on traditional criteria, such as effective control of territory, the Badinter Commission introduced issues of the rule of law, democracy, human rights, especially those of ethnic minorities, disarmament, nuclear non-proliferation (to be used later against Serbia and Iraq). Then having found Croatia wanting in these respects, it nonetheless recommended Croatia's recognition as an independent state, but Macedonia which passed the tests was not to be recognised because Greece objected to the name 'Macedonia' being employed for a new state. Most seriously, the Commission decided that Yugoslavia was a 'state in dissolution', thus opening the way for the recognition of successor states.[25]

The peoples themselves began to take defensive actions, and felt bound to follow their nationalist leaders. The Croat nationalist view, which has become widely accepted, is that a largely Serbian officered JNA, encouraged by Milosevic's vision of a Greater Serbia, moved into Slavonia to take control of that part of western Croatia and carried out the most brutal attack on Vukovar, a town which became, like Srebrenica later in Bosnia and Gracac later still in Kosovo, internationally famous as an apparent witness to Serbian brutality and Milosevic's ambition.

The truth is rather more complicated. First, it should be noted that, as Norah Beloff, a British journalist based in Belgrade, pointed out in her *Yugoslavia: An Avoidable War*, 'In reality, as any study of events in Belgrade will confirm, the Serb leader never used the words "Greater Serbia" except to refute accusations made by outside powers.'[26] Second, the evidence of Croat nationalism is much more telling. Tito had been compelled to act firmly to purge the Croat leadership of Croat nationalists in 1970-71. Franjo Tudjman, moreover, published a book in 1980 arguing that Bosnia-Hercegovina was 'by historical right and geographical logic an integral part of Croatia' and was at that time imprisoned for 'maliciously misrepresenting Yugoslavia abroad'.[27]

The peoples of Yugoslavia were not left to themselves in their troubles. From the start Germany was most heavily involved. The links between Croatian and German industrial interests became obvious to any traveler in Croatia in the 1980s who noticed the billboards advertising German cars, machines and household equipment. The links between their intelligence services were less obvious. I recall Sean Gervasi in the 1980s, then at the Institute for European Studies, retailing bizarre stories of Croatian 'national communists hobnobbing with the Ustashe diaspora, through links made by the German CIA – the BND (Bundesnachrichtendienst or Secret Service). It cannot have been by chance that Klaus Kinkel, who became Genscher's successor as Germany's foreign minister in 1992, announcing within six days of taking office that 'We must bring Serbia to its knees', had been the head of the BND between 1979 and 1982. Whether the weapons that reached Croatia as a result of these contacts arrived with the knowledge of the German government is not revealed by Kinkel's biographer, whose other revelations can be found in Diana Johnstone's *Fools' Crusade*.[28]

What is very evident is that the JNA found itself facing a considerable force, when it tried to move in August 1991 from its garrisons in Croatia to control fighting in the surrounding countryside. On August 25 Croatian forces attacked a JNA base in the Gulf of Kotor, south of Dubrovnik. They were beaten off, but when the JNA moved north and imposed a naval blockade on Dubrovnik it confronted further Croat forces and laid siege to the city.[29] In the outside world we were told that the Serbs had destroyed the beautiful old town, which anyone who has been there since will know was untrue. The Croat government was already being advised by a Washington PR firm and later by Ruder and Finn.[30] A Croat Army was being built up on the basis of the Croat National Guard with the aim of expelling the JNA from all its garrisons in Croatia. The most serious confrontation did occur at Vukovar, a largely Croat town in the middle of the mainly Serbian Western Slavonia. But the reason has to be understood. The Serbs were resisting an attempt by the Croat government to replace the elected regional assembly dominated by Serbs with a governor appointed from Zagreb.[31] For the first time the JNA was drawn in from its civil order function to take the side of the Serbian para-military forces against the Croats. There was heavy fighting and much of the town was destroyed. Pictures were published all over the world. The JNA held the field, but the Croats had won another important public relations victory.

At this point the JNA could have marched on Zagreb but General Panic, the JNA commander, was told by Milosevic in Belgrade: 'We have no job there in Croat populated areas. We have to protect the Serb areas". This was reported by Silber and Little, no friends of Milosevic, in their *Death of Yugoslavia*.[32] So much for the thesis of Greater Serbian ambitions. The JNA was in fact steadily withdrawn under heavy attack, leaving arms and supplies to local Serb militia, who were then joined by volunteers from Serbia, at the proposal not of Milosevic but of Draskovic, the most nationalist of Serbian leaders. This was extremely unfortunate because many of these volunteers were the most despicable thugs, criminals and football hooligans like the gang under the command of the monster Arkan, who was to cause such misery in Bosnia.

Apart from Slavonia the main concentration of Serbs in Croatia was in the Krajina, which had declared itself an autonomous territory. What happened in Gospic in the Lika valley was particularly eerie, because it was here fifty years earlier in 1941 under the German occupation that a Ustashe minister of the newly created quisling 'Independent State of Croatia', Mile Budak, had promised how Croatia would be purified of non-Croatians within ten years. Many hundreds of thousands of Serbs were indeed then murdered or transported to death camps[33] Just fifty years later in Gospic there was a massacre of a hundred or more Serbs – small compared with Ustashe victims. This massacre was not reported at the time, but was picked up by Diana Johnstone from a *New York Times* story six years later of a disgruntled Croat policeman, whose story was subsequently reported to the International Criminal Tribunal.[34] Unlike the massacres attributed to Serbs, such massacres by Croats, as we saw earlier, were ignored by the Tribunal.

The Gospic story of late September 1991 was that the JNA garrison fell to Croat forces, reportedly betrayed by an Albanian Agim Ceku, who rose to high office in the Croatian army, retired to be trained by US military advisers and was to lead the 'operation storm', which emptied the Krajina of its entire 200,000 Serb population in 1995. Ceku went on to command the Kosovan Liberation Army in 1999 and to be chief of the Kosovo Protection Corps under NATO.[35] Back to Gospic in 1991; many Serbs left the town but were persuaded by the Croatian authorities to return and 120, including leading professors and judges, were abducted and executed.[36] Similar stories were reported much later by AIM of massacres in the Pakrac valley, the work of Mercep's gang, the Croatian equivalent of the Serb monster Arkan, and called by an admiring Croat public 'the Croatian knights'.[37] It is no pleasure to say it, but for every Serb horror story there is a Croatian horror to set beside it. As one American wit had it, 'There is nothing much to distinguish Tudjman and Milosevic. Both are absolute bastards. It is just that Tudjman is our bastard'.

Hostilities in Croatia could not be ignored by the International Community, as the governments of the United States and European Union like to think of themselves. Germany unilaterally recognised Slovenia and Croatia on December 23 1991, Chancellor Kohl claiming that recognition would bring a quick end to the fighting by deterring what he saw as Serbian aggression, by which he could claim to grant exemption from the ban on German military intervention.[38] It did not, of course, end the fighting because Serbs defending themselves felt deserted by the loss of Yugoslav protection. Lord Carrington's attempts to mediate in Croatia through the European sponsored International Conference on Yugoslavia thus came to an end. The United Nations was brought in and UN mediator Cyrus Vance after fourteen failed ceasefires achieved a lasting ceasefire agreement signed in Sarajevo on January 2 1992 by Croatian and Serbian military commanders. A UN force of 10,000 peace-keeping troops, later expanded to 17,000, was introduced into the country and UN protected areas were established in the Krajina, north and south, in Pakrac and in Eastern Slavonia.[39]

Peace may have been restored but it was on the basis of the recognition of separatist states and solved nothing in Bosnia-Hecegovina, with its three separate communities. Moreover, it was based on the false assumption that Yugoslavia had been a federation of states, not a federation of peoples who had agreed to come together and to live in six federal republics, with equal rights for all the peoples in each republic. It thus neglected the interests of those who as Serbs wished to continue to live in Yugoslavia, and had expressed this wish in referenda. It also negated the wishes of those from all communities who wished to live in a pluralist society.[40] In July 1991 50,000 people had marched in Sarajevo in support of a united Yugoslavia. I heard of this through our friend

Nada Kraigher's granddaughter Nina, who had been active in organising the march, herself a Slovene married to a Bosnian Muslim. The most harrowing story of such cross-communal relations in Sarajevo was that of the young lovers from different communities who were caught in cross-fire while wading one night through the Miljacka and were found next day dead in each others arms under the shallow running waters of the river.

Croatia had predatory ambitions on Bosnia-Hercegovina and the Muslims became determined to hold their own. President Izetbegovic, a member of the old feudal land-owning Muslim aristocracy, who had once been jailed for his 'Islamic Declaration' published first in 1970 advocating a pure Muslim state, and reprinted for his 1990 election campaign, had spent July of 1991 touring Pakistan, Saudi Arabia and Turkey seeking external support.[41] He did obtain Iranian help in building up his army, but he was still prepared to work together with the Croat and Serb parties in Bosnia-Hercegovina within a revamped Yugoslavia until, according to Diana Johnstone, and also Norah Beloff quoting Crnobrnja's Yugoslav Drama, after he made a trip to the USA he proposed forming a sovereign Bosnian state outside of Yugoslavia.[42] This was wholly unacceptable to the Serbs who withdrew from the coalition government in November 1991 and formed their own Bosnian Parliament.

Fighting was spilling over from Croatia into Bosnia, and the Croatian government decided to intervene. The Bosnian Croat leader was replaced by a strong Croat nationalist, Mate Boban, who proceeded to declare a Croat state of Herceg-Bosna in western Hercegovina.[43] This became virtually part of Croatia. At the same time Boban agreed with Abdic in the Krajina on terms for a settlement there. The prospects for a single Bosnian state, which Izetbegovic was determined to achieve under Muslim leadership, looked dim. A state of emergency was declared, leaving Izetbegovic as sole president in place of the rotating presidency and in January of 1992 the rump of Croatian and Muslim members applied to the Badinter Commission for recognition of the government of Bosnia-Hercegovina. This required a popular referendum, and this was held in February-March 1992.[44]

The Serbs abstained in a widespread boycott of the referendum. Two thirds of those eligible voted (the Bosnian Serbs being the one third missing) and 97 per cent voted for independence, which the Badinter Commission took as qualified support.[45] This outraged the Bosnian Serbs, because their understanding of the Yugoslav constitution was quite correctly that the several *peoples* of Yugoslavia had agreed to come together to form the new post-1945 Yugoslavia. The republics, and particularly Bosnia-Hercegovina, were only administrative units which each contained a mix of peoples. So, the Serbs argued, only the peoples could decide to dissolve Yugoslavia and they had not been asked to do this.

The International Conference was recalled in Lisbon and Lord Carrington appointed a Portuguese minister to find common ground between the three parties. Good progress was made and an agreement was signed for founding a tri-partite state, but within days this was disavowed by both Izetbegovic and Boban. It appeared that they had spoken again to US ambassador Zimmerman, who had encouraged them to go for a unitary state.[46] In April US Secretary of State James Baker recommended acceptance to the European Union. Recognition manifestly failed the Badinter criteria, but it was said that for US political leaders the large Croat expatriate vote in the US 1992 election was a factor.[47] Lord Carrington's comment in an interview for *The Avoidable War* was that 'what the international community – the Europeans, the Americans, the UN – did made it sure there was going to be conflict'.[48]

He was right and the conflict was at one time as violent between Croats and Muslims as between both and Serbs, as each fought to hold territory that was being bargained for in the several UN, American and European Plans for dividing up Bosnia-Hercegovina between the different communities.[49] In May of 1992 Milosevic had ordered the demobilization of the JNA and non-Bosnian troops had withdrawn, arms being inherited by all three factions. By the end of the year Serb forces under the command of Ratko Mladic occupied some 70 per cent of the territory.[50] Given that Serb rural land holdings tended to be larger than any land held by those of the other three, this was only somewhat above the 52 per cent that the plans gave the Serbs, but left major battles over the towns. Croats, who lived mainly in the towns, argued that the Serbs were invaders, although the vast majority were farmers whose families had lived on their land for hundreds of years. In Mostar the Serbs were virtually eliminated in June 1992 by Croat and Muslim forces.[51] Nonetheless, the Europeans and Americans decided that Croat and Muslim unity should be supported and that Milosevic lay behind so-called Serbian aggression. In the same month of June 1992 the UN imposed sanctions on Serbia and introduced the UN peacekeeping force UNPROFOR to Bosnia.[52]

The three UN plans in which Lord Owen, one time UK Foreign Secretary, played a leading role, were designed to establish a Bosnian state which would hopefully comprise all three communities as separate provinces. In fact they were not being treated equally. The USA was increasingly backing Izetbegovic and supported the Muslim-Croat alliance, which was not at all prepared to accept a Bosnia-Hercegovina divided up into separate bits.[53] The Serbs were regarded as the enemy and after 1994 were being bombed by NATO planes. Although Milosevic supported the various UN Plans – against the wishes of the Bosnian Serbs – David Owen complains in his book, *Balkan Odyssey*, that Milosevic might have been more helpful.[54] That seems a bit rich as Milosevic's Yugoslavia was suffering quite seriously from the UN imposed sanctions.

The Plans were moreover, all based on a false premise. These were the Vance-Owen Plan of January 1993 for ten 'ethnic' cantons, three to be Serb, three Croat and four Muslim; the Owen-Stoltenberg Plan of May 1993 for three 'ethnic' states and the Contact Group Plan of March 1994 for two 'ethnic' states, one consisting of the lately agreed Bosnian Croat- Bosniac (Muslim) Federation and the other of Bosnian Serbs, with demilitarized territories in Sarajevo, Gorazde and Zepce/Srebrenica, guaranteed by the UN peace-keeping force (UNPROFOR). The false premise was that certain parts of Bosnia-Hercegovina were supposed to be predominantly populated by one or other of the three communities. If you took large enough territories you could make that work. Or you could take only municipalities as Branka Magas does it in her book[55] and get the same result. The facts are much more complex as Susan Woodward shows in the map and figures in her *Balkan Tragedy*. Out of 109 districts in Bosnia-Hercegovina before the fighting began, only five had a majority of over 90 per cent in one community, only thirty had a majority of over 70 per cent in one community and in less than half was there an absolute majority of one community.[56] As I had discovered when I made my first tours of the country, the norm was a mix of peoples who had lived side by side for generations.

Why then were they fighting each other so bitterly fifty years later? The answer must be a combination of three main factors: first, the rising foreign debt and IMF demands resulting in uncontrolled inflation and the complete breakdown of the Yugoslav national economy, leading all communities to look to their own; second, the appeal of nationalist leaders offering some protection on a communal nationalist basis; third, the widening gap between those from the richer communities in the north and in the social sector on the one hand and on the other the increasingly impoverished farm workers mainly in the south. Most of the Muslims and Croats lived in the towns, most of the Serbs in the countryside.[57] The Serb farmers would hold on to their land, poor as it might be, as the only thing they possessed.

When any group saw someone from another community with *Deutschemarks* or *lire* and they had only worthless dinars, it only needed a Radovan Karadjic or Boban, an Arkan or a Mercep to tell them to take what they could get from a neighbour. And when foreign powers were planning to divide up their country between different communities they would fight for the land they knew to be theirs. It was a witches' brew – concocted by the international community, the Americans in particular – of support for Muslim-Croat unity. Ambassador Holbrooke, in his book *To End a War*, always refers to all Bosnians as Muslims,[58] and the singling out of Milosevic and the Serbs as the enemy, and then, with the imposition of sanctions on Serbia and NATO planes bombing Serbian positions, it was inevitable that Serbian resistance would escalate.

At the same time, the effect of trade sanctions imposed by UN Resolutions from May 1992 on the Federal Republic of Yugoslavia (the rump of Yugoslavia comprising Serbia and Montenegro), though little reported, was very severe.

In 1993 inflation spiraled totally out of control, bringing at least one third of all households, those dependent on dinar purchases, into absolute poverty. Unemployment was the lot of half of all non-agricultural workers. Black markets flourished, in which government ministers, not excluding Milosevic, were involved. The country only survived by consuming its capital, and the government only paid for imports by in effect stealing from private hard currency accounts. Serbia's industry was reduced to operating at about a third of capacity. Cumulative losses of output during the years of sanctions amounted to about two thirds of earlier national income. Annual national income per head fell from about $4000 to$1500, the average for a poor developing country.[59]

In Bosnia and Hercegovina the years 1993, 1994 and 1995 saw the most terrible fighting. There was much exaggeration of the number of deaths and of the rapes reported by spokespersons on either side and by journalists, most particularly pointing the finger at the Serbs. Izetbegovic's government claimed 300,000 dead and 30,000 women raped. UN reports suggested that the dead numbered about a tenth of that figure and rapes of about 2,400 on all sides – a bad enough figure but typical of war.[60] What was less well reported was the effect on men who refused to go and fight. Maja Korac reported a great increase in violence in the home, as some sort of psychological compensation.[61] Large numbers of Serbs called up to the forces fled the country. As many as 200,000 young people are estimated to have left homes in the Former Yugoslavia as permanent émigré's during these years.

It was the one-sidedness of the reporting of the war in Bosnia that was most striking. The pictures of the Serb army's Omarska prison camp spread world-wide and that of the thin man behind barbed wire was regularly dragged out, even though it had been demonstrated that it was the cameraman who was behind the wire.[62] The International Red Cross reported in 'The Avoidable War' film that 'Serbs, Croats and Muslims all ran detention camps, and must share equal blame'.[63] Little was shown of Croat shelling in Mostar, while the world was flooded with pictures of shelling by the Serbs of Sarajevo. And at least some of the bombings of crowded Muslim market places and bread queues were found subsequently to have been carried out by Muslim guns, though blamed on the Serbs to win over world public opinion.[64] According to M. Parenti in his book , To Kill a Nation: The Attack on Yugoslavia, the French general Phillipe Morillon, one-time commander of UNPROFOR 'charged that the Bosnian Muslim government repeatedly refused to let UNPROFOR establish a ceasefire, because it wanted to keep Sarajevo as a focal point for world sympathy'. General Sir Michael Rose was said by Parenti to have come to the same conclusion, while he had found that the Serbs had agreed to all his ceasefire demands.[65]

Once more, far from halting Serb resistance, the proposed recognition of a

Croat-Muslim Bosnia and the bombing of the Serbs as aggressors only made the Serbs in Bosnia more determined – to the point that they went far beyond what Milosevic thought was wise. When the Croat and Muslim forces appeared to be gaining the upper hand, the Serbs still did not give in. To bring them to accept defeat, Izetbegovic pleaded for stepping up the bombing of their headquarters at Pale. He was told that only a terrible massacre by the Serbs could justify that. There is now enough evidence to conclude that this is what he deliberately provoked at Srebrenica. Diana Johnstone quotes the November 1999 UN Report on Srebrenica, which includes the following note:

> Some surviving members of the Srebrenica delegation have stated that President Izetbegovic also told them that he had learned that NATO intervention in Bosnia and Hercegovina was possible, but only if the Serbs were to break into Srebrenica killing at least 5000 of its people.[66]

This idea of a provocation is so contrary to all we were told at the time and to what has been repeated ever since, even by Bill Clinton at an anniversary funeral in 2003 staged for world television coverage, that it needs stronger evidence than the memories of some UN delegates four years later. Diana Johnstone offers a number of considerations[67]:

First, there is the evidence of General Philippe Morillon, the UN commander in Bosnia at the time, who told a French parliamentary inquiry that the Serb commanders had fallen into a deliberate 'trap' which was 'the only way Izetbegovic could get what he wanted – for the International Community to take his side. I'm not afraid to say', he went on, 'that it is Sarajevo that deliberately provoked the dramatic events. It was the Presidency, it was Izetbegovic'.

Secondly, we need to consider the date of the alleged Srebrenica massacre – mid-July, 1995. In May of that year, Tudjman, violating the UN sponsored truce, sent Croat armed forces to recapture western Slavonia from rebels, driving tens of thousands of Serbs from the region and in so doing, as reported by Silber and Little, killing hundreds of civilians who were too old, weak or sick to flee.[68] For this the Croat commander is still wanted by the International Criminal Court (ICTY) for trial, and the Croat government's failure to deliver him up was, until 2003, delaying Croatia's association agreement with the European Union. In retaliation for the action in Slavonia and to try to stop the Croats attacking Serb civilians, Krajina Serbs lobbed two Orcan rockets into central Zagreb, killing seven people. For this Milan Martic, the President of Serbian Krajina was also indicted by the ICTY, although UN envoy Carl Bildt suggested that Tudjman was equally deserving of indictment.[69] Within three months in August 1995, and almost coincident with the Srebrenica 'massacre', the Croatian army strengthened by illegal arms imports and US advisors in 'operation storm' led by the infamous Agim Ceku, mentioned before, drove all the 200,000 Serbs out of the Krajina in northern Bosnia.[70]

Thirdly, Johnstone reminds us that Srebrenica, though termed a UN 'safe haven', was not demilitarized, except for the town centre, and remained, like other 'safe havens' in Bosnia, a base from which Muslim forces made forays into the surrounding Serb villages. The Serbs fled Srebrenica in May 1992 and for the next three years the Muslim commander Naser Oric led forays which burnt and pillaged 192 villages, killing 1300 villagers, the most terrible incident being the Christmas massacre of forty-six Serb worshippers at Kravica, reported in the *Daily Telegraph*[71] and later reported with affidavits to the ICTY – without result.

Disaster followed when an attack by Oric on another Serb village on June 26 1995 led to a Serb army operation which entered the non-demilitarised outskirts of Srebrenica on July 11. To the surprise of the Serbs there was no resistance either from UNPROFOR or from Muslim forces, who appeared to have been deserted by most of their officers. Fearing an ambush the Serb commander, General Ratko Mladic entered the town and had all men of fighting age, including many Muslim soldiers, rounded up and held in a football stadium, while the women and children and old people were evacuated. Undoubtedly, some of the soldiers were killed in revenge for the Oric raids. Others were taken prisoner to be exchanged for Serb prisoners.[72]

The story was then told to the world three weeks later by the US Secretary of State Mrs Albright, waving spy satellite photographs at the UN Security Council, showing the Srebrenica stadium first filled with men and then empty but for marks that might be fresh diggings to reveal, she claimed, that 8000 men had been slaughtered.[73] Her message was that the UN had failed as a peace-keeping force. Only US military might exercised from the air for humanitarian ends could from then on be relied upon. This was just at the moment when the Security Council was due to consider the report that the Croats' 'operation storm' was driving the whole Serbian population out of the Krajina. The Croats were told to stop and respect international law.[74] The Serbs were accused of genocide. What actually happened to all the Muslims rounded up in Srebrenica is not clear. The *New York Times* of July 18 reported that, according to UN officials, some 3000-4000 had escaped from Srebrenica to Bosnian government territory, 2000 Muslim troops to Tuzla.[75] As of 2003, forensic teams had exhumed 2300 bodies in the region, where fighting had been going on for four years. 199 bodies showed that the men had been bound and blindfolded, so the presumption must be that they had been executed.[76] In all conscience that is a terrible number, but it is not 8000 or the 7500 that continued, at least up to 2003, to be accepted by Bill Clinton and by the ICTY, and is now in all the history books, as the number of Muslims massacred by Serbs at Srebrenica.

Izetbegovic got what he wanted. The Serbs gave in to a new wave of NATO bombing.[77] Negotiations were transferred to the USA, to an air force base at Dayton Ohio. Tudjman, Izetbegovic and Milosevic were summoned, Milosevic because the Bosnian Serb leaders, Karadzic and Mladic, had been indicted for war crimes. In what came to be called the Dayton Accords, Bosnia-Hercegovina was recognised as a sovereign state, comprising two entities – a Muslim-Croat federation with 51 per cent of the territory, and a Bosnian Serb republic with 49 per cent. The federation was to include Sarajevo, and a land corridor to Gorazde. Srebrenica and Zepa were to remain under Serb control. There was to be a collective presidency, a Parliament in Sarajevo and a single currency. For a transitional period until elections, subsequently extended indefinitely, the country was to be run by an international administration.[78] The sovereign powers of the new state were extraordinarily limited, not including control over the armed forces or even over the currency, all legislative and executive power lying with the UN High Representative – from 2002 in the person of the former UK Liberal Party leader, Lord Ashdown. Milosevic was given the role of guaranteeing the execution of the Accords, thus neutering the Serbs in Bosnia.[79] That was the end of pluralist Yugoslavia, but nobody believed it was the end of the matter. The problem of Kosovo remained unsolved and the Americans had not finally caught their man and his Serbian army, but they expected to catch them in Kosovo.

The world had become convinced that Milosevic and his Serbians were what *Die Welt* had once called 'barbarians'. What he was doing in Kosovo, the world believed, only proved that *Die Welt* was right. The films made for TV by Norma Percy and Brian Lapping *Death of Yugoslavia* had been among the most influential. When the films' sequel on Kosovo, *The Fall of Milosevic*, appeared in 2002,[80] Alan Little, who had been a war correspondent in Bosnia, greeted the sequel in an article in *The Guardian* with the words: 'At last the truth' and 'the truth [about Bosnia]', he wrote 'was simple. There was a war because a criminalised elite in Belgrade had chosen to have one.'[81] Unfortunately for Little, the first sentence of his review was an invention, which was exposed. It read 'In November 1995 Bill Clinton lent across a desk at an airforce base at Dayton, Ohio and handed a Cuban cigar to Slobodan Milosevic'. Three days later *The Guardian*, in its daily item of 'Corrections', had to explain that Clinton was not at Dayton, but attended the formal signing of the Dayton Accords some time later in Paris.[82] After such inventions, one is hardly inclined to take the reports of such correspondents seriously. But the seriousness of the crisis in Kosovo could not be denied.

6th Century Icon at Decani Monastery, Kosovo

Chapter 12

Kosovo and NATO's War on Yugoslavia, 1996-9

The full-scale war launched by NATO forces against Yugoslavia in March 1999 was the first invasion of a European state for over sixty years since Hitler marched into the Rhineland in 1937. Such an extraordinary affront to all the principles of national sovereignty, without UN authorisation, was justified on a new principle in international relations, that of 'humanitarian intervention'. The war sounded the death-knell of Former Yugoslavia, and the massive aerial bombardment – of factories, houses, hospitals, TV stations, roads, railways and bridges – set back by many years much of the remarkable and painful work of reconstruction in Serbia that the Yugoslav peoples had achieved since they had driven Hitler's armies out of their country. How far this could be justified on humanitarian grounds we shall see, but that such an invasion, both by Americans and by other Europeans, could even have been contemplated requires some prior explanation.

Under pressure from their arms industries, both the United States and the European Union needed some *raison d'etre* for the continued existence of NATO after the demise of the Soviet Union. It was at the same time clear that the United States was seeking to tie Europe into its plans for world hegemony. On March 23, on the eve of NATO's bombing of Yugoslavia President Clinton explained that 'a strong US-European partnership ... is what this Kosovo thing is all about .... If we are going to have a strong economic relationship [with the world] that includes our ability to sell around the world. Europe has got to be a key.'[1 and 2]

NATO air forces had been called in to put an end to the Bosnian civil war but there was still the question of Kosovo.

The 'international community', which is how the USA and European Union saw themselves, was encouraging world opinion to believe that there was unfinished business in Yugoslavia. Milosevic had been brought in to underwrite the Dayton Accords for Croatia and Bosnia-Hercegovina, but the problem of Kosovo remained unsolved and Milosevic was still free to hold down the Kosovo Albanians and cause possible trouble with their fellow nationals in Macedonia. The UN was said to have failed in Bosnia. Unilateral measures were now required. Germany was already involved in the recognition of Slovenia and Croatia, and Chancellor Kohl had persuaded Britain's Prime Minister John Major to fall into line. Germany was providing military peace keeping units in Bosnia and had begun to supply arms to the Kosovo Liberation Army. Germany's interest was both historic and economic. The UN envoy Cyrus Vance had even described the subsequent war in Croatia as 'Genscher's war', and Genscher's successor as German Foreign Minister, Klaus Kinkel, had announced on taking office that he would 'bring Serbia to its knees'.[3]

No less important than that of Germany was the US motive for increased military involvement in Yugoslavia. US military thinking was increasingly moving towards unilateral action, if necessary with UN support, if possible with NATO allies, but in the last analysis on its own. Clinton's Secretary of State, Madeline Albright, was determined to bring Milosevic to court and was asking Colin Powell, the chief of staff, 'what was the good of having that splendid army you are always boasting about if you never use it?'[4] There were long-term US geo-political reasons beyond Milosevic. The ending of the Cold War and the disintegration of the Soviet Union had opened up western Asia with its great natural resources, and especially the undeveloped Caspian oil reserves.

US policy had much earlier been laid down by President Carter's National Security Adviser, Zbigniew Brzezinski, in his book *The Grand Chessboard* – that 'Eurasia is the chessboard on which the struggle for global supremacy continues to be played.'[5] The struggle was still between the USA and Russia, with China an increasingly important player. Russia's strong links with fellow Slavs in Yugoslavia had to be broken and a US base in the Balkans established. When war was launched against Yugoslavia it became possible to establish in Kosovo a secure base for US forces, in what was named 'Camp Bondsteel'§ – the biggest US overseas base since the Vietnam war, built by Brown and Root Services, a subsidiary of Haliburton Corporation, of which Dick Cheney was CEO from 1995-2000 before becoming Vice President under Bush Junior.[6] We are now hearing about Haliburton's contracts in Iraq after the second Iraq war. NATO's remit had thus to be extended eastward, not only in the north through to the Ukraine but in the south on the eastern Mediterranean.

There was some anxiety in American circles that Milosevic was still committed to a socialist economy.[7] There was in fact some evidence for this, but mainly of European capital getting into rump Yugoslavia ahead of the Americans. In the three years between the lifting of UN sanctions against Yugoslavia after the Dayton Accords and the start of NATO bombing of Kosovo economic considerations were activating Europeans in Yugoslavia even more than Americans. A number of giant transnational companies from the West had been welcomed into what remained of Yugoslavia – Serbia and Montenegro. According to reports in the *Financial Times* the National Westminster Bank became the advisor on external debt negotiations and sole financial advisor for the privatisation of Serbia Telecom.[8] By June 1997 a 49 per cent stake in Serbia Telecom had been sold to STET of Italy and OTE of Greece for £565 million, the proceeds of which had to go straight into paying arrears owing to workers and pensioners. UN economic sanctions had reduced much of the Serb economy to bankruptcy.[9]

On prospects for investment in Serbia, the Banque Nationale de Paris commented in 1997, 'We believe state assets will be sold at bargain basement prices. This offers investors some attractive exporting companies in what post [dinar] devaluation Yugoslavia will be amongst Europe's most competitively priced countries.'[10] Early privatisation of power utilities and state oil companies was attracting interest, with British and German companies positioning themselves to buy into Serbia's electricity utility, EPS, and Hoechst taking a majority stake in Technogas. British, French and Greek companies were said to be in talks to buy into Serbia's largest cement producer, while Belgium's Interbrew was buying the Niksic brewery in Montenegro. The same road had already been travelled in Croatia; and there may have been some American business interest in not being excluded from the Balkans by European companies getting there first.

Thus was Tito's socialist Yugoslavia being dissolved, but the United States still§ wanted more and feared Serbia's fraternal relations with Russia. And as for Montenegro, I once asked a Montenegrin what was the population of Montenegro and got the reply, 'We and the Russians are one hundred million.' By the mid-1990s the US military-industrial establishment was moving towards the view that the United Nations was an obstacle to the extension of US military interventions through NATO, where these were required for 'full spectrum US dominance'. UN support had been won for the Gulf War because Saddam Hussein had manifestly aggressed against Kuwait. It might not always be so easy to win (as was proved by the second Iraq War in 2003).

The so-called 'UN failure' to stop ethnic cleansing in Bosnia was used to demonstrate the absolute necessity for US action through NATO to stop Milosevic in his tracks. What was seen by the Serbs as a police operation in Kosovo against an illegal armed revolt by Albanians inside a sovereign Yugoslav state was said by the Americans to require military intervention to prevent a humanitarian disaster. The argument that arose was concerned with the form of intervention, whether bombardment from the air would be enough to bring Milosevic to heel or whether a land force would be required. The most senior US general in the theatre, General Wesley Clark, was convinced that a massive air attack would soon bring Milosevic suing for peace. Others, including Tony Blair speaking for Britain, favoured a supporting land operation.[11]

But committing armies to a land operation had its problems. The use of a regular army with tanks and artillery against an armed uprising is bound to involve civilian casualties, as well as body bags coming home. Civilian casualties may result from misdirected firing but equally from directed firing at houses and buildings where armed insurgents are known or assumed to be sheltering. Whole villages may be burned as reprisal for harbouring insurgents. The result of such destruction leaves people homeless. Some may escape to neighbours or to woods and hills to hide. Others in an area of mixed ethnic population may be tempted to enter what they think of as enemy property, and there are likely in a situation of lawlessness to be marauding armed gangs to encourage them. This was the pattern of civil war in Bosnia. It was repeated in Kosovo, even without a NATO landing.[12] Although there is evidence that the Yugoslav police and army did use very strong measures in dealing with the Kosovan Liberation Army (KLA), measures claimed by Milosevic's prosecutors to have been 'disproportionate', there is no doubt that the greater humanitarian disaster in Kosovo and elsewhere in Yugoslavia took place after, and not before, NATO launched its massive aerial bombardment on the whole country in March 1999.[13] But before they could do that they needed a story to tell like Srebrenica.

The build-up to the NATO bombardment of Yugoslavia has to be understood in some depth. I have tried to reconstruct it from the transcripts of the Milosevic trial.[14] We saw earlier that Milosevic had given support to the Serbs in Kosovo and had seriously reduced the rights of Albanians, degrading Kosovo from the status of a republic to an autonomous province. The result was to encourage the activities of the Kosovan Liberation Army, which had obtained arms from both Germany and the imploded Albanian state and had the military support of disbanded Mujahadeen from Afghanistan after the Russian withdrawal. Heavy handed Yugoslav army reprisals against what the army regarded as a terrorist campaign led to mass evacuation from some Kosovo Albanian villages, and the stories of this were taken up by the world media to indicate a threatened humanitarian disaster. Ambassador Holbrooke on October 13 1998 reached agreement with Milosevic on the withdrawal of army units not normally stationed in Kosovo and of police forces in excess of peace-time establishments – some 6000 men.[15]

This Holbrooke-Milosevic agreement was followed up by a meeting of NATO representatives with Milosevic and his military commanders on October 15 to discuss the military details of the agreement. NATO was represented by

Javier Solana, its General Secretary, and General Naumann, chairman of the Military Committee. Naumann returned to Belgrade ten days later with US General Wesley Clark to see Milosevic and his General Staff because NATO obsevers believed that no action had been taken to withdraw any Yugoslav forces from Kosovo. In his evidence to the Tribunal (ICTY) at the trial of Milosevic, Naumann quoted the words he used at that meeting on October 24: 'Mr.President, we come to deliver a very clear cut, straightforward message. The hammer is cocked, the clock is ticking and you have got 48 hours to deliver' (p. 6978 of the ICTY transcript). Naumann had already made it clear that the sixteen NATO members had been given an 'activation order' on October 16 in response to Holbrooke's request that he needed 'one last convincing argument to obtain Milosevic's agreement' (p. 6968). The General explained to the Tribunal (ICTY) that the nations had already received an 'activation warning' to prepare for military action, followed by an 'activation request' to get their forces ready for deployment. So the 'activation order' meant that they had to go to their Parliament or other national bodies for authority to commit their forces if and when required (pages 6966-7).

Milosevic had rejected the right of NATO to threaten a sovereign state with the use of force and had denied that the Yugoslav police and military were using tanks or artillery against villages and civilians. Naumann confirmed that they had evidence of this. Milosevic in his cross-examination of Naumann claimed the right of any nation to deal with terrorist attacks within its borders, and cited the case of the British in Northern Ireland. Naumann gave the reply which became the standard argument of those who called themselves 'humanitarian imperialists' to justify the bombing of Yugoslavia: 'Sovereignty implies the responsibility of rulers to protect human rights' and to ensure that any 'response to violence against the state is no more than proportionate' (pp. 7043 and 7103). In the event the Yugoslav forces were withdrawn early in November 1998 – a remarkable feat – 6000 men moved in twenty-four hours. The activation order was put on hold, but Naumann claimed that the withdrawal 'did not last for long' (p. 6994).

Milosevic argued that every withdrawal of Yugoslav forces was immediately followed by intensified KLA attacks and Naumann agreed that this was true (p. 7042). Cross examining Naumann (page 6995), Milosevic got him to concede that the 'KLA actions triggered violence in late 1998', but Naumann argued that the disproportionate violence of the Yugoslav forces only generated more violence. Paddy Ashdown, when questioned at the Tribunal confirmed this from his visits to Kosovo at the time, but Milosevic obtained the agreement of both Ashdown (p. 2444) and Naumann (p. 6996) that the KLA could be described as a 'terrorist' organisation. Ashdown had also commented that he was aware that there was arms smuggling, and also drugs smuggling, from Albania. One of the unnamed Yugoslav army witnesses at the Tribunal (K6) averred that the

KLA could have been eliminated in 1996 if plans had been implemented (p. 6594). He had added that by 1998 there were Iranians, Turks, Bosnians and other Islamic elements serving with the KLA (pp. 6613-4). Milosevic claimed that there were *mujahadeen* from Afghanistan, and Naumann agreed that there were in Bosnia, but he said that he did not know about Kosovo (pp. 6911 and 7084).

In considering the problem of which came first, the violence of the Yugoslav army or that of the KLA, the question of arms coming into Kosovo from outside became an important issue at the Tribunal. Milosevic had seized on the point to ask General Naumann why NATO had done nothing to stop arms entering Yugoslavia from Albania. Naumann replied that he did not have authority to do that (p. 7074). This answer tends to confirm the suggestion made in the Percy-Lapping film 'The Fall of Milosevic' that Holbrooke gave Milosevic a wink and a nod that he could safely go ahead with strong-arm action in Kosovo, the inevitable result of which would be to create conditions which could be described as 'ethnic cleansing' and would justify a NATO invasion.[16] It certainly throws a new light on the widely assumed guilt of Milosevic in driving Albanians out of Kosovo. The story of a so-called 'Operation Horseshoe', said to have been initiated by Milosevic to clear Kosovo of all Albanians, was soon to be exposed by General Heinz Loquai of the OCSE in Vienna as nothing but a total fabrication.[17]

Following the Holbrooke-Milosevic agreement, a Contact Group was established to monitor a cease-fire in Kosovo. The Group consisted of the Foreign Ministers of the USA, UK, Russia, Germany, France and Italy. At the same time, a Kosovo Verification Mission (KVM) was set up under the OCSE to be stationed in Kosovo to investigate and report on apparent violations of the agreement. This body of some 1400 persons was placed under the command of Ambassador William Walker, who had become famous as US ambassador in El Salvador and Honduras. His fame rested, as Milosevic in his cross examination at the ICTY pointed out – much to the annoyance of the presiding judge – on his involvement with Colonel Oliver North in supplying aid to the 'contras' resisting the Sandanista government of Nicaragua.[18] It was Walker who announced a 'massacre' at Racak, which, like the massacre at Srebrenica, became the trigger for further American military intervention.

On the fateful day of January 16 1999, Ambassador Walker was called to go to a serious reported crime at Racak. As he described the occasion to the Tribunal (pp. 6791-2) his deputies Generals Drewenkiewicz and Maisonoeuvre had preceded him to Racak, and Walker himself was accompanied by a large body of journalists, cameramen and TV reporters. One American woman reporter had already established connection with her TV company in America. Walker was taken by local people to a gully on a rocky hillside above the village of Racak. Bodies in civilian clothes were strewn over the hillside near to a trench that to

Walker seemed not to have been used recently. Most of the dead were men, several quite old, but there were one or two women and a boy of about thirteen. Many seemed to have been shot in the head or neck and some heads were actually blown off, with multiple bullet holes, as from an automatic weapon. Walker identified twenty-five bodies but another twenty-two were found by those who went up to the top of the gully. Walker said that he saw no sign of spent cartridge cases or other indications of a battle, but he did not go up to the top because he was so disgusted and his gammy leg was troubling him. One of his verifiers did in fact find cartridge cases and an ammunition box further up. Instead, Walker went down to the village to discover what had happened.

The story that Walker was told there was that, after there had been some shelling in the village during the previous day, Yugoslav police had come into the village and rounded up a number of villagers and marched them up the hillside and shot them. It had been reported to Walker by the Yugoslav General Loncar that there had been some fighting in this area on January 15, and fifteen KLA soldiers and one or more Yugoslav policemen had been killed. Walker had an Albanian interpreter with him but no Serb. Loncar had declined to come with him to the site and his Serb interpreter was, according to Walker, too frightened to come. Walker decided on the spot that Loncar's story was false and returned to Pristina to a press conference, but according to videos played by Milosevic to the Tribunal Walker first spoke to Holbrooke and Wesley Clark by cell phone from Racak itself, saying that there had been a massacre (pp. 6895-6). Certainly, the story was all over Europe and America in no time.

Milosevic's case was that the whole story had been rigged. Walker did not tell what he knew, that there had been a major shoot out above Racak on January 15. The bodies could have been gathered together in the gully to give the impression of a massacre. A KLA commander giving evidence to the Tribunal stated that the KLA had a base in a house at the edge of the village of Racak (p. 6366), that they had bunkers and trenches above Racak and that this was a crucial area for the KLA to hold because it lay between Pristina and Prizen and the Albanian border. There had been other clashes in and around Racak between the Yugoslav forces and the KLA in late 1998 according to one inhabitant who gave evidence (p. 6269). Other inhabitants who gave evidence tended to deny that there were any KLA members in Racak but to agree, when pressed by Milosevic, that they had relatives in the KLA.

The prosecutor several times warned the Tribunal that the witnesses were in an extremely nervous state, but one of the judges commented that much of the evidence including that of Walker and of the English police officer Hendrie, who accompanied him, was hearsay and should have been introduced with the words, 'I was told'. There was an interesting incident in the Jeremy Paxman programme about Milosevic in July 2002, when one of the witnesses from Racak was interviewed by a BBC researcher at the site. He described how delighted he had been at seeing Milosevic on TV being questioned at the Tribunal, but horrified when he got to the Hague to tell his story to find that he had to be cross-examined by the 'monster' himself. Evidently Kosovo TV was somewhat selective in its coverage of the Tribunal.[19]

The main arguments employed by the prosecution against Milosevic's case that the massacre was rigged and that the bodies were not of civilians but of soldiers who had been in battle were the following: there were no signs of a battle; the bodies were not in uniform; there were old men, a woman and a boy among the bodies, and there were blood stains on the grass where they lay; they appeared to have been shot from close range. Answers given by Milosevic were: that the KLA commander questioned by the Tribunal stated that there had been a battle on January 15, and this was confirmed by a Yugoslav police officer who had been there and spoke later on the Percy-Lapping 'Fall of Milosevic' film;[20] that the police had retaken lost positions by the evening (p. 6914); that the KVM's own verifiers had found empty ammunition cases and spent cartridges in the gully above where Walker went; that the KLA did not always wear uniforms, as several witnesses confirmed (pp. 4047, 6271 & 8889); that there were often 60 year olds, women and boys among those fighting (as the KLA commander confirmed – p. 6391); that there was not as much blood around the bodies as could be expected in an execution (Hendries' replies to Milosevic's questioning, p. 6476).

The question of the distance from which the firing took place was the subject of intense inquiry by forensic experts. The leader of the Finnish forensic team, a dentist Dr Helena Ranta, gave her opinion at the time at Walker's press conference that the wounds indicated 'criminal action', but the conclusions of the team's investigations were 'delayed' and not in fact published until 2001, in an article in an international forensic journal, revealed by Diana Johnstone in her *Fools' Crusade*.[21] This article made it quite clear that there was no execution at close range, but the bullet holes were more likely to have arisen from long distance firing, as in a battle.

So the trigger for the war that ruined Yugoslavia was a rigged massacre. It was enough for Ambassador Walker to report killings in January 1999 as a massacre for Louise Arbour, the ICTY prosecutor, to announce after four days of consultation with NATO officials that this was a war crime.[22] The NATO bombing of Kosovo began on March 24. Such announcements were carefully timed. A week later Ms. Arbour announced the indictment of Serb para-military leaders for crimes committed in Bosnia, with evidence which she had prepared two years earlier. When in May 1999 NATO turned to attacking civilian targets in Yugoslavia, Arbour announced on May 27. the indictment of Milosevic for Serb killings in Kosovo based on data provided by US Intelligence (the Inter-Agency Balkan Task Force, housed at the CIA). Madeline Albright, US Secretary of State, then felt able to state that 'the indictments make clear to the world and the public in our countries that this (NATO) policy of bombing is justified.'[23] Methinks, she did protest too much!

The US by then thought they had got their man and started their war. If Racak was the trigger for the NATO bombing of Yugoslavia, the Rambouillet 'peace conference' provided the priming. Three weeks after the supposed 'massacre' at Racak the Contact Group called a conference under the joint chairmanship of the British and French foreign secretaries to bring together at Rambouillet Palace outside Paris representatives from the Yugoslav government and the Kosovars to try to reach an agreement on a peaceful settlement of the issues between them. The two parties stayed in separate rooms at first, but after some days the Yugoslavs agreed to meet the 'terrorists'. Milosevic did not attend but his vice-president Sainovic did, together with Ratko Markovic, Minister of the Interior, and the Serbian President Milutinovic. The Albanian Kosovars' representatives included both the moderate pacifist Rugovar and the KLA leader Thaci.[24]

The Rambouillet story was revealed to the Tribunal by the evidence and cross-examination of the Austrian diplomat Wolfgang Petritsch, who had been his country's ambassador to the Former Yugoslavia from 1997-1999, and from October 1998 to July 1999 the European Union's special envoy to Kosovo. He became one of the three chief negotiators at Rambouillet together with Chris Hill of the USA and Boris Maiorsky from the Russian Federation. Petritsch is the author of a book on Kosovo, which Milosevic quoted from in his cross-examination to try to show some pro-Albanian prejudice on Petritsch's part.

In his evidence to the Tribunal, Petritsch made much of the fact that the Yugoslav government had agreed to an international conference, having previously insisted that Kosovo was an entirely internal Serbian affair (p. 7218). He thought that this was a good augury for the success of the negotiations. The basis for an agreement was the substantive autonomy of Kosovo within the Yugoslav Federation, and negotiations proceeded for establishing clear principles governing the legislature, executive, judiciary, human rights and so on (p. 7222). Petritsch recalled that much progress was made in the first two weeks, but the question of the implementation of the agreement remained to be solved. The proposal of the Italian Foreign Minister, Lamberto Dini, that UN forces should be employed for this purpose received a sharp response from Mrs Albright: 'The whole point is for the Serbs to accept a NATO force.'[25]

Implementation certainly meant military provision, including the withdrawal of Yugoslav forces and the decommissioning of the KLA. The Kosovan delegates, horrified at the prospect of disarming, demanded a NATO presence and not an enlarged and lightly armed OCSE, which was being discussed (p. 7299). Markovic was said by Petritsch to have agreed to the possibility of 'a military presence' (p. 7230), but, according to Milosevic, Markovic asked three times whether 'in addition to the documents, or rather proposals, there were not some others that were not tabled.' Petritsch denied knowledge of this (p. 7264).

It was clear to Petritsch that Milosevic would not accept NATO forces in Kosovo. The draft agreement referred to 'the participation of the OSCE and other international bodies, if that is indispensable' (p. 7298). Petritsch confirmed to Milosevic's cross-examination that the military sections of the draft agreement were only handed over after the last day of the negotiations (p. 7257) and explained that 'the prerequisites of the political agreement were negotiated and this was the time to hand over the military part of the agreement.' In answer to further cross-questioning, Petritsch stated that this part was 'only given to the Yugoslav side, because of the fact that a military agreement, of course, can only be concluded with a government and not with a group like in the case of the Kosovo Albanians.' (p. 7259)

At the signing ceremony the Kosovan Albanian delegation signed up, but the Yugoslav delegates referred back to Belgrade because of their earlier inability to consider the military sections. Of the three mediators Petritsch and Hill signed but Maiorsky was recalled to Moscow, having said that he would sign if the Yugoslavs did (p. 7292). That left no signed agreement, and Petritsch and Hill flew to Belgrade to make what they called 'one last ditch effort' on March 22 to persuade Milosevic to sign. The Yugoslav Parliament had agreed on March 23 without seeing the military appendix. In seeking to defend this appendix, Petritsch argued that it was no more than had been agreed to by Milosevic himself in the Dayton Accords for Bosnia. Recalling this, Milosevic reminded the Tribunal of what was actually said in section 8 of the military appendix:

'NATO personnel shall enjoy, together with their vehicles, vessels and aircraft and equipment free and unrestricted passage and unimpeded access throughout the Federal Republic of Yugoslavia, including associated airspace and territorial waters. This shall include but not be limited to the right of bivouacs, manoeuvres, and utilisation of any areas or facilities as required ... use of airports, roads, rails and ports ...' and under item 15 'the whole spectrum of electro-magnetic frequencies, communications ... etc, etc ...' (quoted on p. 7261).

Questioning the relevance of the Dayton Accords as a precedent, Milosevic asked, 'How can you equate Bosnia and Hercegovina, in which there was civil war as a whole throughout the territory of Bosnia and Hercegovina, and the conflict between the forces of government and terrorists in a sovereign state?' (p. 7254). Milosevic had a strong point here because Bosnia was being established under Dayton as a newly independent state to end the fighting for Bosnian leadership between Serbs, Croats and Muslims, whereas Yugoslavia was a long established state facing an insurrection in part of its territory. In a later exchange Milosevic was able to quote George Kenney, a one-time US State Department official saying that 'the bar was deliberately set too high' for the

Serbs to be able to accept the terms imposed (p. 10261).

On the breakdown of the Rambouillet talks there was an interesting exchange at the Tribunal between Milosevic and Ambassador Vollebaek, the Norwegian who headed up the OSCE in 1998-9 and to whom Ambassador Walker was responsible. Milosevic probed his relations with NATO and especially with Javier Solana, NATO's Director General at that time. Vollebaek firmly denied taking orders from NATO, but under pressure admitted that any military force required to support the Rambouillet political agreement would need to have a 'strong NATO component' (p. 7703). The Tribunal judge tried to stop Milosevic pursuing this argument as being irrelevant to Vollebaek's original submission, but Milosevic had made a crucial point, underlining Mrs Albright's outburst quoted above. Thaci for the Kosovo Albanians had been promised a NATO presence as the only way to get them to sign the agreement (p. 7303).

Since the Russians and Chinese would certainly have vetoed any resolution in the Security Council to impose a settlement on Yugoslavia by force, the Americans had no UN support for military intervention, but could rely on NATO. General Naumann offered an interesting justification for NATO action without UN authority. In answer to one of Milosevic's gibes at Naumann about his constant reference to 'the international community' when he meant NATO or the United States and not the United Nations, the General was recorded saying:

'Yes, of course the United Nations are the supreme international authority. They are the only authority which can authorise the use of force. And only in cases – and we had such a case – where the Security Council fails to do its duty and to authorise military action, although the risk of considerable loss of life is imminent, one may come to different conclusions, as did the 16 nations of NATO in the case of the Kosovo intervention' (p. 7034). Milosevic was not allowed by the presiding judge to explore this interesting definition of the 'duty' of the United Nations.

Ambassador Petritsch referred in his evidence to a discussion he had at Rambouillet with a member of the Yugoslav delegation, a certain Vladimir Stambuk about the probable result of a breakdown of negotiations. He quoted Stambuk as saying that 'if there is bombing... this will mean massacre in Kosovo' and he meant massacre of Kosovo Albanians by the Yugoslav army and police (page 7233). General Wesley K. Clark, both chief of United States European Command and NATO's supreme allied commander, writing in his book, *Waging Modern War*, explains that he was convinced from his experience of the US bombing of the Bosnian Serbs which led to the Dayton Accords that Milosevic would give in if not at the threat of bombing then as soon as the bombing started.[26] For all his boasting about knowing his man, Clark got Milosevic wrong and thereafter began to demand a full-scale land invasion.

Bombing Yugoslav positions in Kosovo failed to move Milosevic but did fulfil Stambuk's fearful warning. A NATO invasion designed to prevent a humanitarian disaster served to create one. Tens of thousands of Kosovans, though not the hundreds of thousands the media reported, fled from their villages and towns into the hills or aimed for Macedonia and Albania.[27] Witnesses were called to the Tribunal to describe what happened, and Milosevic did his best to suggest that they were fleeing from NATO bombing rather than from any action by the Yugoslav forces.

Members of human rights organisations all described what the refugees told them – that they were fleeing from the destruction of their homes and at the orders of the Yugoslav forces. Of course, they would say this to win the sympathy of outsiders, but Milosevic's attempts to lift the blame from his forces' actions after the bombing began do not carry the same conviction as his earlier argument in defending his forces before the NATO bombing, in villages where they were engaged in rooting out centres of KLA activity (see several witnesses pp. 3300-4030). Many witnesses called to the Tribunal did vindicate the claim that after NATO's bombing began, Serb forces – both military and police – not only drove Kosovo Albanians out of Kosovo, burning and looting their villages, even relieving them of their money and documents in the process, but in some cases carried out summary executions. Accusations of rape by Serb soldiers were often thrown in for good measure. The long list of names of Albanian men (only very rarely women) in the indictment of Milosevic, who, it is alleged, were killed by Milosevic or his agents, must certainly include large numbers who died in fighting. It is not said, but it is implied, that they were all civilians.

Milosevic claimed that 40 per cent of NATO bombs fell on Kosovo (p. 3492), which, given the relatively small area of this part of Yugoslavia, must have been fairly terrifying. It became well known that some harmless Kosovans were killed in error as a result of bombers flying at great height to avoid anti-aircraft gunfire, and Milosevic returned to these stories on several occasions in the Tribunal's hearings. When Wesley Clark, having started off as a strong advocate of bombing to bring Milosevic to heel, began to argue that only a land army could do the job, he got the support of Tony Blair. He got no support from President Clinton, whose basic policy was that there should be no body bags with dead American soldiers coming back to the USA. Wesley Clark's standing both with the White House and the Pentagon had slumped.[28] The only alternative for the Pentagon was to switch the high level bombing to Serbia proper, targeting government facilities, communication networks, road and rail bridges, the electric grid, oil refineries, vehicle factories and basic infrastructure. Wesley Clark swore that he would 'systematically attack, disrupt, degrade, devastate and ultimately destroy' Milosevic's fighting capability until he gave in.[29]

The first result of this open aggression was a great increase in Milosevic's popularity in Serbia, which rendered ineffectual the brave efforts of many non-governmental organisations led by Milos Nikolic, our old friend from the Cavtat Round Table meetings, to rally others in neighbouring countries around a proposal for an all-Balkan peace pact. But, as life became increasingly intolerable for the Yugoslav people under daily bombardment, the desire grew for peace at almost any price.

Targets for air strikes had to be vetted by the several members of NATO involved, much to the irritation of Wesley Clark.[30] But, nevertheless, what was euphemistically called 'collateral damage', including civilian Yugoslav deaths, mounted up, however much the egregious Jamie Shea, NATO's spokesman tried to explain them away. From mid-May onwards 85 per cent of Serbs were without electricity.[31] My elderly friends in a high-rise apartment in Belgrade had no lift, and food was becoming scarce, as transport from agricultural areas broke down.

Still Milosevic did not give in, until finally a Russian initiative produced a formula for an agreement, which would involve several powers including Russia monitoring peace in Kosovo. Milosevic agreed, and a NATO peace-keeping military force, KFOR, was immediately established in Kosovo. An armoured brigade from the Russian peace-keeping forces in Sarajevo then raced across Yugoslavia to occupy Pristina airport. Wesley Clark ordered the KFOR commander to block the runways to prevent Russian reinforce-ments and received the now famous reply from General Sir Michael Jackson, 'I am not starting World War Three for you!' Though junior in rank to Clark, Jackson knew that Clark had lost his bosses' support.[32] It was Clark's ultimate humiliation. In the event it proved impossible for any peace-keepers to control the violent outbreak of revenge killings by Kosovo Albanians of the Serbs in Kosovo, and most of the latter fled as the Kosovo Albanians returned. The KLA was disbanded but immediately reincarnated under US auspices as the Kosovo Protection Corps.[33]

What then was left of the rump of Yugoslavia after the bombing and the years of economic sanctions? 'Operation Allied Force', as the NATO war on Yugoslavia was called, lasted for 78 days, during which 38,000 sorties were flown, including over 10,000 strike sorties, expending over 28,000 weapons amounting to 12,000 tons of munitions. It was claimed by NATO to have been 'the most precise and lowest-collateral damage air campaign in his-tory'. No airmen were killed, but at least 500 Yugoslav civilians died and very much larger numbers were injured.[34] More will unfortunately follow as cluster bombs, mines and shells with depleted uranium take their toll. The Amnesty International Report on the Yugoslav war concluded that 'There were viola-tions of the laws of war by NATO during Operation Allied Force.'[35] This was surely a case of 'disproportionate action'. But no charges were laid against

NATO before the courts.

The destruction of the TV stations, oil refineries, factories, of the many bridges over the big rivers and even of hospitals and the Chinese Embassy was shown everywhere on television. What was only revealed by Neil Clark from Belgrade in September 2004 was that only socially owned companies and not any foreign or privately-owned companies were targeted.[36] Apart from Amnesty International there was no demand for NATO to be brought to trial. What was hardly shown on the world's television screens was the Yugoslav army withdrawing from Kosovo with its tanks, armoured cars, guns and vehicles largely intact. The many tanks reported destroyed by bombing raids turned out to have been plywood dummies. NATO's war had hit civilian targets; the military was hardly affected.[37]

But the war was won. President Clinton reported to the American people 'that we have achieved a victory for a safer world, for our democratic values and for a stronger America. In Kosovo we did the right thing. We did it the right way. And we will finish the job.'[38] It has to be understood that this is modern war, as explained by Col. John A.Warden of the US Air Force. 'Fighting is not the essence of war', he writes, 'nor even a desirable part of it. The real essence is to make the enemy accept our objectives as his objectives ... by causing such changes to one or more part of the enemy's physical system that the enemy decides to adopt our objectives, or we make it physically impossible for him to oppose us.'[39] This was quoted by Ken Coates in his introduction to the Spokesman publication of Collateral Damage or Unlawful Killings. So the war ended with an election in Yugoslavia in 2000 in which Milosevic was defeated. After that he was kidnapped by foreign agents and brought to trial at the Hague on charges of crimes against humanity and violations of the laws and customs of war before the International Criminal Tribunal for the Former Yugoslavia.

Map of Former ex-Yugoslav States, 2000

Closure: What is Left of Yugoslavia after Sixty Years?

In place of the single Former Yugoslavia of 1944 we have six or, depending how you count them, eight or nine, separate entities. Slovenia is a recognised sovereign state, at the top of the list for membership of the European Union. Croatia is also a sovereign state moving towards EU membership when it agrees to hand over its indicted war criminals for judgement at the International Criminal Court for Former Yugoslavia. Bosnia-Hercegovina is a single state, recognised as such but made up of two parts – a Muslim-Croat Federation and a Bosnian Serb Republic. For the time being it is in effect a UN protectorate. Serbia and Montenegro form a single state, sometimes referred to as 'Solana' after the European Union's chief representative, Javier Solana, who negotiated this new union to replace the Yugoslav Federation.[1] The union was to last for three years until Montenegro could have a referendum to decide on self-determination. 'Solana' is not yet recognised by the EU or the UN. Serbia contains an Autonomous Region of Voyvodina and also, for the time being, Kosovo. The status of this last was the face-saving concession offered by the Russian negotiator to the Serbs, so that the NATO war with Yugoslavia could be ended. But Kosovo is in fact a UN protectorate, and is likely to remain so because an independent Kosovo would certainly join Albania and attract the Albanian population of Macedonia also into a 'Greater Albania'. This would be quite unacceptable to Greece and upset the convenient arrangement for the USA of maintaining a large military base, Camp Bondsteel, in Kosovo. For these reasons also, Yugoslav Macedonia is a state, but with a large US military presence.

These several entities which once made up Former Yugoslavia have not only quite different status in their international recognition but a very different mix of populations. Slovenia is virtually a one-nation state of two million people, although some Italians on the Trieste border remain inside and a dwindling number of migrant workers from other parts of Former Yugoslavia. Croatia's population of 5 million now consists almost entirely of Croats, the other half million Serbs having been expelled and about a quarter of a million Croats from Bosnia absorbed.

It is a very different story in the other successor states of Former Yugoslavia. Bosnia-Hercegovina was ostensibly created to establish the principle of viable multi-ethnic statehood, in practice to support the Muslim community, which the United States had decided to adopt as its protégé against any rival claims by the pariah Serb community. By combining in one Federation the Muslims and Croats, who had been fighting each other in the war, this was a larger entity than the Serb Republic, which became the other half of Bosnia and Hercegovina. It gave the Muslim leader Alija Izetbegovic the chance to be Bosnia's President until his death.

Serbia and Montenegro has a total population of 9 million, which comprise not only Serbs but also Hungarians, Croats and Romas in the Vojvodina, Muslims in the Sandzak and Novi Pazar (southern Serbia) and, while Kosovo is attached to Serbia, Albanians as well. Thus even without the Albanians, Serbia, contrary to general world opinion, is a truly multi-ethnic state. Macedonia's two million include a quarter of a million Albanians. In Kosovo there were once 200,000 Serbs out of Kosovo's population of a million and a half, but few of them remain. Former Yugoslavia was a mosaic of different peoples, and a long article with maps in Le Monde Diplomatique (August 2003) suggests that the smallest minorities who lived peacefully among the others until 1941 have suffered most.[2] The Nazi occupation had almost eliminated the Jews. Thereafter, by emphasising the common struggle against the enemy occupation and then for rebuilding a shattered economy, Tito had created a united country. As we have seen, it was the widening gap between the rich north (Slovenia and Croatia) and the poor south (especially Bosnia-Hercegovina, Montenegro, Macedonia and southern Serbia, including Kosovo), under the pressure of foreign debt that destroyed this unity.

The economic gap even widened as a result of civil wars and the massive NATO bombardment. Slovenia and Croatia were actually able to increase their industrial output between 1992 and 1998, although in Croatia's case with a great increase in unemployment and with massive foreign debts, only in part covered by international loans. Serbia suffered not only UN economic sanctions between 1992 and 1996, but further sanctions in 1998 and the NATO aerial bombardment in 1999. The economy effectively stood still for seven years, a loss equivalent to two thirds of Serbia's total output in 1994.[3] Even before the bombing Serbia's industry was estimated to be working at 35 per cent of capacity. Inflation in 1993 at over a thousand per cent reduced the value of the dinar to nothing. The black economy came to represent one half of the gross national product. Unemployment in the non-agricultural sector rose to 50 per cent. At least 200,000 young people left the country. The effects of the bombing have been estimated to have cost 20 billion euros. 372 industrial installations were hit, including the Zastava car plant at Kragujevac, leaving hundreds of thousands jobless. Only social sector plants were hit, none that were foreign or privately owned.[4] The destruction of roads, railway lines and bridges and of power stations left people in the towns and cities with serious food shortages and often no light or water. On top of all this, cases of cancer greatly increased as the result of NATO's use of depleted uranium tipped shells and the bombing of the Pancevo chemical complex.[5]

This situation had hardly improved much by 2002, according to my friends in Belgrade. The demands made by the IMF on the government for public spending cuts in return for aid were being widely blamed. Food prices had risen three or fourfold and 170,000 families in Belgrade were reported in the local press to be unable to afford to pay their electricity bills.[5] Electricity prices were increased at the command of the IMF, which at the same time required the dismissal of 800,000 workers in public services and state run enterprises. Workers have been striking and occupying factories to protect them against the privatisation required by the IMF, but they are finding that there are no assets available even for payments from pension funds. Governments come and go, the latest in 2004 being a coalition including representatives of Milosevic's old party.

Conditions in Bosnia-Hercegovina and in Kosovo, especially in areas where there was the heaviest fighting, were even worse, and Macedonia and Montenegro suffered from the great influx of refugees. It is a terrible story in these areas and after all the relief and rehabilitation work had taken the people back to where they were in 1944. In many ways the situation was worse than sixty years ago. In part this is because of the internecine fighting, but equally because the work of reconstruction had been taken out of the hands of the people themselves. The actual amount of foreign aid was immense – some $50 billion for Bosnia-Hercegovina in the first three years after the Dayton Accords. At $1200 a head this was taking one third of the US foreign policy budget, which can be compared with $3 per head of US aid for Africa.[6] With UN support, aid for Bosnia-Hercegovina continued at that rate thereafter. The whole country had literally lived on it – not for two or three years, as with UNRRA in 1945-7, but already for seven or eight years.

How could that be? The first answer must be the cutting off, by sanctions and by destruction of the transport links, of Bosnia's dependence on the Serbian bread basket. The second must be the absolute absence of the Titoist enthusiasm and egalitarian ethos of fifty years ago: the sheer joy then of liberation and rebuilding together anew. But why such apathy today?

The failure of political or economic recovery in Bosnia-Hercegovina after the Dayton Accords is explained by some as the end result of a long history of ethnic and religious differences, by others as the result of the recent horrors of war. The people were, it is said, quite simply shell-shocked. Both conditions existed fifty years earlier. The German occupation had set ethnic groups against each other and there had been terrible massacres of Muslims, Serbs and others by the Croat Ustashe forces and by some Serbian Chetnik bands. But the response when the wars ended was quite different on each occasion. Comparisons between the situation in Bosnia in the mid-1940s and in the mid-1990s can provide the clue. In 1945 the Axis occupation was ended and peace established by Tito's Partisans, who were drawn from all ethnic groups. Those guilty of direct collaboration with the Germans and Italians were tried and condemned to death. As I have explained in earlier chapters, in 1945-7 the Bosnian authorities – Serbs, Croats, Muslims – were wholly responsible for the organisation and distribution of UNRRA supplies. As UN representatives, we only monitored the distribution and provided technical advice where it was needed. The Yugoslav peoples were in charge, not a 'High Representative' from another land.

By contrast, the Dayton Accords were imposed from outside by the US and UN, and aid for relief and reconstruction was managed entirely by outside bodies. The list of these was formidable. Beneath the overall authority of a UN High Representative, under whose direct control was the police force, NATO was made responsible for all military and boundary questions, the IMF for the Central Bank, the OSCE for regional stabilisation and elections, UNESCO for preservation of national monuments, while finance for relief was placed under the European Bank for Relief and Development and for reconstruction under the World Bank. In addition, representatives of the UN organisations, the FAO, the WHO, the International Children's Fund, hold key positions in the respective ministries for food, health and child welfare.[8] As so often in the aid to Third World countries, a large part of the aid goes to the high salaries of all these foreign bodies. By contrast, in 1945-7 there were very few of us in UNRRA and our salaries were quite modest.

It is hard to believe that the poor Bosnians are getting much benefit from the great number of expensive outside consultants. Graham Hancock has shown in his authoritative *Lords of Poverty* what a small proportion of UN and US aid actually reaches those for whom the aid is intended.[9]

David Chandler in his book *Bosnia: Faking Democracy after Dayton* drew up the most devastating indictment of what amounted to colonial rule over the country.[10] He quoted a Cato Institute author writing in the *Washington Times* (24.10.97) to sum up the position:

'The US-led democracy mission in Bosnia has become a grotesque parody of democratic principles ... we are teaching ... the virtues of democracy by showing ... that an outside power, if it possesses enough military clout, has the right to overrule court decisions, establish political purity tests for candidates for public office and suppress media outlets that transmit politically incorrect views.'[11]

Chandler summarised his own studies as showing that 'elected Bosnian institutions of government ... at [all] levels ... had a largely formal existence', that 'the framework of human rights protection ... weakened the peace-building and integrative capacity of Bosnian political and judicial institutions', that ' international regulation of political competition and media output ... restricted the democratic mandates of elected politicians', that 'support given to small unrepresentative civil groups tended to downplay the importance of democratic debate ... doing little to encourage popular involvement in the political process'. Moreover, he added in relation to building civil society that 'the unintended consequence of creating civil society NGOs, which are reliant on external support, has been that they are never forced to build their own base of popular support or take on the arguments or political programmes of the nationalists.'[12]

The explanation for all this was that Bosnians were assumed to be incapable of managing their own affairs and were still in thrall to nationalist leaders. Evidence for this last was soon found in the first elections, in which over 84 per cent of the population voted for one or other of the nationalist parties. That was understandable in the immediate aftermath of civil war, but the position thereafter scarcely improved, despite or perhaps as a result of all the efforts of the UN authorities to push forward alternative parties. The evidence is that up to 1999, not one single law put to the state Parliamentary Assembly, according to the International Crisis Group, had been drafted and ratified by Bosnian representatives. The Council of Ministers has very little supporting structure outside the office of the High Representative. As Chandler quotes the Council of Europe, heavily involved in the process: 'Since the High Representative is effectively the supreme legislative and executive authority in the country, this means in the final analysis that Bosnia and Hercegovina is not a democracy.'[13]

The first High Representative was Carl Bildt, who had been a peace negotiator in Croatia and Bosnia. He was accused of being pro-Serb, because he had dined and wined with Milosevic and had stated that Croats, and especially Tudjman, and Muslims as well as Serbs should be indicted for ethnic cleansing.[14] He was succeeded by Carlos Westendorp and then by Wolfgang Petrisch the Austrian diplomat, who we met as the chief negotiator at the Rambouillet conference. Both were accused of extreme high-handedness, dismissing numbers of elected Bosnians – mayors, governors, ministers and deputies.[15] Their successor, Paddy Ashdown, onetime UK Liberal Democratic Party leader, has tried to act more diplomatically, and to insist that his job is to make his job redundant. In opinion polls he appears to be twice as popular as even the most favoured of Bosnian politicians. That must be partly because voters' loyalties are still divided between the three nationalist parties and partly because many nationalist politicians are seen as mere puppets attached to the strings of leaders behind the scenes, who are indicted criminals still wanted for war crimes. It is also because Ashdown is prepared to work with less liberal types favoured by voters to bring peace, democracy and economic development to a divided country.[16]

In an interview with *Financial Times* correspondent John-Paul Flintoff, Ashdown made a very important concession, 'We held elections all over the place and, as soon as we could, for all levels of government. What we should have done was put law and order first. Once that is in place you have the foundations for a real democracy.'[17] Ashdown recognises himself as a raj in a colonial set-up. He was born in India, and that is perhaps where he learnt his respect for law and order. Unfortunately it is also the country where the British practised their skills of dividing and ruling. The continuing separation of Bosnia-Herceovina into two entities – the Serbian Republic and the shot-gun marriage of the Muslim-Croat federation – only perpetuates the division and justifies the refusal of many refugee families to return to their original home across the border. Others return to their homes only because they believe that they will be protected by their own people. Segregation is perpetuated.

Between the two entities the balance of outside favour is very unequal. Whereas links between the Serbian Republic and Belgrade are banned, those between the Muslim-Croat Federation and Croatia are encouraged. As architect of the Federation the US takes a special interest in its development, exercising a strong influence over the parties. The hunting down of indicted war criminals is confined almost entirely to Serbs. In the three main cities of Bosnia-Hercegovina – Sarajevo, Mostar and Brcko – administration is in the hands of a European Union Envoy, who manages the elections, and is himself often nominated by the US. In other towns the OSCE chooses the mayor and other officials. The stick of dismissal and the carrot of foreign aid are used to ensure the result that outside bodies desire. The fact that what they desire is often a pluralist balance rather than a nationalist outcome may appear admirable, but has the exact opposite effect to what is desired. Non-nationalist candidates are seen as nominees from outside.[18]

The belief of those representing the 'international community' that Bosnians are incapable of democracy is self-fulfilling. OSCE officials confided to David Chandler that many of them did not accept this approach, but they had difficulty in getting this over to their international superiors. 'Civil society and democratic values did once exist', they said, 'Bosnia had a multicultural society, good nationalities policy and progressive policies regarding women'.[19] One up for Tito's Yugoslavia! At the top, with the possible exception of Ashcroft, the UN officials' view of Balkan peoples as barbarians prevailed. David Owen, at the beginning of his *Balkan Odyssey*, wrote: 'History points to a tradition in the Balkans of a readiness to solve disputes by the taking up of arms.... It points to a culture of violence ... dark and virulent nationalism'.[20] It hasn't occurred to such people that the arms were introduced by occupying forces, Turks, Italians, Austrians, Hungarians, Germans, Americans. Between such invasions they lived peacefully and happily side by side.

What has actually been happening in Bosnia-Hercegovina is in absolute contradiction to what is said to be the policy of the United Nations. In the Secretary General's *Agenda for Democratisation* issued in 1996 for guidance in such experiments as the Bosnian mandate, it is written that it would be a mistake to impose a model of democratisation:

> Indeed to do so would be counter-productive to the process of democratisation which, in order to take root and to flourish must derive from society itself. Each society must be able to choose the form, pace and character of its democratisation process. Imposition of foreign models not only contravenes the [UN] Charter principle of non-intervention in internal affairs, it may also generate resentment among both the Government and the public, which may in turn feed internal forces inimical to democracy and democratisation.[21]

After comparing that statement with the reality, as it presents itself in Bosnia-Hercegovina, it is not surprising that David Chandler called his book *Faking Democracy After Dayton*.[22] One is bound to wonder whether there was ever any intention of establishing a great experiment in supporting democratisation in Bosnia, except as a propaganda exercise to win public support in America and Europe for what came to be called "humanitarian intervention" or 'benign imperialism'. Noam Chomsky in his book *Hegemony or Survival* has reminded us that there is a long history of such deceptions, not only used to cover invasion in the British Empire but similar imperialist actions by the United States – in the Philippines, Cuba, Haiti, Viet Nam, Nicaragua, Panama, Grenada and now Iraq.[23]

Such a thought leads us naturally to look at the condition of Kosovo, the last of the successor states of Former Yugoslavia. Nominally, Kosovo remains an autonomous Yugoslav province, but all Serbs except for a few sick and aged have left, the currency is the mark, the flag has gone and, more importantly, the state owned power plants, telephone system and the rich Trepce mines have been expropriated. Kosovo is in fact a UN protectorate like Bosnia Hercegovina, under a UN High Authority with an Executive Committee having no Kosovan members. Elections were held in November 2001 and after three separate ballots the moderate Rugova was elected President against Hashim Thaci, the Kosova Liberation Army leader.[24]

Law and order is still absent in Kosova. The police force – the Kosova Protection Corps – consists of ex-KLA officers and members. This force together with 48,000 NATO troops failed to protect the Serb population, some 250,000, from expulsion; not surprising perhaps because there are frequent clashes between NATO's KFOR and the KLA.[25] The country is divided into five regional sectors, one each under respectively French, Italian, German, British and American control. The original proposal for a Russian sector was dropped. Armed clashes still take place on the border of southern Serbia and northern Kosova. Amnesty International has reported human rights abuses and general absence of systems of justice, despite the huge resources of money and personnel pumped into the province.[26] Corruption is said to be rife among the international officials and the drug trafficking based in Albania is a constant problem. Most of the remaining Albanian Kosovan population has benefited not at all. Some two thirds are reported by the International Committee of the Red Cross to be living below the poverty line.[27] A widely held American view is that the country will have to be given its independence, but without evacuating the US base at Camp Bondsteel, which has a 99 year lease, or abandoning US oil company plans for developing a terminal for a trans-Balkan oil pipeline at Durres in Albania.[28]

The lessons to be drawn from UN protectorates in both Bosnia-Hercegovina and Kosovo can well be applied to Afghanistan, Iraq and wherever is next. There never was any intention to establish democracy there. That was for the Michael Ignatieffs, David Rieffs, Branca Magases and Mary Kaldors of the world to promulgate their belief in a 'benign imperialism'.[29] It was never to be. Poor Yugoslavia! Once more divided and conquered by an occupying force, which this time has broken cover from what was hoped to be the internationalism of the United Nations. The destruction of Yugoslavia is not just the shattering of a South Slav dream[30] but the destruction of a practical attempt with all its human weaknesses to build a pluralist society, which put real economic democracy before a sham political democracy. *Requiescat in Pace!*

The brave experiment in pluralism that was Former Yugoslavia was always weakened by a failure to develop political democracy alongside economic democracy. This failure must be accepted, even by its most enthusiastic admirers. The weakness of capitalist societies is the other way round – political without economic democracy. What destroyed Yugoslavia and divided the several peoples against each other was, however, as so often before in their history, the intervention of powerful outside forces with their own interests. This time, it was first the demand for fundamental changes in Yugoslavia's socialist system made by the financial institutions from which the Yugoslavs had borrowed money for economic development. Then it was the abrupt cessation of loans when Yugoslavia was no longer seen as a bulwark against the Soviet Union. Thereafter, it was direct military intervention from outside in support of nationalist leaders who could see personal advantage in the independence of separate nation states. Milosevic was more the victim than the victor in that tragic process.

We have come full circle back to the trial of Milosevic and the other indicted war criminals at the Hague. Crimes should certainly be punished, and criminals as far as is possible made aware of their guilt and helped to reform. Demonising them may only reinforce their worst emotions and those of their families and friends. More seriously, the trials do little or nothing for the victims. Some feelings of the justice of revenge may be satisfied, but the lesson of Tito's Partisans was that when the suspicions of those having other faiths and of other national communities had been played on by outside forces, this could only be assuaged by all taking on the common tasks of reconstruction and rehabilitation. The Partisans' successes should be recognised and the foreign meddlers should get out. After the devastation caused by NATO's bombing financial recompense is needed, but without the foreign advisors. It is a lesson which could be learned elsewhere – in Iraq for example.

References

Chapter One: *The Trial of Slobodan Milosevic*

1. For the trial transcripts, see www.un.org/icty/milosevic
2. Susan Woodward, *Political Economy of Yugoslavia, 1945-90*, Princeton 1995; *Balkan Tragedy*, Brookings Institution, 1995.
3. Diana Johnstone, *Fools' Crusade*, Pluto Press, 2002.
4. Edward S.Herman, *The Milosevic Trial*, Byronica, PO Box 355, CH1211, Geneva 4.
5. Diana Johnstone, op.cit., p. 99.
6. Ibid., p. 96.
7. David Chandler, *Bosnia Faking Democracy*, Pluto Press, 2000.
8. Johnstone, op.cit., p. 95.
9. Ibid., p. 93.
10. Michael Scharf, *Washington Post*, 3.10.99.
11. Johnstone, op.cit., p. 103.
12. Herman, op.cit.
13. Ibid., quoting AP World stream, 31.07.2001.
14. Johnstone, op.cit., p. 31.
15. Ibid., p. 32.
16. UN doc. PRP.I.S./510E
17. Johnstone, op.cit., p. 104.
18. Charles Trueheart, *Washington Post*, 20.02.2000.
19. Ian Black, Brussels, *Guardian*, 01.08.03.
20. Ian Traynor, Zagreb, *Guardian*, 29.09.03.
21. *Le Monde*, February 4, 2004, p. 17.
22. Johnstone, op.cit. p. 69.
23. Ibid., p. 70.

24. Ibid., p. 71.
25. Ibid.
26. *Guardian*, 01.08.03.
27. David Rieff, *Slaughterhouse*, Vintage 1998.
28. Johnstone op.cit. p. 186.
29. Ibid., p. 181.
30. Ibid., p. 190.
31. Michael Ignatieff, *Warrior's Honour*, Chatto & Windus, 1998
32. Mary Kaldor, 'One Year after Dayton', *Dayton Continued*, Helsinki Citizens'Assembly.
33. Johnstone, op.cit., p. 10.
34. Colin Powell, *My American Journey*, Random House, 195, p. 576.
35. Woodward, *Balkan Tragedy*, op.cit. pp. 384-5.
36. Peter Gowan, 'The Twisted Road to Kosovo', *Labour Focus on Eastern Europe*, 1999.
37. Johnstone, op.cit., p. 193.
38. Ibid., p. 25.
39. Ibid., p. 44.
40. Ibid., p. 34.
41. Ibid., p. 45.
42. Johnstone, p. 119.
43. Ibid., p. 265-6.
44. David Owen, *Balkan Odyssey*, Indigo, London, 1996.
45. Johnstone, op.cit., p. 141.

Chapter Two: *Sarajevo, April 1945*

1. and 2. The whole chapter as well as the Annexe is taken from Michael Barratt Brown, *Historical Monograph on the UNRRA Regional Office for Bosnia and Hercegovina at Sarajevo*, UNRRA Yugoslav Mission, Belgrade April 1947.

Chapter Three: *Yugoslavs in Exile, Egypt, 1943-4*

1. A. Tegla Davies, *History of the Friends Ambulance Unit, 1939-46*, Allen & Unwin, 1947.
2. Michael Barratt Brown, April 1947, op.cit.
3. Davies, op.cit.
4. James Burnham, *The Managerial Revolution.*
5. Laurence Durrell, *Alexandria Quartet*, Faber.
6. P. Auty and R. Clogg, (eds.) *British Wartime Policy Towards Resistance in Yugoslavia and Greece*, MacMillan, 1975.
7. Basil Davidson, *Special Operations Europe*, Gollancz, 1980.
8. Michael Barratt Brown, *Historical Monograph of the Office of the Chief of Mission*, UNRRA Yugoslav Mission, Belgrade, June 1947.
9. P.I.C.M.E. *The National Liberation Movement of Yugoslavia.* A Survey of the

Partisan Movement, June 1942-March 1944, PIC/276, Bari, June 1944.

10. Basil Davidson, *Partisan Picture*, Bedford, 1948.
11. Noel Malcolm, *Bosnia: A Short History*, Macmillan, 1994.
12. Davidson, *Partisan Picture* op.cit.
13. Michael Barratt Brown, *Historical Monograph of the Office of the Chief of Mission, UNRRA Yugoslav Mission*, Belgrade, June 1947.
14. Ibid.
15. PICME op.cit.

Chapter Four: *War Relief Planning for Yugoslavia – Bari, Italy, 1944-5*

1. PIC ME op.cit.
2. UNRRA-AML Agreement of April 3, 1944 quoted in Michael Barratt Brown, op.cit., June 1947.
3. Barratt Brown, op.cit.
4. Ibid.
5. Ibid.
6. Ibid.
7. Ibid.
8. Ibid.
9. Ibid.
10. Ibid.
11. Ibid.
12. Ibid.
13. Martin Gilbert, *Churchill, Road to Victory*, Macmillan,
14. Basil Davidson, op.cit.
15. Teodor Shanin, *The Awkward Class*, Macmillan.

Chapter Five: *UNRRA Relief in Bosnia and Hercegovina, 1945-6*

1. Michael Barratt Brown, op.cit. April 1947.
2. Ibid.
3. Ibid.
4. Ibid.
5. Arthur Calder-Marshall, *The Watershed*, Contact, 1947.
6. Dr. Eleanor Singer, Historical Monograph on *The Work of the Save the Children Fund Unit in Bosnia and Hercegovina*, UNRRA Yugoslav Mission, May 1947.
7. PIC ME, op.cit.
8. Woodward, *Political Economy*, op.cit., p. 60.
9. Calder Marshall, op.cit.
10. Barratt Brown, April 1947, op.cit.

Chapter Six: *UNRRA Rehabilitation, Belgrade, 1946-7*

1. Allied Conference on Reparations, 1946 quoted in Michael Barratt Brown,

op.cit., June 1947.

2.   Barratt Brown, June 1947, op.cit.
3.   Ibid.
4.   Ibid.
5.   Ibid.
6.   Ibid.
7.   Ibid.
8.   Michael Barratt Brown, *Yugoslav Pictorial,* unpublished 1949.
9.   Vladimir Dedijer, op.cit.
10. Misha Glenny, op.cit.
11. Noel Malcolm, op.cit.
12. Duncan Wilson, *Oliver Franks,* Oxford University Press, 1983.
13. Woodward, *Political Economy,* op.cit, p. 101.
14. Doreen Warriner, *Jugoslavia Rebuilds,* Fabian Research Series, 1946
15. Mosha Pijade, *About the Legend that the Yugoslav Uprising owed its existence to Soviet Assistance,* London, 1950. (Quick & Co. Clacton)
16. Edward Kardelj, 'Struggle for the Fulfilment of the First Five Year Plan', *Privredni Problemi FNRJ,* Cultura, Belgrade, April 1948.

Chapter Seven: *Tito's Break with Stalin, 1948-57*

1.   Documentation became available in Central Committee of the CPY, *The Correspondence between the Central Committee of the Communist Party of Jugoslavia and the Central Committee of the All-Union Communist Party (Bolsheviks),* Jugoslav Books, Belgrade 1948.
1.   James Klugmann, *From Trotsky to Tito,* Laurence & Wishart, 1951.
2.   James Klugmann, *Yugoslavia Faces the Future,* Britain Yugoslav Friendship Association, London 1947.
3.   Tito, 'The Foundations of the Democracy of a New Type', *The Communist,* no. 2, Central Committee of the CPY, Beograd 1947
4.   Klugmann, 1947, op.cit.
5.   Gilbert, op.cit.
7.   Dedijer, op.cit.
8.   Woodward , *Political Economy,* op.cit. p. 84.
9.   Ibid., p. 144.
10. Ibid., p. 134.
11. Milovan Djilas, *The New Class,* Thames & Hudson, 1957.
12. Woodward , *Political Economy,* op.cit. p. 189.
13. Ibid., p. 124.
14. Dorian Cooke, (ed. and trans.) *Selected Speeches and Articles by Tito, 1941-61,* Naprijed Zagreb 1964.
15. Woodward, op.cit., p. 246.
16. Ibid., p. 283.

Chapter Eight: *Workers' Self-management, 1958-74*

1. Michael Barratt Brown, 'Yugoslavia Revisited', *New Left Review,* nos. 1 & 2, 1960.
2. Ernest Gellner, *Nations and Nationalism,* Blackwell, 1983.
3. Michael Barratt Brown, 'The Yugoslav Model', *Models in Political Economy,* Penguin, 1984 and Second Edition, 1995.
4. Barratt Brown, *New Left Review,* op.cit.
5. Michael Barratt Brown, *The Yugoslav Tragedy,* Spokesman, 1996.
6. Woodward, *Political Economy,* op.cit., p. 189.
7. Tito, *Tenth Congress of League of Communists of Yugoslavia,* Belgrade, 1975.
8. B.Boscovic (ed.) *Socialist Self-management in Yugoslavia,* Belgrade, 1980.
9. M. Drulovic, *Self-management on Trial,* Spokesman, 1978.
10. 10. J. Vanek, (ed.) *Self-Management,* Penguin, 1975.
11. Woodward, *Political Economy,* op.cit., p. 262.
12. Benjamin Ward, 'The Firm in Illyria: Market socialism in Yugoslavia', *American Economic Review,* 49, no. 4, 1958, pp. 568-9 and 'Marxism-Horvatism: A Yugoslav Theory of Socialism' *American Economic Review,* 57, 1967, pp. 509-23.
13. Woodward, *Political Economy,* op.cit. p. 215.
14. Ota Sik, 'Socialist Marker Relations and Planning' in C.Feinstein (ed.) *Socialism, Capitalism and Economic Growth,* Cambridge University Press, 1967.
15. Oscar Lange, ?
16. Pierro Sraffa, *Production of Commodities by Means of Commmodities*
17. Edward Kardelj, speech at the Congress of Self Managers, 1971.
18. Woodward, *Political Economy,* op.cit., p. 226.
19. J. Moravic, 'Twenty Years of Yugoslav Economy', *Medjunarodna Stampa,* Belgrade, 1967.
20. Woodward, *Political Economy,* op.cit. p. 269.
21. Ibid., p. 205, Table 6.1.
22. Ibid., p. 284.
23. Michael Barratt Brown, *Africa's Choices,* Penguin.
24. Nicola Mincev et al. *Yugoslav Survey* – from 1960, Jugoslavia, Belgrade.

Chapter Nine: *Socialism in the World, 1975-85*

1. Michael Barratt Brown, *After Imperialism,* Heinemann, 1963.
2. Michael Barratt Brown (ed.) *The Anatomy of Underdevelopment,* Spokesman, 1972.
3. Ragnar Frisch, 'A Multinational Clearing Agency'. *The Economics of Planning,* vol.7 no.2, Norwegian Institute of International Affairs, Oslo, 1967.
4. Hart, Kaldor & Tinbergen, 'The Case for an International Currency Reserve', UNCTAD, 1964.
5. Andreas Goseco, 'A Supplementary Payments Mechanism', *Indian Journal for Agricultural Economics,* Vol. xix, No. 2, Delhi, 1975.
6. Woodward, *Political Economy,* op.cit. 222 ff.
7. Jose' Mencinger, 'The Yugoslav Economy: Systemic Changes, 1945-1985',

Russian and East European Studies, No. 707, Pittsburgh, 1989.
8. Milos Nikolic et al. *Socialism in the World*, No. 1, IC Komunist,
   Beograd, 1977
11. Ibid.
12. Ken Coates, 'Prospects for Socialism in Britain', *Socialism in the World*, op.cit.

Chapter Ten: *Nationality and Nationalism, 1986-90*

1. Ivo Andric, *Bridge over the Drina*
2. Basil Davidson, *The Black Man's Burden,: The Curse of the Nation State,* Times
   Books, 1992.
3. Michael Barratt Brown, Historical Monograph, April 1947, op.cit.
4. Michael Barratt Brown, *Yugoslav Tragedy*, op.cit.
5. Ibid.
6. Ibid.
7. Ibid.
8. Ivo Andric, 'A Letter from 1920', in Celia Hawksworh's edition of Andric's short
   stories, published by Forest Books, London and Dereta, Belgrade, 1992.
9. Glenny, op.cit.
10. Woodward, *Political Economy*, op.cit., fn. 345.
11. ICTY web site.
12. Ernest Gellner, *Nationalism*, Phoenix, 1998.
13. Mencinger, op.cit.
14. OECD, *Economic Survey of Yugoslavia*, 1989.
15. UN Economic Commission for Europe, *Economic Survey of Europe, 1989-90*,
    UN, 1990.
16. Woodward, *Political Economy*, op.cit.,
17. Michael Barratt Brown & Pauline Tiffen, *Short Changed: Africa in World Trade*,
    Pluto, 1992.
18. Michael Barratt Brown, *Africa's Choices: After 30 Years of the World Bank*,
    Penguin, 1995.
19. Branka Magas, *New Political Economy*, vol.2.3 1997.
20. Branka Magas, *The Destruction of Yugoslavia,* Verso, 1993.
21. Woodward, *Political Economy*, op.cit.
22. Woodward, *Balkan Tragedy*, op.cit., 15.
23. Michael Barratt Brown, 'The Role of Economic Factors in Social
    Crisis', *New Political Economy*, vol.2.2, 1997 and 'Restating My Case: A Reply to
    Magas and Keerns', *New Political Economy*, vol.2.4, 1998.
24. Magas, *New Political Economy*, op.cit.
25. Johnstone, op.cit. p. 68.
26. Noel Malcolm, *Short History of Kosovo*, Macmillan, 1998.
27. Woodward, *Balkan Tragedy*, op.cit. pp. 215 ff.
28. Ibid., p. 383.
29. Ibid., p. 341.
30. Johnstone, op.cit., p. 30.
31. Norma Percy & Brian Lapping, *Death of Yugoslavia & Fall of Milosevic* – films

32. Johnstone, op.cit., p. 16.
33. Ibid., p. 19.
34. Michael Barratt Brown, *Models in Political Economy*, Penguin.

Chapter Eleven. *Descent into War: Croatia and Bosnia, 1991-5*

1.   Diana Johnstone, op.cit. and Susan Woodward, *Political Economy of Yugoslavia*, op.cit. and *Balkan Tragedy*, op.cit.
2.   Woodward, *Balkan Tragedy*, p. 1.
4.   Johnstone, op.cit. p. 68.
5.   Johnstone, op.cit. p. 35.
6.   Woodward, *Balkan Tragedy*, p. 98.
7.   Ibid., p. 120.
8.   Ibid., p. 122.
9.   Robert.Thomas, *Serbia under Milosevic: Politics in the 1990s*, Hurst 1999, p. 426.
10. Woodward, *Balkan Tragedy*, op.cit. p. 122.
11. H. Poulton, *The Balkans: Minorities and States in Conflict*, London, 1991, pp. 65-6.
12. F.Singleton, *Twentieth Century Yugoslavia*, Basingstoke, 1976, p. 177.
13. Woodward, *Balkan Tragedy*, op.cit. pp. 172-3.
14. M.Crnobrnja, *The Yugoslav Drama*, New York, 1994, p. 152.
15. Ibid. p. 167.
16. Ibid. p. 149.
17. Woodward, *Balkan Tragedy*, op.cit. p. 157.
18. Ibid. p. 161.
19. Ibid. p. 158.
20. Ibid. p. 149.
21. Ibid. p. 183
22. Ibid. p. 212
23. Ibid. p. 136
24. Ibid. p. 174
24. M. Almond, Europe's Backyard War: the War in the Balkans, 1994, p. 226
25. Woodward, Balkan Tragedy, op.cit. p. 250
26. Norah Beloff, Yugoslavia: An Avoidable War, 1997, p. 25
27. L.Benson, Yugoslavia; a Concise History, 2001, p. 139
28. Johnstone, op.cit., p. 186
29. Almond, op.cit., p. 211
30. Johnstone, op.cit., p. 69
31. Crnobjrna, op.cit., p. 149
32. quoted in Silber & Little, Death of Yugoslavia, pp. 186-7
33. Johnstone, op.cit., p. 28
34. Ibid., p. 29
36. Ibid.
37. Ivica Djikic, AIM Zagreb, 14.10.2000
38. Woodward, Balkan Tragedy, op.cit., p. 146

39. Ibid., p. 188
40. Ibid. p. 169
41. Johnstone, op.cit. pp. 59-62
42. Beloff, op.cit., p. 97
43. Woodward, Balkan Tragedy, op.cit., p. 194
44. Ibid., p. 195
45. Ibid., pp. 213-4
46. David Binder. Zimmerman interview, New York Times, 29.8.93
47. Woodward, Balkan Tragedy op.cit. p. 283
48. Peter (Lord)Carrington, interview for George Bogdanic & Martin Lettmayer film, Yugoslavia: The Avoidable War, 2000
49. Woodward, Balkan Tragedy, op.cit., p. 255
50. Ibid., p. 312
51. Johnstone, op.cit., p. 51
52. Ibid., p. 66
53. Ibid., p. 159
54. David (Lord) Owen, Balkan Odyssey, op.cit.
55. Magas, op.cit., p. xvii and map on p. 177
56. Woodward, Balkan Tragedy, op.cit., pp. 226-7
57. Johnstone, op.cit., p. 151
58. Ibid. p. 158, quoting Richard Holbrooke, *To End a War*, Random House, 1998
59. Figures taken from a report prepared by Dr. Phil Wright from the Management School, Sheffield University, for an International Conference on "The Yugoslav Crisis" held at Bradford University, March 24-26, 2000
60. Tim Judah, The Serbs, History, Myth and the Destruction of Yugoslavia, New Haven 1997
61. Maja Korac, Linking Arms: Women and War in Post-Yugoslav States, Life & Peace Institute, Uppsala, June 1998
62. Johnstone, op.cit. p. 80
63 Bogdanic & Lettmayer, film, op. cit..
64. C.G.Boyd "Making Peace with the Guilty", Foreign Affairs vol. 74, 5
65. M.Parenti, To Kill a Nation: The Attack on Yugoslavia, London, 2000
66. Johnstone, op.cit., p. 112
67. Ibid., p. 117
68. Silber & Little, op.cit.
69. Owen, op.cit., p. 355
70. Johnstone, op.cit., p. 109
71. London *Daily Telegraph*, 08.01.93
72. Johnstone, op.cit., p. 115
73. Tim Weiner, *New York Times*, 31.10.1995
74. Johnstone, op.cit., p. 115
75. Chris Hodges, *New York Times*, 18.07.1997, p. 7
76. Johnstone, op.cit., p. 115

77. Ibid. p. 119
78. Woodward, *Balkan Tragedy*, op.cit. , p. 315
79. Ibid., p. 330
80. Norma Percy & Brian Lapping, The Fall of Milosevic, film 2002
81. Alan Little, *The Guardian*, 06.01.03
82. Corrections *The Guardian*, 09.01.03

Chapter Twelve: *Kosovo and NATO's War on Yugoslavia, 1996-9*

1. Reported in the *Washington Post* 24.03.99
2. Commented on by Andrew Sullivan in "Clinton's War Strategy is Hit and Hope", *Sunday Times*, 28.03.99
3. Diana Johnstone, op.cit. p. 186
4. Noam Chomsky, Hegemony or Survival, Hamish Hamilton, 2003
5. Zbigniew Brzezinski, The Grand Chessboard, Basic Books, 1997
6. John K. Cooley, Unholy Wars, Pluto, 2000
6. Johnstone, op.cit., quoting Le Figaro Magazine, 09.06.2000, pp. 30-34
7. Financial Times, Yugoslav Supplement, 20.10.97
8. Phil Wright, Sanctions and Yugoslavia, Paper presented to an International Conference on 'The Yugoslav Crisis' at Bradford University, 24-26 March 2000
9. Ibid.
10. Wesley K.Clark, Waging Modern War, Bosnia, Kosovo and the Future of Combat, 2001 quoted in A.J.Bacevich, The American Empire, Harvard, p. 185
11. Yugoslav Red Cross, Report, Belgrade, February 2000
12. Johnstone, op.cit. pp. 247-8
13. International Criminal Court for Former Yugoslavia, Transcript op.cit. Page numbers in brackets hereafter are pages in the transcript.
14. General Klaus Naumann quoted in Alan Little and Laura Silber, Death of Yugoslavia, film, BBC 12.03.2000
16. Norma Percy & Brian Lapping, "Fall of Milosevic", film, op.cit.
17. Johnstone, op.cit. p. 306
18. Ibid. p. 237
19. Jeremy Paxman, Newsnight, BBC TV, July, 26, 2002
20. Percy & Lapping, op.cit.
21. Johnstone, op.cit. 243, quoting Forensic Science Journal, no. 116, 2001, pp.171-185
22. Johnstone, op.cit. p. 119
23. Johnstone, op.cit. p. 104
24. Johnstone, op.cit. pp. 245-6
25. Quoted by James Rubin, *Financial Times*, 30.09.2000 and see 07.09.2000
26. Wesley Clark, op.cit., quoted in Bacevich, op.cit. p.183
27. Johnstone, op.cit. p. 248
28. Bacevich, op.cit., p. 188
29. Ibid., p. 184
30. Ibid., p. 186

31. Amnesty International, 'Collateral Damage' or Unlawful Killings, Violation of the Laws of War by NATO during Operation Allied Force,   reprinted in Ken Coates (ed.) *The Spokesman* No. 69, 2000

32. Bacevich, op.cit., p. 181

33. Johnstone, op.cit. p. 255

34. Ibid., p. 250

35. Amnesty International, op.cit.

36. Johnstone, op.cit. p. 250

37. Ibid. , p. 231

38. Quoted by Ken Coates,introducing Collateral Damage or Unlawful Killings, Spokesman, no.69, 2000

Closure: *What is Left of Yugoslavia after Sixty Years?*

1. *The Guardian*, 01.01.2002

2. Le Monde Diplomatique, 02.08.2003 and 16.11.2003

3. Phil Wright, op.cit.

4. Amnesty International op.cit.

5. Tanjug, Belgrade, 24.01.2002.

6. *The Guardian*, G 2, 11.10.2002, p. 3

7. Ibid.

8. Graham Hancock, *Lords of Poverty*

9. Chandler, op.cit., 155-6

10. *Washington Times*, 24.10.97, quoted by Chandler, op.cit., p.158

11. Chandler, op.cit., p. 155

12. Ibid., p. 204

13. Johnstone, op.cit. p. 109

14. Chandler, op.cit., p. 202

15. John-Paul Flintoff, "The Liberal Imperialist", *Financial Times Magazine*, 25.10.2003

16. Ibid.

17. Chandler, op.cit., p. 203

18. Ibid., p. 148

19. Owen, op.cit.

20. Chandler, op.cit. , p. 36

21. Ibid., 180

22. Chomsky, Hegemony or Survival, Hamish Hamilton, 2003

23. House of Commons, Foreign Affairs Committee, Fourth Report, 20.03.2001

24. UNHCR/OSCE Report, November 1999-2001, p. 14

25. Amnesty International, op.cit. and Misha Glenny, 'The Forgotten Land', Guardian, 19.07.04

26. International Committee of the Red Cross, Emergency Appeal, 2000, Federal Republic of Yugoslavia, 29.08.03

27. Guy Spitaels, Improbable Equilibre, reviewed in Le Soir, 22.01.03

28. David Rieff, *Slaughterhouse: Bosnia and the Failure of the West*, Vintage, 1995; Michael Ignatieff, *The Warrior's Honour: Ethnic War and the Modern Conscience*,

Chatto & Windus 1998; Mary Kaldor, 'One Year after Dayton', Dayton Continued in Bosnia-Hercegovina. Vol. 1., The Hague: Helsinki Citizen's Assembly; Branka Magas, op.cit.
29. Francis R.Jones & Ivan Lovrewnov, *Reconstruction and Deconstruction*, Form Books, Ferhadija 30/iii, Sarajevo, no.15 2002
30. Kate Hudson, *Breaking the South Slav Dream: The Rise and Fall of Yugoslavia*, Pluto, 2003.

INDEX

(n = note; p = picture)

Abdic, Fikret, 137
Abramowitz, Morton, 12
Afghanistan, 135, 156, 157
Africa, 123, 128
Agriculture, 38p., 58, 109p
  see also droughts
AIM (Alternative Information Media),
  136, 142
Akashi, Yasushi, 129
Albania, 155, 157, 164, 167, 176
  map 168p.
Albanians, 9, 56, 96, 124, 130, 156,
  separatism 16, 130-1, 138, 154, 157,
  162, 163
Albright, Madeleine, 5, 8, 9, 12, 144, 154,
  160, 161, 163
Almond, M., 185n.
Al Qaeda, 6, 165
Allied Military Liaison (AML), 2, 3, 24,
  37, 39, 40, 41
  later ML (Yugoslavia) 42, 43, 45, 46,
  48, 49-50
Amnesty International, 165-6
Andric, Ivo, 122-3, 126
Apostolski, P., 81
Saudi Arabia, 144
  Gulf War, 14-15
Arab-Islamic opinion, 14
Arbour, Louise, 160
'Arkan', 18, 142, 146
arms culture, 135
Ashdown, Paddy, 9, 150, 157, 173-4
Australia, 90
Austria, 2, 13, 97-8, 107, 123, 126-7 map
  168p

Austro-Hungarian empire, 139, 175
Auty, Phyllis, 180n.
Avala, 77
AVNOJ, 120p.
Axis see Germany

Babic, Major, 23, 66
Bacevich, Andrew J., 187n.
Badinter, Robert, 140-1, 149
Bailey bridge, 45, 83
Baker, James, 139, 146
Balkan federation, 90, 123
Balkan Mission – see UNRRA
Balkan wars, 130
Bandoeng powers see Third Bloc
Banja Luka, 62, 66
Barbarism, 15
Bari, 37, 39, 40, 42, 44, 46, 47, 63
Barratt Brown, Christopher (son), 68
Barratt Brown, Michael
  After Imperialism, 111
  Bari, 39
  Belgrade, 73, 77, 83
  Cairo, 29
  Cavtat, 115, 117
  Claridges, 46-7
  Communist, 87, 89, 97
  Quaker, 31
  Sarajevo, 23ff. 59, 62
  UNRRA reports, 26
  on Yugoslavia, 130
Begic, Mauricette, 64
Belgrade, 50, 55, 56, 62, 73, 89, 98, 102,
  129, 135, 141, 171 Map 168
Beloff, Nora, 141, 149

Ben Bella, 111-2
Benn, Tony, 113
Benson, L., 185n.
Beria, 89
Berlin wall, 132, 135
Bertrand Russell Peace Foundation, 32, 114
Bicanic, Rudolf, 35, 43, 49
Bihac, 100
Bildt, Carl, 148, 173
Binder, David, 186n.
Black, Ian, 178n.
Blair, Tony, 8, 156, 160
Blunkett, David, 116
BND, 11
Boban, Mate, 141, 146
Bobetko, Janko, 7
Bolton, John, viii
Boscovic, B., 182n.
Bosna river, 57
Bosnia-Hercegovina, vii, 1, 2, 4
    agriculture, 38p., 60, 68, 69
    Bosniaks, 5, 98, 144, 146
    cantons, 145
    civil war, 135ff.
    Commerce ministry, 59, 69
    and Croatia, 141, 170
    Dayton Accords, 6, 10, 12, 150, 154, 162
    destruction 1941-5, 58-9, 79
                1992-5, 171
    development after 1945, 83, 92, 105
    elections, 137
    genocide, 6, 7
    Herceg-Bosna, 142
    liberation 1945, 37, 40, 55-6
    map, 168
    nationalism, 117-8, 126
    unemployment, 107, 128
    UN rule, 150, 171, 173-4
    referendum, 144
    Serbs, 144, 145, 169, 174
Boyd, General Charles, 70
Bratunac, 10
Brcko, 174
British Military Mission, 31, 39, 45, 47, 78
British Red Cross, 31, 33, 76
British Yugoslav Friendship Association, 46, 78, 88
Brookings Institution, 125, 135

Brzezinski, Zbigniew, 154
Budat, Mile, 142
Bukharin, N., 89
Bulgaria, 88, 90 Map 168p.
Bureaucracy, 104
Burnham, James, 32
Bush, George W., 154

Calder-Marshall, Arthur, 180n.
'Camp Bondsteel', 154, 169
Canadians, 33-4
Carrington, Lord, 10, 103, 144, 145
capitalism, 89, 108, 114, 176
    investment in Yugoslavia, 3, 128, 132, 155, 166
Caserta (AFHQ), 45
Casese, Antonio, 5
Caspian oil, 154
Castro, Fidel, 111, 113
catholics in Bosnia, 62, 65, 66, 121,124
Cato Institute, 172
Cavtat 'round table', 114-5, 117, 165
Ceku, Agim, 142, 146, 188
Chandler, David, 5, 172-3
Chetniks, 26, 33, 34, 52, 68
    see also Mihailovic
Cheney, Dick, 154
Children, 58, 68, 98
China, 115, 154, 163, 166
Chomsky, Noam, 175
Churchill, Randolph, 32, 33, 40
    Winston, 32, 51, 74
Clark, Neil, 166
Clark, Ramsay, 6
Clark, General Wesley, 16, 156, 159, 163, 164-5
Clinton, Bill, 5, 14, 148, 149, 153, 164
Clogg, R., 180n.
coal mining, 106, 112
Coates, Ken, 114-5, 140
COCOM, 91
Cold war, 115-6, 135
collaborators, 66
'collateral damage', 156, 164, 165-6
collectivisation, 82
Combined Chiefs of Staff (CCS), 42, 43, 45, 47
COMECON, 90
COMINFORM, 82-3
Commerce ministry, 24 see also Zavod
Commerce, Chambers of, 102

Common Market, 112, see also European Union
Communism, 32, 88, 89-90, 97
  see also Yugoslav Communist Party
concentration camps, 8-9
constitution of FRJ, – first, 144
  of 1953, 70, 92
  of 1974, 125, 131
Contact group, Bosnia, 146
  Kosovo, 159
Cooke, Dorian, 182n.
cooperatives, 51, 80
  see also zadruge
coordination, economic, 103
Corley, J.K., 187n.
Crnobrnya, 144
Croatia, vii, 1, 3, map 168p.
  Croat-Muslim federation, 144, 146, 149, 150
  collaboration with Nazis, 63
  Dayton Accords, 158, 163
  development after 1945, 116
  elections (CDU), 137
  ethnic cleansing, 3-4
  exports, 145
  German support for new Croatia, 11, 15
  at Gospic, 7
  and income distribution, 92
  Krajina, qv.
  liberation from Axis occupation, 37
  Mostar, 99
  nationalism, 118, 120p., 121ff., 124
  'operation storm', 149
  para-militaries, 142
  Partisans, 81, 120p.
  population, 170
  PR, 8, 135
  prison camps, 8-9, 147
  recognition, 9, 12, 29, 139-40, 143, 145
  unemployment, 107, 113,128
  Ustashe, 11, 24, 26, 60, 66, 127, 134, 141, 142, 172
Croats, armed attacks, 3, 179
  diaspora, 17
  on trial, 2, 7
Crossman, Richard, 111
Cuba, 175
Czechoslovakia, 49, 70, 79, 88, 90

Dalmatia, 23, 34, 48, 50, 55, 56, 59, 67, 75, 100
Danube river, 24, 57, 73-4
Davidson, Basil, 33, 123
Davies, A. Tegla, 179n.
Dayton Accords, 6, 10, 12, 150, 154, 162, 163, 171
Deakin, William, 33
Dokmanovic, Slavko, 3
debt, foreign, 128, 137, 170
decentralisation, 83, 92-3, 97, 102, 104, 107
Dedijer, Stefan, 34
  Vlado, 32, 70
Dedinje, 73
Del Ponte, Carla, viii, 6-7
Democracy
  democratic centralism, 32, 35, 37, 56
  in Bosnia, 173
  industrial, 2, 92, 114
  lack of political, 133, 140, 176
development, economic, 82, 93, 115, 116
Der Spiegel, 139
developing countries, 108, 112, 125
Die Welt, 139, 150
Dini, Lamberto, 161
distribution, see UNRRA
Djikic, Ivica, 185n.
Djilas, Milovan, 91, 104, 120p.
Draskovic, Vuk, 131, 138, 142
Drenica, 16
Drewenkiewicz, General, 158-9
Drina river, 57, 61, 98
drought, 74
drugs, 157, 176
Dubrovnik, shelling of, 19, 29
  port (Gruz), 44, 45, 49, 56, 93, 99
Durrell, Lawrence, 179n.

education, 93
EFTA, 112
Egypt, camps in, 23, 29ff., 34, 37, 50
  UNRRA in, 37, 41
electrification, 93-4, 99
Elliot, Air Vice-Marshal Walter, 44
emigration, 147
equality, 70
ethnic cleansing, 1, 3-4, 5, 6, 7, 10, 127, 155
Europe, 115, 124, 132, 135

European Union, 7-8, 10
  and Bosnia, 174
  and Croatia, 148
  Eurocorps, 13
  federation, 117
  free trade, 111-2
  and Kosovo, 154
  Parliament, 139
  and USA, 11, 14

Fascism, 77, 89
Fischer, Joschka, 12
fishing, 75, 115
Foca model, 93-4, 98, 99, 106
  regulations, 66
foreign investment in Yugoslavia, 1ff., 3,
  18, 128, 132, 155, 166
foreign trade, 80-1, 90, 105, 106
Flintoff, J –P, 188n.
Fotic, Constantin, 36
France, 8, 24, 123, 155, 158
Frankfurter Algemeine Zeitung, 129
Franks, Oliver Lord, 82
Franz Ferdinand, Archduke, 55
Fraser, Gordon, 32
Friends Ambulance Unit (FAU), 29, 31,
  32, 37, 49, 64, 82, 172
Frisch, Ragnar, 112
full spectrum dominance – see USA

Gale, General, 77-8
Gellner, Ernst, 98, 127
Geneva Convention, 6
genocide, 2, 6, 16, 17
Genscher, Hans Dietrich, 11, 141, 154
Genscher's war, 154
Germany
  Alamein battle 29
  Axis occupation vii, 2, 17, 24, 25ff.,
    55ff., 61, 99, 127, 138, 170, 175
  Croat support, 11, 20
  immigrants, 107
  interest in Yugoslavia, 12-13, 14, 97,
    103, 141, 155
  and Kosovo, 17, 20
  offensives against Partisans, 2, 34, 35,
    39, 99
  recognition of Slovenia, Croatia, 154
  Stalingrad defeat, 34
Gervasi, Sean, 141
Gilbert, Martin, 180n.

Glenny, Misha, 33, 81, 126-7
Gligorov, 138
Goldstone, Richard, 4
Golnik sanatorium, 86p.
Gorbachev, Mikhail, 135
Goseco,Andreas, 112
Gospic, 142
Gotovina, Ante, 7-8
Gowan, Peter, 12, 15
Greece, 37, 41, 49, 130, 141, 155, 168
  map,169
Greens, 12

Haliburton corporation, 154
Hall, Alan, 41, 49
Hancock, Graham, 172
Harriman, Averil, 127
Harrod, Roy, 112
Hart, Charles, 112
Health, 31, 33, 93
Hendrickson Mr., 49
Hercegovina, 56
  see also Bosnia
Hendrie, Sergeant, 159-60
Herman, Edward S., 178n.
Hill, Chris, 161-2
Hitler, Adolf, 2, 3, 4, 5, 11, 89, 153
Hodges, Chris, 186n.
Holbrooke, Richard, 12, 146, 156, 158,
  159
Holland, Stuart, 116
Holy Roman Empire, 13
Hudson, Kate, 189n.
humanitarian intervention, 12, 13, 149,
  156, 164, 175
Hungarians, 2, 18, 88, 89, 92, 112, 130,
  138, 145
Hussein, Saddam, 139

Ignatieff, Michael, 12, 176
Imber, Vivien, 68
Ilic, Zoran, 10, 19
incognito, 18
income redistribution, 92-3
industry, nationalisation, 51, 147
  see also social sector
industrialisation, 81
inequality, 92-3, 103, 170
Institute of Workers Control 113
'International community', 2, 10, 16, 157
International Court of Justice, 5-6

International Criminal Court, 5
International Criminal Tribunal for
Yugoslavia (ICTY), vii, viii, 1, 2, 3, 4, 5,
7, 8, 18, 20, 125, 142-3, 148, 159, 164,
169
  hearsay evidence, 7, 159
International Crisis Group, 175
International Monetary Fund (IMF), 82,
90, 112, 124, 135, 137, 171
International Post-war Requirements
Bureau, 35
International Red Cross, 8, 10, 147, 176
Iraq, 154, 155, 176
Iranians, 158
iron & steel, 96p.
Italy, 2, 34, 39, 81, 158, 175
Izetbegovic, Alija, 7, 14, 120p., 137, 144,
148, 149, 170

Jackson, Commander, 49
Jackson, Sir Michael, 165
Jajce, 10, 33, 124
Japan, 115
Jews, 17, 120p., 123, 130, 170
Jugoslav National Army (JNA), 132, 135,
139, 141, 142, 145
Johnstone, Diana, vii, 3, 8, 11, 12, 14,
135, 141, 142, 144, 160
Jones, Francis R., 189n.
Jovi, Borisav, 19
Judah, Tim, 186n.

'K' rations, 24, 25, 65-2, 68
Kaldor, Mary, 12, 176
Kaldor, Nicholas, 112
Kalinovik, 56
Karadzordzevo, 19
Karadzic, Radovan, 18, 70, 137
Kardelj, Edvard, 81, 83, 93, 106, 127
Kenney, George, 162-3
Ketzmanovic, President, 59
Key (kljuc), 81, 121
Khruschev, Nikita, 89
Kidric, Boris, 93
Kinkel, Klaus, 5, 11, 17, 141, 154
Klugmann, James, 31, 32, 39, 46, 88-9
Kohl, Chancellor Helmut, 12, 142, 154
Korac, Maja, vii, 147
Kosovo, vii, 1, 2, 3, 117, 124, map 168
  civil war, 127, 130
    Decani monastery, 152p.

'ethnic cleansing', 4, 6, 16, 150
  German interest, 13, 17, 20, 154
  Kosova Liberation Army (KLA), 6, 9,
  11, 12, 15, 138, 142, 154 ,156 157, 158-
  9, 160, 176
  language, 131
  and Milosevic, 131-2, 156
  polje, 130
  population, 16, 170
  Protection Corps, 175 see also Rambouillet
  S.S. Skanderbeg, 13, 16
  unemployment, 92, 105, 113, 131
  UN Protectorate, 135
  US interest, 13, 17, 154
  Verification Mission see OSCE
  War, 153ff.
Konjic, 57
Kostov, 88, 90
Kotor, Gulf of, 142
Kraigher, Boris, 83-4
Kraigher, Nada, vii, 8, 33-4, 107-8, 118, 144
Krajina, 7-8, 10, 19, 138, 142, 145, 148-9
Kranj, 101
Kucan, Milan, 120p., 137

land reform, 51
Lange, Oscar, 106
La Guardia, Fiorello, 77
Lapping, Brian, 150. 158, 160
Lehman, Governor Herbert, 36, 46, 47,
67
Leith-Ross, Sir Frederick, 35
liberal reformers, 102-3
Little, Alan, 150
Ljubjana, 74, 101, 113, map 168p.
Loncar, General, 159
Loquai, General Heinz, 155

Macedonia, 76, 82, 92, 107, 113, 117,
118, 120p., 124, 130, 138, 141, 164,
map 168, 171
MacLean, Sir Fitzroy, 38p., 45
MacDonald, Gabrielle Kirk, 5
Magas, Branka, 129-30, 176
Maitland-Wilson, General, 41
Maiorsky, Boris, 101-2
Maisonoeuvre, General, 158
Major, John, 12, 154
malaria, 76
Malcolm, Noel, 35, 81
Mandel, Michael, 87

market competition, 100, 103, 135
Markovic, Ante, 19, 20, 137, 138, 161
Markovic, Ratko, 4
Martic, Milan, 48
Martin, Kingsley, 46
Marshall Aid, 82
Marx, Karl, 51, 106
Marxists, 114
Matthews, Sir William, 31, 46-7
May, Judge Richard, 1, 7
medical supplies, 64, 76
Mercinger, Jose, 193n.
Middle East Relief and Refugee
    Administration (MERRA), 30ff., 35
Mercedes cars, 103
'Mercep', 142, 146
Mestrovic, 115
migration, 105, 108
Mihailovic, 34, 83
Milosevic, Slobodan, ix p.
    Dayton Accords, 154, 162
    defence, viii, 6
    demonised, 1ff., 121, 129, 136, 146, 150
    election, 3, 137
    illness, vii, 7
    and JNA, 142, 145
    and Kosovo, 131, 154, 156, 160, 161,
        176
    and Rambouillet, 162-3
    and socialist economy, 155
    Socialist Party, 137, 171
    support for UN plans, 145
    surrender, 164-5
    trial, vii, viii, 1ff., 15ff. 127,
Milutinovic, Jilan, 4
Mincev, Nicola, 183n.
Mladic, Ratko, 10, 26, 145, 149
Molotov, 82
Monde Le, 8, 170
Montegro, 37, 73, 100, 107, 120p., 124,
    155, 168 map, 169, 170
Moon, Penderel, 64
Moravic, J., vi, 182n.
Morillon, General Philippe, 148
Mostar, 23, 57, 99, 145, 147
MUP, 17
Muslims, Arab-Islamic support, 14
    in Bosnia, 62, 65, 66, 98, 100, 121, 137
    in Communist Party, 117
    conversion, 127
    and Croat Federation, 145-6, 174

and Dayton, 154, 162
ethnic cleansing, 10, 17
and Germany, 172
inter-marriage, 144
in Kosovo, 130-1, 138
as nation, 124
prison camps, 8, 147
as witnesses, 9, 15
at Srebrenica, 7
on trial, 2, 7

Nadj, Josta, 81
narod, 124
Nasser, Abdel, 111, 113
nationalism, 94, 115, 117, 118, 121ff.,
    125, 137-8, 175
nationality, 124
nation state, 124-5
North Atlantic Treaty Organisation (NATO),
    3, 6, 9, 13, 143, 145, 146, 149
    in Kosovo, 175-6
    and rules of war, 165-6
    war on Yugoslavia, 153ff., 155, 156,
        158, 160, 161, 163, 164, 165, 170, 176,
Naumann, General Klaus, 16-17, 157,
    163
Nehru, Pandit, 11, 117
Neretva river, 54p., 57, 79, 99
Neubauer, Robert, viii, 43, 46, 84, 97-8
New Left Review, 97
Nice, Geoffrey, 1
Nicaragua, 158
Nicolic, Milos, 114, 165
Nixon, Richard, 47
Nkrumah, Kwame, 111, 113
non-governmental organisations (NGOs), 76,
    118, 132, 173
    see also BRCS, FAU, SCF
North, Colonel Oliver, 158
Novi Pazar, 170
Nuremberg trials, 4

OFFRO, 35
oil, 154, 176
Orthodox church, see Serbia
Omarska camp, 8, 147
one party state, 82, 91, 132
'Operation Horseshoe', 158
Oric, Naser, 149
OSCE, 158, 162, 163, 174, 180

Oslobodzenja, 11, 24
Ottoman empire, see Turks
Owen, David, 9, 11, 18, 145, 174
  see also Stoltenberg and Vance

Panic, General, 142
Parenti, M., 147
Partisans, vii, 2, 16, 24, 25, 27, 28p., 116
  AVNOJ, 120p.
  and collaborators, 81
  dancing and singing, 64-5
  delegates at UNRRA talks, 43-4
  German offensives, 30, 34, 39, 77
  German retreat, 55-6
  mix of nationalities, 81, 120p.,122
  National Liberation Council (NLC),
    36, 42, 124
  1941 rising, 59, 74
  organisation, 31, 41, 121-2
  recognition by British, 33, 34, 35
  unity, 124, 176
Paxman, Jeremy, 4, 159
peace movement, 116, 165
Peake, Charles, 38p.
peasants, 81
Percy, Norma, 150, 158, 160
Petritsch, Ambassador, 9, 161-2, 173
Pickard, Sir Cyril, 35, 45
Pijade, Moshe, 66, 81, 120p.
Powell, Colin, 13, 154
planning, 92-3
plastic surgery, 77
pluralist society, 51, 64
Popovic, Milentije, 32
Poulton, H., 185n.
prices, world, 107, 128
Pristina, 159
protecsia, 87

Qassim, 111, 113
Quakers, 31, 87

Racak, 9, 158-9, 161
railways, 45, 58, 72p.
  youth, 68, 78
Raj, Kosta, 88, 90
Rambouillet conference, 9, 161-2, 163
Rankovic, Alexander, 91, 120p.
Ranta, Helena, 160
rapes, 147, 164
Reagan, President Ronald, 135

redistribution, 79, 92
refugees, 50
Ribar, Ivo, 81, 120p.
Rieff, David, 11, 176
relief observers, 45-8, 50-1, 61-2
  see also UNRRA
rehabilitation, 68, 69
Rigg, Sir John, 34, 35
Rijeka, 73
Robinson, Joan, 112
Rogatica, 56, 61, 67
Romanija, 56, 57, 61, 62, 98
Romas, 130, 176
Roman Empire- East-West, 14, 66
Roosevelt, Franklin D., 51, 89
Rose, General Sir Michael, 157
Rozman, 81
Ruder Finn, 8
Rugova, Ibrahim, 138, 161, 175
Rukovina, 81
Russia, 154, 156, 158, 161, 162, 165, 176

SACMED, 43-45, 77
  see also Maitland-Wilson
Sandjak, 18, 123, 176
Sarajevo, 10, 11, 22p. 23ff., 55, 57, 58,
  59, 63, 67, 98, 118, 128, 137, 142, 147
  map 168, 174
Sava river, 57, 2, 74
Save the Children Fund (SCF), 31, 33,
  64-5
Scharf, Michael, 5
Schroeder, Chancellor Gerhardt, 13, 16
Serbia, Serbs, 120p., map 168p.
  agriculture, 62, 70
  in army, 2, 132, 141
  Bosnian Serbs, 20, 122, 123, 145, 146,
    147, 174
  and Croatia, 140
  Dayton Accords, 150, 162
  decentralisation, 92
  elections, 137
  expulsions from Croatia, 3, 8
  foreign investment, 155
  federation, 124, see also Solana
  genocide accusation, 17
  and Germans, 16, 55
  'Greater' Serbia, 17, 141
  industry, 147, 170
  and Kosovo, 131, 161, 170
  nationalism, 118, 122, 132

NATO bombing, 153, 170
Pravo-Slavs (Orthodox church), 64, 65, 121,124, 130
para-militaries, 10, 17, 142
prison camps, 8-9, 147
population, 170
Republica Srbska, 174
sanctions, 147
Socialist Party, 135, 171
trials of, 1, 3
unemployment, 107, 113
Sergeichic, Mihail, 47, 61, 67, 73
Seselj, Vojislav, 131
Shanin, Teodor, 180n.
Shea, Jamie, 7
shipping, 96p., 100
Sik, Ota, 105-6
Silber, A., 185n.
Singer, Dr. Eleanor, 33, 64, 65, 75, 78, 123
Singleton, Fred, 185n.
Slansky, 98
Slav peoples, 2, 124
Slavonia, 5, 141, 143, 147
Slovakia, 14
Slovenia, 3, 14, 19, 37, 81, 120p., 124, map 168
  armed forces, 139
  elections, 137
  nationalism, 118, 124
  population, 170
  secession, 140, 143
  unemployment, 113, 125
socialism, in Yugoslavia, 51, 111ff, 128
  in Western Europe, 113-4
Social Democrats, 12, 13, 16
social sector, 103, 195, 107, 166
  bombing of, 171
Society of Socialist Economists, 105
Sokolac, 6, 61, 67, 98
Solana, Javier, 9, 157, 163, 170
Solana, State of, 170
Sontag, Susan, 11
Soros, George, 5
Soviet Union, 32, 34, 36, 59-60, 76, 82-3, 115, 123
  and Afghanistan, 135
  Red Army, 89
  trade bloc
  and Yugoslavia as bulwark, 113, 132
  aid to Yugoslavia, 82-3, 87

Special Operations Europe (SOE), 31, 33, 34, 39 see also British Military Mission
Spitaels, Guy, 189n.
Split, 26, 34, 46, 48, 49, 100
Sraffa, Piero, 106
Srebrenica, 7, 10, 108-9
Stambolic, Ivan, 4
Stalin, 82-3, 84, 88-9
Stalingrad, 89
Stambuk, Ivaan, 163-4
statistics, 76, 78-9, 84
Steele, General 38p.
Stoltenberg, Thorwald, 9-10
Subasic, Dr., 41
Sukarno, 111
Sullivan, Andrew, 187n.
Sweden, 91, 116-7

Tait, Nikki, viii
tax system, 102
Teheran agreement, 51
Territorial Defence Forces, 18, 138
Third Force, 111
Tinbergen, Jan, 112
Thaqi, Hashim, 161
Tito, Josip Broz, 38p., 120p.
  Belgrade, 73, 74-5
  Communist Party, 81, 193
  Croat, 115
  death, 137
  and federation, 124, 138
  and Khruschev, 83
  Kumrovec, 116
  Partisans, vii, 2, 39, 87, 176
  regime, 2, 3, 170
  in Sarajevo, 59
  and Stalin, 82-3, 87ff., 93
  Third Force, 111-2
  and UNRRA, 36, 41, 42, 45, 46, 47
  turn to West, 90,93
  and working class, 103-4
Titoism, 111, 126, 171
Titolik, 75
tourism, 94, 102, 103
trade unions, 91, 113, 117
training schemes, 77
transnational companies (TNCs), 117, 155
transportation, 80, 88, 94, 109p.
  see also railways

Traynor, Phil, viii
Trieste, 34, 40, 77, 78
Trotsky, Leon, 88
Trueheart, Charles, 178n.
Tucan, Ivica, 8, 120p.
Turks, 2, 14, 74, 126-7, 134, 144, 157
Tusla, 57, 63, 149
typhus, 64

unemployment, 92, 105-6, 107, 113, 128,
   130, 170-1
United Kingdom (UK),
   British army in Yugoslavia 33, 34, 35,
   77
   in Greece, 37
   see also British Military Mission
   British Empire, 89, 175
   devolution, 117
   Foreign Office, 45, 47
   foreign trade, 117
   Labour government, 111
   unity, 124
   Yalta agreement, 51
United Nations (UN),
   UN Association, 117
   Charter, 5, 175
   and democratisation, 175
   Economic Commission for Africa, 112
   Economic Commission for Europe, 79,
   184fn.
   Conference on Trade and Development
(UNCTAD), 112
   'failure', 155
   forces in Bosnia, 79, 143
   General Assembly, 6
   Kosovo, 163, 169
   UNPROFOR, 145, 149
   sanctions, 146, 170
   Security Council, 8, 149, 163
United Nations Relief and Rehabilitation
Administration (UNRRA), 23, 24, 26,35
   agreement with Yugoslavia, 36, 49-50
   aid to Yugoslavia total, 78-9, 171
   Belgrade office, 62, 73
   Bosnia relief, 55ff.
   chief of mission, 73-6, 77
   food exchange with army, 60
   in Greece, 37
   milk from London, 59
   mission to Yugoslavia, 36, 37, 39ff., 47,
   48, 63, 116, 172

PR exhibitions, 64, 74
rationing, 60-1
rehabilitation, 72p., 73ff
relief functions, 40ff., 62-3, 77
Sarajevo office, 63-4, 123
UK and US staff differences, 63, 74
Washington office, 44-6, 74, 75-6

United States of America (USA)
   aid to Bosnia, 171, 174
   airmen, 56,82
   Americans in UNRRA, 63, 76
   attitude to WWII, 77
   banks, 3
   Belgrade embassy, 76
   'camp bondsteel', 154, 169, 171
   elections, 145
   exports, 128
   food relief, 25, 70
   'full spectrum dominance', 89
   intelligence, 160
   interest in Yugoslavia, 12-13,14,51,132,
   175
   and Kosovo, 54-5, 164
   loans, 51, 92
   recognition of Bosnia, 145
   recognition of Slovenia, 140
   support for Muslims, 11
   support for Tito, 90, 113
   TV in Kosovo, 158
   union, 124
   US army, 2
   Yalta agreement, 51
uranium, depleted, 171
Uzice, 59

Vallance, Aylmer, 46
Vance, Cyrus, 9, 11, 143, 154
Vance-Owen plan, 145
Vanek, J., 182n.
Velebit, General, 41, 47, 78
Velebit mountains, 57
Victory Day, 59
Vietnam, 175
Vis, 36, 39, 41
Visegrad, 61, 122
Vlasenica, 56, 61
Vojvodina, 130, map 168, 169
Vollebaek, Ambassador, 9, 163
Vukovar, 3, 19
Vukmanovic-Tempo, 92

Waldheim, Kurt, 17
Walker, Ambassador William, 9, 158-9
Ward, Benjamin, 105
Warden, Colonel J.A., 166
Warriner, Doreen, 181n.
Warsaw Pact, 138
Washington Post, 5, 7
Washington Times, viii
Weiner, Tim, 186n.
Westendorp, Carlos, 173
Wladimiroff, W., 6
Woodward, Susan, vii, 3, 12, 15, 92, 106,
  107, 129, 135, 145
working class, 81
workers' self-management, 86p., 90,
  97ff., 100
  payment systems, 98-9, 101-2
  social sector, 103
World Bank, 90, 113
World Health Organisation(WHO), 172
Wilson, Duncan, 181n.
Wright, Phil, viii, 147, 155

Xoxe, 88

Yalta agreement, 51
Yugoslavia, army (JNA), 17, 19, 132, 138,
  139, 141
  break-up, 3, 10, 14, 19, 121ff., 126, 127,
  135
  bulwark v. Soviet Union, 113
  constitution, 124, 130, 138, 140, 142,
  144, 170
  destruction by Germans, 74
  elections, 137
  map, 168
  NATO destruction, 153, 165
  occupation, vii, 74, 176
  peoples, 3, see also Croats, Muslims, Serbs,
  Slovenes
  socialism, 108, 111ff
  Stalin, break with, 88ff
Yugoslav Communist Party, 81, 87, 88-9,
  90, 118
  League of Communists 103-4,
  116, 131, 135, 137
Yugoslav government, AVNOJ, 51
  Commerce ministry, 59, 69, 75
  egalitarian, 79
  federal presidency, 139
  Five Year Plan, 80, 85, 9, 93

Foreign ministry, 98
  foreign trade, 80-1, 90, 103
  intelligence services, 78, 87
  Marshall Plan, 82
  Popular Front, 83, 87
  purges, 83
  re-arming decision, 83, 90
  Socialist Alliance, 97, 103
  Tito-Subasic agreement, 46, 49, 50
Yugoslav Reform Party, 20, 138
Yugoslav Royal Government, 35, 36, 41,
  43, 47, 52, 82, 127
  monarchy abolished, 52
Yugoslavia (rump of Serbia & Montenegro),
  146, 155, 161, 162, 170

zadruge, 51
Zagreb, 3, 11, 35, 98, 100, 116, 148, map
  168
Zavod, 75
Zemun, 73, 98
Zenica, 46, 69
Zilliacus, Konni, 78, 88
Zilavka, 99
Zimmerman, Warren, 14, 137, 139, 144,
  145